CW00554538

# THE CITY THAT REFUSED TO DIE

# THE CITY THAT REFUSED TO DIE

Glasgow:
the politics of urban
regeneration

**Michael Keating**

ABERDEEN UNIVERSITY PRESS

First published 1988
Aberdeen University Press
A member of the Pergamon Group

© Michael Keating 1988

**British Library Cataloguing in Publication Data**

Keating, Michael, *1950-*
    The city that refused to die: Glasgow:
    the politics of urban regeneration.
    1. Scotland. Strathclyde region. Glasgow
    inner areas. Social development
I. Title
    307′.14′0941443

    ISBN 0 08 036412-8

Printed in Great Britain
The University Press
Aberdeen

# Contents

# Preface

At the turn of the century, Glasgow, in its own proud boast, was the second city of the British Empire, the centre of a booming industrial region. For the last fifty years, its name has been associated with urban decay, poverty and industrial decline. Such images are almost always misleading and Glasgow is no exception. Its growth was rapid, its period of glory short and its economic decline prolonged, but in the last century poverty and squalor went along with expansion while in the late twentieth century visitors are surprised at the quality of life which it offers. A city is a complex phenomenon, continually changing and developing, subject to the forces of nature, the world and national economy, demographic trends, technological progress and political choice and conflict. This book is about the efforts by public authorities to tackle the appalling social, economic and environmental problems, which the city undoubtedly has faced, and guide the process of urban change for the better. I have attempted to examine the extent of the problems, assess the solutions proposed and undertaken and judge their effectiveness. The origins of policy initiatives are traced and the forces moulding them assessed. As a political scientist, I am primarily interested in the struggle for control of the process of urban change and the interests and ideological assumptions which underlie it.

The first chapter looks very generally at the growth and development of Glasgow and at politics and policies in the post-war period. The rest of the book is largely about events since the early 1970s, a critical time in which assumptions which had guided urban policies since the war were overturned, new directions taken and the system of urban government radically reformed, with the creation of regional and district councils and the Scottish Development Agency. Chapters 2 and 3 are about the government and politics of the city since 1975 and, while Scottish readers may find much of chapter 2 familiar, I have assumed that the background material will be essential for other readers. There follows a series of chapters on policy areas—housing, a perennial Glasgow problem, planning and transportation, anti-poverty strategies and policies for economic regeneration. Many of the developments have had their origins beyond Glasgow and Scotland and, to avoid too parochial a perspective, the national background has been sketched in briefly where appropriate. I have tried also to capture not only the broad thrust of policy change but some of the minutiae of politics on the ground. Clearly in a city as large and complex as Glasgow, not everything can be covered in this detail (nor would this be of interest to readers) so I have used case studies which typify certain types of problem, allowing us to tease out the complex pattern of interests and values underlying issues such as highway development, housing or the problem of the Glasgow periphery. The assessment of policies is largely contained within the individual chapters but the conclusion attempts a general overview, is perhaps more opinionated than the rest of the book and speculates on the future of Glasgow.

I have received a great deal of help in preparing this work. The University of Strathclyde's Research and Development Fund paid for the services of a short-term research assistant, James Mitchell, whose efforts are reflected particularly in chapter 6. Members and officials of both local councils and the Scottish Development Agency have been extremely generous with their time and advice and without their cooperation the work would have been impossible. The Mitchell Library, Glasgow, and its staff have been a major source of information. I owe a great deal, too, to colleagues at Strathclyde University with whom I have collaborated on previous projects and on whose advice I have drawn—in particular, Robin Boyle and Urlan Wannop. Jack Geekie, Duncan Sim and Gerry Stoker read and commented on draft chapters. Elizabeth Harvey drew the maps and John Bochel helped with electoral data. My partners in the survey of Glasgow councillors were Roger Levy, Jack Geekie, Jack Brand and Gilles Leydier; Roger Evans helped process the data. Needless to say, none of these bears any responsibility for errors of fact and judgement into which I may have fallen.

Michael Keating
Glasgow

# 1 The Development of Glasgow

## Glasgow up to 1945

Glasgow traces its origins to the settlement of Kentigern, also known as St Mungo who, around 543, came to preach Christianity to the kingdom of Strathclyde. It then largely disappears from history until the twelfth century, when the present cathedral was commenced. Achieving burgh status under the bishop in the same century, it grew slowly as a trading centre, under the jealous eyes of the neighbouring burghs of Rutherglen and Dumbarton. In 1451, under a papal bull, the university was founded and in 1492 the see was raised to the status of an archbishopric. Municipal politics in the early days were dominated by the rivalry between the traders and the craftsmen, resolved to some extent in 1605 when the Dean of Guild (for the craftsmen) and the Deacon Convenor (for the traders) were given seats on the council, a privilege which they retained until recently. In 1611 the city was raised to the status of a royal burgh.

The growth of trade and the shallowness of the river Clyde at Glasgow led to the foundation of Port Glasgow near Greenock on the lower Clyde. As we shall see, in the late twentieth century, history has repeated itself, with trade moving down river to deeper water. It was the Treaty of Union in 1707, giving Scottish traders access to English imperial markets, which stimulated Glasgow's first economic take-off. As the American colonists were themselves prohibited from trading directly with Europe, Glasgow became an important entrepôt, notably for the tobacco trade. The Clyde was dredged and channelled to allow trade up to the city itself and the Glasgow 'tobacco lords', with their fine mansions and scarcely less grand warehouses, became a byword for opulence. When the American war of independence put paid to the tobacco traffic, the cotton industry took off. Another crisis was provoked by the American civil war but, from the early nineteenth century, the heavy industries for which the Clyde was to achieve world fame had started their ascent. Local deposits of coal and iron ore together with the strategic location as the lowest point at which the Clyde could be bridged, favoured the growth of industry especially, after the development of the iron hull, shipbuilding.

With the railway boom from the mid nineteenth century, locomotive manufacture, too, became an important element of the local economy. From the formation of the earliest railway companies in the 1830s, the network was expanded until the 1860s, with connections down the Clyde to Greenock

(1841), across central Scotland to Edinburgh (1842) and to London (1848)—though the development of four separate terminals not only caused considerable damage to the city landscape, sweeping away much of the pre-Victorian city, but left a legacy of unconnected systems to twentieth century transport planners. The earliest railway works were established in 1836 and in 1900 the major manufacturers came together to form the North British Locomotive Company, the largest in Europe, whose plants at Springburn and St Rollox employed 8,000 men and supplied locomotives to Britain and the Empire. Production had already peaked by 1900 but continued at a slightly lower rate of about 500 per year up to 1914 (Orr and Orr, 1958).

Other important industries established in the late nineteenth century included publishing, chemicals, optical instruments and carpet manufacture— the last being responsible for the extraordinary building on Glasgow Green designed for Templeton's to imitate the facade of the Doge's Palace in Venice. In 1896, the Arrol-Johnston motor car factory commenced, later moving to Paisley and then Dumfries. In 1899, Albion started making cars, moving over to the production of lorries in 1912 and in 1905 the Argyll firm was founded, producing cars in Glasgow and nearby Alexandria up to the First World War. In the early 1880s, the American Singer company founded what was to become the world's largest sewing machine factory at Clydebank and in 1895 and 1910 another American firm, the engineering giant Babcock and Wilcox, moved into Renfrew and Dumbarton (Lindsay, 1972).

It is shipbuilding, however, which was to give Glasgow its image in the world. By 1903, the city's thirty-nine shipyards were producing 370 vessels a year, with a combined tonnage of over 750,000 tons (Robb, 1958) and, on the eve of the First World War, accounted for a third of British and a fifth of world production (CVRPAC, 1946). Around 60,000 men were employed in the shipyards, with another 40,000 dependent on the industry (Daiches, 1982). At this time, too, the Clyde appeared able to keep up with the pace of technological change, adapting to steam turbine and diesel propulsion and pioneering several of the new techniques. In 1906, Yarrow's yard moved from the Thames to the Clyde, prompting fears of a 'drift north' of industry (Oakley, 1975).

Shipping, too, was booming by the end of the century, with a series of new docks being excavated to replace the river-side wharfs. Kingston dock was the first, in 1867, followed by the ever-larger Queen's dock, Princes dock (1900) and Rothesay dock (1907). Tonnage handled rose accordingly up to the First World War (see Table 1.1). In terms of shipping registered, Glasgow was the third British port, behind London and Liverpool.

Iron and, later, steel manufacture were booming by the end of the century. A and J Stewart was founded in 1862 and its 1903 merger with Lloyd and Lloyd of Birmingham was seen more as an expansion of Scottish interests than a sell-out to the English. Beardmore's was another famous name established in the late nineteenth century and by 1900 their Parkhead Forge could be described as a 'steel works, forge and armour manufacturing establishment second to none in the country' (Oakley, 1975, p.162). Colville's, founded in

TABLE 1.1   TONNAGE AT PORT OF GLASGOW

| | |
|---|---|
| 1860 | 1,200,000 |
| 1870 | 1,900,000 |
| 1880 | 2,700,000 |
| 1890 | 4,800,000 |
| 1900 | 7,200,000 |
| 1910 | 10,097,000 |
| 1920 | 7,028,000 |

Source: J. Cunnison and J B S Gilfillan (eds.), *Third Statistical Account of Scotland, Glasgow* (Glasgow: Collins, 1958).

1872 at nearby Motherwell, was by 1900 the largest steel-making plant in Scotland, employing 2,000 men.

By the turn of the century, however, natural resources for the heavy industries were already nearing exhaustion, as the figures for Lanarkshire iron ore production make clear (see Table 1.2). At the same time, coal mining was moving from the western fields of Lanarkshire—which in 1890 was producing two-thirds of Scottish output (Cairncross, 1958)—and Ayrshire, to Lothian and Fife in the east (Harvie, 1981). Production in Glasgow's major industries had peaked between 1900 and the First World War but rearmament, war demand and the short-lived post-war boom masked the fundamental problems of the local economy, dependent on a relatively narrow and vulnerable range of industries. Checkland's (1976) powerful metaphor of the upas tree shows the heavy engineering of Glasgow killing off anything that sought to grow beneath its branches. A less tangible element is the failure of business leadership to take the sort of initiative which had allowed the city to weather the storm of the loss of the American trade over a hundred years earlier.

Premonitions of doom, though, were confined to the prescient few for in 1913 Glasgow was still the 'second city of the Empire' and Britain the 'workshop of the world'. The population, a mere 77,000 in 1801, had grown to over 300,000 by mid century and on the eve of the First World War had

TABLE 1.2   LANARKSHIRE IRON STONE PRO-
DUCTION (tons)

| | |
|---|---|
| 1880 | 2,200,000 |
| 1890 | 700,000 |
| 1900 | 600,000 |
| 1913 | 590,000 |
| 1920 | 280,000 |
| 1929 | 25,000 |

Source: C A Oakley, *The Second City*, 3rd edition (Glasgow: Blackie, 1975).

passed the million mark (Figure 1.1). Immigration brought large numbers from the Scottish Highlands and from Ireland. In 1851, following the Great Famine and exodus, some 20% of the city's population was Irish by birth. In 1911, the Irish-born still comprised 7% of the population and many more, of course, were of recent Irish descent. At the same time, Glasgow had become the centre of a large industrial conurbation, extending well beyond its own boundaries. In addition, a number of free-standing towns, of which the largest were Paisley, Greenock, Hamilton and Motherwell, flanked it to the west and east. Substantial populations, settled in smaller communities, had also developed in the mining areas of Lanarkshire and Ayrshire (Figure 1.2).

Rapid industrialisation and growth had produced a city of contrasts. The wealth of industry existed side by side with some appalling social conditions, notably overcrowding and ill health. In 1861, after the wave of Irish immigration, no less than 63.2% of the population lived at densities of more than two persons per room. By 1921, there were still some 40% of the population living at this density (Baird, 1958). Nineteenth-century immigrants had congregated in the old parts of the city where warrens of 'back lands' (cramped dwellings) were developed in the gardens and closes of the existing tenements

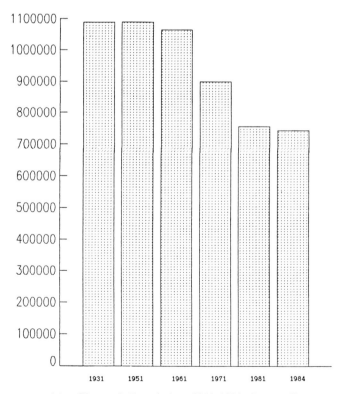

FIGURE 1.1   Glasgow's Population, 1931-1984. *Source*: Census.

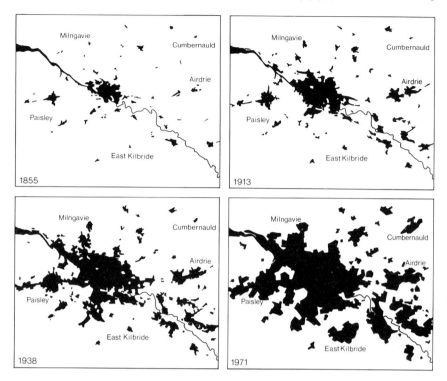

FIGURE 1.2   Growth of the Conurbation. *Source*: West Central Scotland Plan.

(Worsdall, 1979). The earliest attempts at controlling densities and over-crowding were through the 'ticketing' system whereby the city authorities posted on each house the maximum number of persons permitted to sleep there. In 1866, the City Improvement Trust was set up, its powers being transferred to the corporation (city council) in 1895. The trust's early work appears to have been more by way of demolition than rebuilding, with some of the worst areas cleared to widen streets and make new ones. Along with the slums, too, much of old Glasgow was swept away. It is a telling comment on the spirit of mid-Victorian industrialism that the ancient university, with its fine college buildings and gardens, said to be comparable to the best of Oxford and Cambridge, was demolished to make way for a railway goods yard! The university itself was moved to more spacious quarters in the developing western suburb. In another ironic twist of history, the university, finding itself hemmed in the west end during the expansionary phase of the 1960s and 1970s, was to acquire a new reputation for civic vandalism, while its younger neighbour, Strathclyde university, with an embarrassment of land in the now-depopulated city centre, was developing fast towards the site of the (now abandoned) goods yard.

The 1870s and the years between 1885 and the First World War saw the greatest boom in Glasgow tenement building, with Dalmarnock, Springburn, Govanhill and Maryhill expanding working-class housing outwards (Worsdall, 1979) and middle-class tenements springing up in Hyndland, Langside and Pollokshields. The expansion of population gave rise to a protracted series of skirmishes between the corporation of Glasgow, anxious to extend its boundaries to take in the whole built-up area, and the surrounding authorities. The General Police Acts of 1850 and 1862 had made it fairly easy for communities to accede to the status of independent burghs, with their own town councils, and by the mid nineteenth century a profusion of small burghs had sprung up around the city. A boundary extension of 1846 brought in the burghs of Calton and Anderston, most of the Barony of Gorbals and parts of the adjacent counties. After minor extensions in 1872 and 1878, a second major expansion in 1891 took in the burghs of Govanhill, Pollokshields, Pollokshields East, Hillhead and Maryhill, with the areas of Mount Florida, Shawlands, Kelvinside, Possilpark and Springburn. This followed an abortive attempt by a royal commission to extend the city to include 'the whole continuous area of which the present city is the centre.' A bill to give effect to this was rejected by the House of Lords in 1891. So it was not until 1912 that the burghs of Govan, Partick and Pollokshaws, with parts of Lanarkshire, Renfrewshire and Dunbartonshire were taken over; and even then Rutherglen managed to slip through the net. In 1926 and again in 1938 large areas of unbuilt land including Knightswood, Nitshill, Easterhouse, Drumchapel and Darnley, were taken to meet Glasgow's needs for housing and green space, doubling the geographical size of the city (Gilfillan, 1958b). The last boundary extension, in 1975, is covered in the next chapter.

The economic optimism of pre-1914 Glasgow disappeared with the postwar slump which on Clydeside continued into the 1930s depression. Unemployment peaked at 130,000 or 30% in 1932 and on the eve of the Second World War was still running at 68,000, or 15% of the insured population. Tonnage of shipping launched on the Clyde rose briefly with the need to replace war losses and new yards were even laid down in the frenetic boom of the years immediately after the First World War. In 1924, the Clyde was still producing 37% of British and nearly a quarter of world mercantile tonnage but output fell away in the 1920s and slumped to 56,000 tons in 1933, to recover slowly with rearmament in the late 1930s. Symbolically, the liner Queen Mary lay rusting at Clydebank for two years until government help enabled her to be completed in 1933. The opening of the King George V dock in 1931 did little to stimulate trade, given the condition of Glasgow's export-based industries. Locomotive manufacture was hit particularly hard by the loss of export markets and by the beginning of the 1930s one works had to be closed and at the other production was slashed (Orr and Orr, 1958). A general decline of heavy industry was accompanied by a 'drift south' of much of what remained, typified by the move of Stewart and Lloyd's steel works to Corby in the English Midlands.

Nor was Clydeside able to share in the expanding industries of the inter-

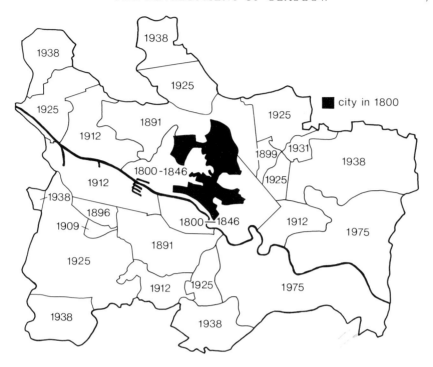

FIGURE 1.3    City Boundary Extensions. *Source*: Robin Boyle.

war period. In 1932, for example, 626 factories were opened in England and 132 closed, a net gain of 496. In Scotland, 20 were opened and 36 closed. In the following year, England's net gain was 69 and Scotland's loss 15 (Thomson, 1935). Over the period 1932-7, of 3,217 factories opened in Great Britain, only 127 were in Scotland and these were more than counterbalanced by 133 closures (Johnston, 1971). As a result, Scotland's share of British industrial production fell from 9.9% in 1924 to 8.2% in 1935 (Oakley, 1937). The car industry, after a promising start before the the First World War, failed to take root, with Argyll going to the wall in 1914 and Arrol-Johnston, having moved to Dumfries, failing in 1920. Other new industries of the 1930s, such as electrical engineering and chemicals, tended to go to the south of England while existing Scottish firms came under English control. Scott and Hughes (1980) claim that the proceeds of sales of Scottish firms were not put back into local industry but went into investment trusts which in turn placed their funds in government stock or stable companies in England or Scotland. The entrepreneurial culture of the early period had all but disappeared, with the attention of the remaining big industrialists concentrated on cartelisation, protection and monopolisation, though national protectionist policies have been criticised as particularly inappropriate for the export-oriented industries

TABLE 1.3    % OF TOTAL EMPLOYMENT IN THE WEST OF SCOTLAND

|  | 1924 | | 1930 | | 1939 | |
|---|---|---|---|---|---|---|
|  | no. | % | no. | % | no. | % |
| coalmining | 69,500 | 11.5 | 40,500 | 7.1 | 30,000 | 4.2 |
| shipbuilding, marine | | | | | | |
|    engineering | 55,500 | 9.2 | 48,500 | 8.5 | 47,500 | 6.5 |
| service industries | 178,000 | 29.6 | 200,000 | 35.1 | 274,000 | 37.8 |

Source: CVRPAC (1946).

of the Clyde (Harvie, 1981). The Second World War, with its insatiable demand for the products of heavy industry, restored full employment but again hid the underlying problems.

On the other hand, the inter-war period did see, in Glasgow as elsewhere, a major expansion of service industry. The steep rise in service employment is in sharp contrast to the slump in two of the most characteristic heavy industries (see Table 1.3).


## Politics in Glasgow

Nineteenth-century Glasgow was dominated by the Liberal Party until the split over Gladstone's Irish Home Rule Bill in the 1880s. Thereafter, sectarianism entered Glasgow politics, giving the Unionist Party (who did not change their name to Conservative until 1965) an advantage among a Protestant population largely hostile to Irish aspirations (Miller, 1985). The first Labour councillors were elected in 1898, forming an alliance with Irish councillors elected from the immigrant population and organised by the United Irish League. By 1914 there were nineteen on a council of 113 but the sectarian factor prevented Labour from mobilising its full expected vote in what has always been an overwhelmingly working-class city. A series of major industrial disputes and rent strikes during the First World War created the legend of 'Red Clydeside' and a myth about the radical bias in Glasgow politics which persisted until quite recently. A particularly vivid folk memory is of the tanks in George Square in January 1919 during the strikes called in the engineering industry to demand a forty-hour week. In left-wing circles, it is still widely believed that Glasgow at this point was on the brink of a workers' revolution. Recent scholarship has cast great doubt on this interpretation of history (McLean, 1974; 1983; Kendall, 1969). The mainspring of the industrial militancy during the war was in fact protest by the skilled industrial workers against 'dilution', the bringing in of unskilled men and women during the wartime labour shortage. McLean (1983) also points out that the leaders of Red Clydeside were overwhelmingly Protestant, fired by visions of the seventeenth-century Covenanters, with little involvement by the Irish Catholic element in Glasgow, given that Catholics were effectively barred from apprenticeships in the skilled trades. Revolutionary rhetoric was widely employed but the number of real revolutionaries was small and these were often middle-class professionals like the legendary John Maclean, an enduring hero of the Scottish left but whose achievements in life were few. As for the incident of the tanks in George Square, the place of this in 'the heroic annals of the labour movement can be attributed jointly to police misconduct on 31 January and to the Government's exaggerated and panicky reaction to the strike as it developed' (McLean, 1983, p.120). Red Clydeside, according to the revisionist view of history, was an invention of over-optimimistic revolutionaries and an alarmist government. Myths, though, can be powerful forces in politics and the myth of Red Clydeside was to influence the view of Glasgow of a wide variety of people in the years to follow.

Labour's electoral advance in the city did not start in earnest until after 1920, when the Irish political machines, after a period in which they had reserved the right to endorse whichever candidate promised strongest support for Irish Home Rule, joined the Labour camp. As the Irish population was overwhelmingly working class, this might appear a natural development, but both divisions within the working class between the skilled and the unskilled workers and the wider considerations of the Irish had posed major obstacles. The settlement of the Irish question by the 1920 Treaty was a key element in permitting the new alignment, as was Labour's downplaying of the prohibition question. In 1920 Labour's Scottish conference had voted for prohibition. The local elections that year were held together with local veto polls which allowed local prohibition under an act of 1913. With the public house playing a central role in the Irish community but Labour candidates pledged to 'no licence' policies, it is not surprising that 'wet Irish' candidates had some success against Labour (McLean, 1983). Thereafter, Labour kept quiet on the issue.

The other factor bringing in the Irish was the Education (Scotland) Act of 1918 which gave Catholics in Scotland their own schools, paid for and maintained by the elected local school boards. In alliance with Labour, the Irish could control the boards and safeguard Catholic schools. Labour, for its part, had to agree to maintain the separate Catholic school system, despite the misgivings of some of its Protestant or secularist leaders. By 1921, the Labour-Irish alliance was cemented and the Irish press was advising its readers to back Labour candidates. At the same time, Labour was making considerable political mileage out of the housing issue, calling for the continuation of war-time rent controls. In 1922, the first fruits of all this were apparent, with the election of 10 Labour MPs out of 15, against just one in 1918 (Labour's share of the vote went up from 32% to 43%). These included a number of the famous 'Clydesiders', such as Jimmie Maxton, John Wheatley, Campbell Stephen, Neil Maclean and John McGovern, who were to make a dramatic impact on their arrival at Westminster but whose long-term influence, with the exception of Wheatley, was to be slight.

The long-term effects of the manner of Labour's rise in Glasgow were to be profound. While the myth of Red Clydeside persisted and grew, the reality of Labour politics was very different. The Irish had brought to Labour the benefits of a well-organised political machine and machine politics were to remain an important element in the life of the city for decades to come. At the same time the Irish connection was the cause of some tension within the party. Scotland is the only European country in which the Catholic vote goes overwhelmingly to an ostensibly left-wing party and conflicts between conservative Catholic social doctrines and the liberal and secular views of many Labour activists have been frequent. They have surfaced in the 1970s and 1980s over the abortion issue. There were even tensions over the issue of the Spanish civil war, with the left supporting the republican government but the Catholic element worried about its anti-clericalism and swayed by the Church's support for Franco's rebellion. So Labour in Glasgow, in its years of dominance was not to be the revolutionary force envisaged by the perpetuators of the Red Clydeside myth but, on the contrary, a rather conservative influence. Another legacy of these years is identified by McLean (1983) as the deep concern with low-rent housing, a concern which was to inform the city's housing policies with some disastrous consequences in the years to come.

While Labour gained a majority of Glasgow's parliamentary seats in 1922, it was not until 1933 that it first won control of the corporation. Indeed, of major British cities, only in Birmingham and Liverpool did it have to wait longer to gain power. This has been attributed (McLean, 1983) partly to the Irish effect. As school boards were not taken over by the corporation until 1929, the Irish machines had less motive to mobilise votes in corporation than in school board and parliamentary contests. Turnout levels are in any case always lower at local elections, with differential voting favouring middle-class interests. The anti-Labour coalition at local level went wider than the Conservative Party which was its principal opponent at parliamentary elections with Moderates (later called Progressives) drawing in Conservatives, Liberals, anti-Irish forces and some independent and business interests. Organisation was loose and candidatures decided on by a committee of existing councillors; candidates paid their own expenses and organised their own campaigns. Working-class Protestant voters were wary of Labour's association with Catholic Irish interests and a substantial working-class 'Orange' vote supported the Conservatives until very recently. In 1931 and 1932, a short-lived Scottish Protestant League split the working-class vote, though in 1933—taking a quarter of the vote—they did more damage to the Moderates, allowing Labour to take control of the corporation. Despite the sectarian undertones of much of Glasgow politics, however, the influence of the religious factor was in the long run less than in Liverpool or Edinburgh, let alone Belfast. Protestant extremists received no sympathy from the Unionists or right-wing councillors, who saw in sectarian politics as much of a threat to themselves as to the Labour Party. Nevertheless, the Orange vote continued to prevent Labour occupying the whole of its expected class constituency for many years.

Since 1933, Labour has consolidated its hold on Glasgow. At the general election of 1945, Labour won 55.8% of the vote, reflecting its national triumph, but the Conservatives were able to recover almost to equal the Labour vote in 1955. This brought them seven out of the fifteen parliamentary seats, a success not to be repeated. In 1959, against the national trend, the Conservatives lost support in Glasgow and commenced a steady decline which was to leave them with no parliamentary seats at all by 1981. Labour climbed steadily to 60.3% of the vote in 1966 and, when they began to falter, it was the smaller parties, the Scottish National Party and Liberal/Social Democratic Party Alliance who were to benefit (Table 1.7).

In local politics, Labour formed the administration—that is, they were the ruling party, taking the chairs of the committees—in the corporation for the entire period between 1933 and the reorganisation of local government in 1975 except for 1948-51 and 1968-71 when the reaction against Labour governments nationally led to heavy losses. Folk legends continued to maintain the picture of Glasgow as a very left-wing city. This was distinctly misleading. Labour's high level of electoral support went along with a low membership and an organisation which at times was quite moribund. Its increasing vote must be attributed to demographic change (the migration of the middle classes) together with the gradual decline of the religious factor, although the latter continued to affect politics up to the 1970s. A strong correlation was established between religion and voting in Scotland at the 1959 General Election and in surveys of the Glasgow divisions of Cathcart and Govanhill in 1964 (Budge and Urwin, 1966). Indeed, in Govanhill, religion completely displaced class as the determinant of voting behaviour while in local elections in the ward the same effect was observed. Brand (1968) and Budge, Brand et al. (1972), too, found a strong correlation between religion and voting in Glasgow. Middle-class Protestants divided 60-22 between Conservative and Labour, while for middle-class Catholics the proportions were almost exactly reversed, at 23-61. Among all categories of the working class there was majority support for Labour but in the case of the Catholics the proportions were 78-6, while among the Protestants they were just 52-33 (others were Liberals, independents etc.). The effect, however, diminished among the younger age groups, indicating that the religious factor was dying out. The result of this is that Labour was able, without any undue effort on its own part, to occupy more of its 'natural' constituency among a working class which was itself becoming more preponderant in the city's population.

In the areas of the city where Labour was best established (the older working-class areas), political 'machines' had developed with local bosses able to control council nominations and, to some extent, other forms of patronage (jobs in council departments for teachers and manual workers, trade union positions). In the large council-owned estates developed around the edge of the city in the 1950s, 1960s and 1970s—the 'peripheral schemes' whose growth is discussed below—political activity of all sorts was weak and party organisation very thin on the ground. The Glasgow 'machines' do not compare with the scale of operations of bosses in North American cities in the late nineteenth and early twentieth centuries but it was a type of politics which put little emphasis on active participation and a great deal on party and personal loyalty. The basic unit of organisation was the parliamentary constituency, whose committee was made up of delegates from ward branches, trade unions and a small number of affiliated bodies like the Fabian Society. There was also a city party for the whole of Glasgow, comprising delegates from constituencies and trade unions (the structure has changed somewhat since 1975, as we shall see in chapter 3). Party membership figures for this period are impossible to gauge accurately because of a rule requiring local constituency parties to affiliate to the national party on the basis of a minimum of 1,000, whatever the real membership. The effect was that some constituencies rarely managed to raise the necessary fee while those that did were credited with 1,000 members. Certainly, no constituency in Glasgow could produce anything like this number of real flesh-and-blood members, with the exception of Cathcart which made membership of the licensed Labour club in the otherwise almost entirely 'dry' Castlemilk estate conditional on the purchase of a party card (neighbouring constituencies with strong temperance traditions gratefully accepted the fraternal cheques sent by the Cathcart party at election time). Frequently, constituency parties were unable to pay their national affiliation fees (for the notional 1,000 members) and so were unable to send a delegate to the annual national conference. Indeed, at one point, Labour's national executive committee stepped in to suspend the City Labour Party (covering the whole of Glasgow).

Glasgow's politics were remarkably inward-looking. Its civic leaders made no impact nationally or within the Labour Party as a whole and its members of Parliament followed the same mode. Of 28 Labour MPs elected in the city 1945- 70, just three gained ministerial office in twelve years of Labour government, none at Cabinet level (Keating, 1975). Indeed, in the whole of the post-war period, Glasgow has produced just one Cabinet Minister, a Secretary of State for Scotland, an extraordinary under-achievement for a major city. The recruitment cycle played an important role here. Glasgow's Labour MPs have usually been selected from the ranks of local councillors— not the council leaders who have preferred to stay at home, but the long-serving backbenchers. Their average age is higher on first election than that of MPs as a whole. One MP elected in 1945 at the age of 55 went on for 28 years while the candidate for the bye-election caused by his death in office was a 59 year old councillor—he lost the bye-election but came back in the subsequent general election. In the case of another Glasgow parliamentarian of the 1950s, a comprehensive scrutiny of *Hansard* in the course of another research project failed to reveal a single parliamentary intervention during his 14 years in the Commons—he had, prior to his election at the age of 61, spent no less than 30 years on Glasgow corporation (Keating, 1975).

The ideology of the Labour Party on Glasgow corporation can best be summed up as 'municipal labourism', a concern with a limited range of policy issues with an immediate impact on their constituents—notably housing matters—but little consideration of wider policy issues. Municipal ownership and control of major services was often seen as an end in itself, making questions about the control and use of the services irrelevant. The eternal verities of Labour politics—nationalisation, 'Clause 4' and the welfare state—were taken for granted but their contemporary meaning rarely debated. Allied with this was a moralism born both of Catholic and Calvinist influences most clearly seen in the liquor question. Temperance had been an important influence in the early Scottish labour movement as well as the radical wing of the Liberal Party, with a substantial prohibitionist wing developing. In 1890, a Corporation resolution barred the sale of alcohol on council property, a ban which affected not only municipal entertainment halls but virtually the whole of the peripheral housing estates where the council owned almost everything. Although the prohibition policy had been toned down to avoid alienating the Irish vote, the local veto polls introduced after the First World War allowed local prohibition by polling districts. With large areas of the city thus 'dry', the borders of the 'wet' areas (such as Shawlands, the east side of Rutherglen or the city centre) attracted large numbers of pubs, most of an extremely low standard (and often all-male), with a tide of population flowing to them during the restricted opening hours then permitted under Scottish law. The view that drink was sinful and to be taken, if at all, in dingy, unlit bars was a reaction to the drunkenness of nineteenth-century Glasgow but served only to perpetuate the social habits which it attacked while the patronising view that alcohol should not be available in the working-class estates betrayed a lack of confidence in the socialist ideal that, with better living conditions, people would be able to handle liquor in a sociable and civilised manner.

In short, Glasgow Labour was neither on the radical left nor on the revisionist right of Labour politics in the 1950s and 1960s. Indeed, the 1966 survey by Brand *et al.* (1968) shows—in contrast to our findings twenty years later—that most councillors in these years came into political activity and stood for office as a result of local group influences and contacts rather than because of an ideological motivation. Such an 'apolitical' group could contribute very little to the battles over policies and programmes within the Labour Party in this period. This system was maintained not only by Labour's demographic advantages but also by the lack of effective political competition over much of the post-war period. After their success in the late 1940s, the Progressives lapsed in the 1950s. In the mid 1950s, the Scottish National Party (SNP) made a big effort with 27 candidates in 1957, but to no effect. On the left, the Independent Labour Party had been fatally weakened by the decision of its remaining members of Parliament in the late 1940s to rejoin the Labour Party, while the Communists, though wielding some influence in the trade unions, the Trades Council and the Scottish Trades Union Congress, made no headway in electoral politics. Nor did smaller groups like the Social Credit Party or the Modern Labour Party which sprang up in the early 1960s fare any better.

Labour's hegemony was vulnerable, though, to any group which could establish an electoral machine of sorts and present a credible, non-Conservative challenge. In 1968, a considerable dent was made by the Scottish National Party (SNP), capitalising not only on the unpopularity of the Labour government in London but also on local grievances, including the disruption of the redevelopment programme, the management of council housing and corruption scandals (like most of Glasgow's corruption scandals, these were on a rather unimposing scale) in the corporation. Twelve Scottish Nationalists were elected to the corporation in 1968 and the resulting 'shake-out' of the Labour group removed some of the major figures of the older generation and was an important factor in bringing in younger councillors, less committed to the old policies and old style of governing, when Labour started to recover the lost seats in the early 1970s. As for the Scottish Nationalists, many were inexperienced in local affairs and their party had never worked out a strategy for local government. Indeed, there was some uncertainty within the SNP as to why they should be contesting local elections at all, given their strategic aim of achieving independence for Scotland through Parliament. None of them succeeded in being re-elected and the SNP disappeared from Glasgow municipal government, to make a brief reappearance in the late 1970s. On the right, the Progressives continued to be the main force until the late 1960s, forming a minority administration dependent on the SNP in 1968. It was in the late 1960s that the Scottish Conservatives, following a reorganisation of party structure, decided to contest local elections under the party label. Progressives were given the choice of joining the Conservative group on the

TABLE 1.4    SEATS WON, GLASGOW CITY COUNCIL, 1949-73

|      | Labour | Progressive | Conservative | SNP | Other |
|------|--------|-------------|--------------|-----|-------|
| 1949 | 19 | 18 | — | — | — |
| 1950 | 18 | 19 | — | — | — |
| 1951 | 17 | 20 | — | — | — |
| 1952 | 27 | 10 | — | — | — |
| 1953 | 23 | 14 | — | — | — |
| 1954 | 23 | 14 | — | — | — |
| 1955 | 22 | 15 | — | — | — |
| 1956 | 23 | 14 | — | — | — |
| 1957 | 23 | 14 | — | — | — |
| 1958 | 23 | 14 | — | — | — |
| 1959 | 23 | 14 | — | — | — |
| 1960 | 21 | 16 | — | — | — |
| 1961 | 23 | 14 | — | — | — |
| 1962 | 25 | 12 | — | — | — |
| 1963 | 22 | 15 | — | — | 1 |
| 1964 | 23 | 14 | — | — | — |
| 1965 | 18 | 19 | — | — | — |
| 1966 | 18 | 19 | — | — | — |
| 1967 | 19 | 17 | 1 | — | — |
| 1968 | 6 | 16 | 2 | 12 | — |
| 1969 | 14 | 15 | 7 | 1 | — |
| 1970 | 22 | 8 | 7 | — | — |
| 1971 | 29 | 4 | 4 | — | — |
| 1972 | 28 | — | 9 | — | — |
| 1973 | 26 | — | 11 | — | — |

Source: Miller (1985); Craig (1984).

TABLE 1.5    PARTY % OF TOTAL VOTE AT PARLIAMENTARY ELECTIONS, GLASGOW

|  | Conservative & allies | Labour & ILP | Liberals & Social Dem. | SNP | Other |
|---|---|---|---|---|---|
| 1918 | 62.7 | 31.8 | 6.1 | — | — |
| 1922 | 30.4 | 42.9 | 25.3 | — | — |
| 1923 | 34.0 | 48.1 | 14.8 | — | 2.8 |
| 1924 | 48.5 | 48.5 | 2.7 | — | — |
| 1929 | 43.4 | 52.9 | 3.2 | — | — |
| 1931 | 56.2 | 41.2 | — | — | 2.4 |
| 1935 | 45.9 | 53.8 | 0.2 | — | — |
| 1945 | 42.5 | 55.8 | 1.0 | — | 0.5 |
| 1950 | 44.2 | 51.9 | 3.0 | — | 0.4 |
| 1951 | 48.8 | 51.2 | — | — | — |
| 1955 | 48.1 | 51.6 | — | — | — |
| 1959 | 45.1 | 52.5 | 0.5 | — | 1.6 |
| 1964 | 38.6 | 58.7 | 1.5 | 0.8 | 1.0 |
| 1966 | 34.6 | 60.3 | — | 3.2 | 1.5 |
| 1970 | 35.8 | 55.5 | — | 7.6 | 1.1 |
| 1974F | 30.6 | 47.6 | 0.4 | 20.6 | 0.7 |
| 1974O | 20.2 | 49.0 | 4.2 | 26.3 | 0.3 |
| 1979 | 26.7 | 57.4 | 4.1 | 11.1 | 0.7 |
| 1983 | 18.8 | 52.0 | 21.0 | 7.6 | 0.6 |
| 1987 | 12.5 | 62.5 | 15.0 | 10.0 | 0.3 |

TABLE 1.6    PARLIAMENTARY SEATS, GLASGOW

|  | Conservative & allies | Labour & ILP | Liberals & Social Democrats |
|---|---|---|---|
| 1918 | 14 | 1 | — |
| 1922 | 5 | 10 | — |
| 1924 | 7 | 8 | — |
| 1929 | 5 | 10 | — |
| 1931 | 10 | 5 | — |
| 1935 | 6 | 9 | — |
| 1945 | 5 | 10 | — |
| 1950 | 7 | 8 | — |
| 1951 | 7 | 8 | — |
| 1955 | 7 | 8 | — |
| 1959 | 5 | 10 | — |
| 1964 | 2 | 13 | — |
| 1966 | 2 | 13 | — |
| 1970 | 2 | 13 | — |
| 1974F | 2 | 11 | — |
| 1974O | 2 | 11 | — |
| 1979 | 1 | 12 | — |
| 1983 | 0 | 10 | 1 |
| 1987 | 0 | 11 | — |

council and standing as Conservatives or facing a Conservative opponent at the next election. Most of them opted to join the party, though a few left local policies altogether and by 1972 there were no Progressives standing for the council. Table 1.4 gives the results of the local elections between 1949, when new boundaries were established, and 1973, the last elections for the old corporation before local government reform. There were three councillors per ward, with one coming up for election every three years, so that changes in control could take more than one year to effect.

## The Postwar Economy

The Second World War, like the First, stimulated demand for the heavy industries of the Clyde, a demand which persisted into the 1950s as continental competitors sought to rebuild their war-torn economies. In the long post-war expansion, Glasgow's unemployment remained at historically very low levels, a sharp contrast to the 1930s experience. Only at the end of the 1950s did economic development again become a major priority and the question of Glasgow's industrial structure come under the spotlight. The debate over whether it was the specialisation in heavy industrial sectors or other factors which were at the root of sluggish growth rates for the older industrial areas then resumed. By 1958, Cairncross (1958, p.229) pinpointed the problem;

> This preponderance of heavy industry would be of little significance if the heavy industries were still themselves in the course of expansion; and it is the fact that those industries have had long order books since the war that had accounted for the revival of industry on Clydeside much more than the arrival of new firms and industries. The fact appears to be, however, that the older heavy industries are likely to play, in the world of the future, a much less important role than they did in the nineteenth century; an area specialising in those industries must adapt its industrial pattern in line with this long-run trend or run the risk of participation in the general stagnation or decline.

This sort of concern had been expressed immediately after the war and inspired some of the planning proposals aimed at preventing a return to the 1930s. In terms of practical activity, however, the economic problem for a while took second place, while attention was focused on physical planning and, above all, a solution to Glasgow's appalling housing conditions.

## Planning and the Housing Crisis

Inter-war Glasgow had seen a drift of population to England and overseas and, especially in the 1930s, some movement from the city to the surrounding suburbs and smaller towns. This latter development was on a smaller scale than in most English cities and, with a high natural rate of population growth, Glasgow's overall population had remained stable. Housing renewal failed even to keep up with rising official standards. The 1921 Royal Commission on Housing in Scotland had found that, defining overcrowded as more than three persons per room, 17.7% of all Glasgow houses were overcrowded. On the more generous English standard of more than two persons per room, the figure would be 39.4% (Baird, 1958). The Housing (Scotland) Act of 1935 laid down new standards of acceptable densities as follows:

| 1 room | 2 adults |
|---|---|
| 2 rooms | 3 adults |
| 3 rooms | 5 adults |
| 4 rooms | 7.5 adults |
| 5+ rooms | 10 adults |

Each child between one and ten years was to count as half an adult. Using this standard, a survey found that half of all houses in the central area were overcrowded. In 1944, the Scottish Housing Advisory Committee again raised recommended standards. With all children counting as individuals, the tolerable densities were:

| 1 room | 0 persons |
|---|---|
| 2 rooms | 2 persons |
| 3 rooms | 4 persons |
| 5 rooms | 8 persons |

Each house should have a living room not used for sleeping purposes. On this standard, using the 1931 census, 59.9% of all houses were overcrowded. Reworking the figures with the 1951 census, Baird (1958) shows that, in that year, 44.2% of all houses were still overcrowded. Pre-war boundary extensions, taking in unbuilt land, gave a misleading impression of densities for the city as a whole but in the central area, in 1945, some 700,000 people lived on 1,800 acres at an average gross density of 400 persons per acre. In some areas, densities were as high as 700 per acre, with one-seventh of Scotland's population compressed into three square miles (Robertson, 1958).

Some progress had been made in the inter-war years but, while in much of England the 1930s had seen a private house-building boom, in Glasgow most of the work had been undertaken by the corporation (the council) which had built some 50,000 houses under a series of legislative provisions starting in 1918. Inspired by the 'garden suburb' ideal, the earlier developments—such as Knightswood and Mosspark (1921-3)—consisted of semi-detached houses with gardens, a deliberate break with the tenement tradition, but later cost restrictions led to a cheap form of tenement building for the remainder of the 1920s and 1930s. Such schemes as Blackhill and Calton (1933-38) were associated with slum clearance under a 1935 Act and attracted a social stigma from the outset (Butt, 1983).

By 1945, the existence of a housing crisis in Glasgow was universally accepted; there was a need for more houses, for a reduction in city centre densities and for an improvement in standards. There was not, however, a consensus on the solution, despite a series of plans and proposals. The main dispute was over whether Glasgow could accomodate its redevelopment programme within its existing municipal boundaries. Largely for reasons of muncipal pride, the corporation instinctively tended to the view that this could be done. On the other hand, the predominant view of the British planning profession at this time was that urban densities should be reduced and city sprawl controlled by 'green belts' of unbuilt land, with surplus populations being taken beyond the green belt and accommodated in self-contained new towns. In Glasgow, the issue hinged on the densities at which redevelopment could or should be achieved and on the use of the land around the edge of the city brought within the boundary by the inter-war extensions which might form part of the green belt. First in the field was the report of the Clyde Valley Regional Planning Advisory Committee (CVRPAC, 1946) set up during the war by the Secretary of State for Scotland and bringing together eighteen local authorities in the region with representatives of central government. CVRPAC's report boldly asserted the need for regional planning to guide the necessary reconstruction. Of the conurbation, it stated:

> Here, at the hub of the region, the problems of urban plannings (sic) are focused and exaggerated. Here, in an incredibly small area, some 15 miles by 10 miles, live and work more than two million people, crowded together at densities hardly touched elsewhere in Great Britain. It is here that in the past the industrial enterprise of Scotland reached its maximum output (it is doubtful whether ever again employment can be found for such numbers in this Region) and six generations of immigrants have flooded the land to saturation point. Physically, the cycle has been rapid—growth, stagnation and decay: the blight of unplanned industrialisation has swept over the area; whole districts are obsolescent and past the possibility of reconstruction to modern standards, alike for industry, commerce and housing; not only are the buildings out of date, the whole con-structional arrangement of many of these areas, frequently thrown together in haste, added to piecemeal again and again, is so inadequate to meet the needs of modern life that large-scale surgical treatment is now, belatedly, recognised to be the only possible solution. Civic pride, so conspicuous in other directions, has lamentably failed to maintain even a tolerable standard of town planning (CVRPAC p.159).

What was needed was a regional plan by a planning authority encom-passing the conurbation and surrounding countryside. Urban growth should be limited by a green belt around Glasgow and the other towns and urban densities reduced by 'overspill' of population to new towns and communities beyond it. Over half a million people would have to be moved in Glasgow, to reduce densities and permit rebuilding of the slums, with substantial numbers for the other Clydeside towns as shown in Table 1.7.

The smaller towns should be allowed to expand away from Glasgow, preserving the green belt and preventing them becoming part of a continuous urban sprawl. Glasgow could not, itself, do this and, as it could accommodate

TABLE 1.7    ESTIMATED DECENTRALISATION OF POPULATION FROM REDEVEL-
OPMENT AREAS

|  | 1946 population | population to be decentralised |
|---|---|---|
| Glasgow | 1,127,948 | 550,000 |
| Airdrie | 27,860 | 3,500 |
| Clydebank | 47,912 | 17,500 |
| Coatbridge | 45,045 | 10,000 |
| Dumbarton | 22,214 | 10,000 |
| Greenock | 81,297 | 39,000 |
| Hamilton | 39,305 | 11,000 |
| Motherwell & Wishaw | 67,693 | 11,000 |
| Paisley | 91,167 | 28,500 |
| Port Glasgow | 19,785 | 9,500 |
| Rutherglen | 25,441 | 9,000 |
| Barhead | 12,265 | 6,000 |
| Johnstone | 13,882 | 4,000 |
| Milngavie | 6,400 | nil |
| Renfrew | 16,509 | 7,000 |

Source: Clyde Valley Regional Planning Advisory Committee, *The Clyde Valley Regional Plan* (Edinburgh: HMSO, 1946).

only some 250,000 of the 550,000 at acceptable densities within its boundaries on new and redeveloped land, would have to disperse its surplus population further afield. The topography of the Clyde valley limited the scope for such new developments, with the Campsie Hills to the north, boggy moorland to the south and the built-up areas of Paisley to the west and Motherwell and Hamilton to the south-east. Four new town sites were identified, at Cumbernauld to the north-east, East Kilbride to the south and Bishopton and Houston, close together between Paisley and Greenock to the west. These, with some expansion of the existing small towns in the region, could accommodate some 200,000 people, leaving 100,000 to be dispersed away from Clydeside altogether.

It was not only population which CVRPAC wanted to disperse. Industry would have to go as well to reduce industrial congestion, allow modernisation and re-equipment on proper sites and provide jobs for the dispersed population. To this end, industrial incentives should not merely encourage industry to move to the areas of highest unemployment; they should be part of a planned movement of industry to accompany population dispersal while taking account of natural industrial relocation (for example, the shift of coalmining from the west to the east of Scotland). One massive piece of industrial relocation was specifically recommended. The iron and steel industry of Lanarkshire, which had grown up around the now exhaused coal and iron ore deposits, should be shifted to a new site on the Clyde near Erskine, where its need for imported materials could more easily be accommodated.

On the other hand, Glasgow's future as a major port and centre of ship-building was confirmed. Other recommendations concerned railway elec-trification, the coordination of public transport and the building of a motor-way system.

This philosophy proved anathema to the corporation (city council) of Glasgow and, when, in 1947, the first new town was duly designated at East Kilbride, it was in the teeth of opposition from the city. CVRPAC collapsed shortly afterwards, when Glasgow withdrew. Glasgow's objections to the exercise were based partly on suspicion of the notion of regional planning as an encroachment on its municipal independence but focused specifically on the proposals for overspill and the consequent loss not only of industry and rateable value (the local tax base) but of the cherished status of 'second city of the British Empire.' By a resolution of 1946, the corporation declared its belief that the whole of its redevelopment programme could be accom-modated within its own boundaries, though this would mean building at high densities and in areas designated in the Clyde Valley Plan as green belt.

Glasgow's own planning scheme, however, was to have an inauspicious start in the First Planning Report by the city engineer, Robert Bruce. Reflect-ing the professional bias of its author, this extraordinary document was dominated almost exclusively by engineering considerations. The entire cen-tral area of the city was to be rebuilt within a system of urban motorways and expressways, sweeping away commercial and residential buildings, the main railway terminals and the 'outdated' city chambers (a magnificent nine-teenth-century building). Obsessively tidy-minded, the report wanted to seg-regate land uses, divide the city into 'communities' bounded by main roads and sweep away everything that was old. A vision is given of the traveller who, arriving at the new railway terminal, will not, as now, be 'debouched into a maze of uncoordinated streets flanked with closely-packed buildings' but will instead be greeted by the open sweep of the new civic centre and the modern office buildings. Even multi-storey car parks appealed to the author's modernistic aesthetic sense:

> with regard to the type of off-street parking structures erected in America, some are very simple and consist only of a ground floor, first floor, and second floor, without containing walls, and having no roof. The appearance of these structures, which are constructed in reinforced concrete, is not displeasing (Bruce, 1946, p.34).

Further changes would be needed if the helicopter were to develop as a major means of urban transport or, indeed, 'a vehicle combining the properties of the motor car and aeroplane' became practicable, for then buildings would have to be designed with flat, reinforced roofs, with height restrictions. Public transport should be provided by frequent electric train services on existing lines and on new lines built along the central reservations of the new highways, with complicated systems of flyovers and elevated roundabouts at stations and interchanges.

The new city would be cleaner, safer, more efficient, with all the require-ments of modern living but there was one group for whom it had no place—

the poor. 31% of the inner core was occupied by residential accommodation, for 75,000 people. As Bruce put it:

> Unfortunately, most of the residential property is of an aged character, the people dwelling in the bulk of the residential buildings being there by virtue of the low rental which pertains to such buildings. If the new city centre is to be developed satisfactorily, then it would appear to be necessary that it be given an improved character throughout its area. This cannot be done if the domestic buildings which are to be provided are to house persons whose means are insufficient to enable them to pay rents appropriate to the nature of such build-ings . . . it would appear desirable that the new forms of residential development which may be raised in the inner core of the city should be of such a standard as to secure their occupancy by persons fitted to pay relatively high rentals (Bruce, 1946, p.49).

Such a strategy would also remove the anomaly that 'poor people live on dear land' (Bruce, 1946, p.50). For the privileged residents of the new city centre, on the other hand, there would be the advantages of modern housing, open space and safety, clean air, new roads, electrified railways and reduced travel time to work.

For the displaced masses, there was only one solution. They would have to be accommodated in high density developments around the periphery of the city, building in tenement style and using land acquired in the pre-war boundary extensions which CVRPAC had recommended as green belt. If this were done, Bruce was adamant that Glasgow could solve its housing problems within its own boundaries and that overspill was unnecessary and undesirable. Specifically, there was a disagreement with CVRPAC about fourteen sites, including 921 acres at Drumchapel where the Corporation had declared that it wanted to build 7,882 houses and 1,153 acres at Castlemilk, where it wanted to build 6,500 houses (these were later to develop into two of the largest peripheral schemes).

So the strategic choice was clear. There was the CVRPAC strategy of low-density redevelopment, preservation of the green belt around the city and overspill of surplus populations to self-contained new towns at some distance; and there was the Bruce philosophy of high density redevelopment right up to the boundary. There was indeed considerable debate over these alternatives, a debate which continues in academic and professional circles to this day; but, as we shall see, the decisions which in practice were made often represented short-term responses to the pressures of the moment rather than any strategic vision. It is arguable that, as a result, Glasgow got the worst of both worlds. On its publication, the Bruce plan aroused considerable opposition from business interests concerned at the cost and disruption proposed, though little of the left-wing protest which one would expect nowadays. Most members of the corporation appear not to have held fixed views on the matter, though it soon became clear that the general scheme was financially unrealistic. It did, however, leave its mark on Glasgow's planning policies. The city's development plan, statutorily required under post-war legislation, dropped major elements of the Bruce plan and Bruce himself resigned in 1951. It did, however, incorporate the major highway proposals and a scaled-down version of the ambitious plans for building within the city, listing sites for 35,717 new corporation houses, 7,600 private houses and 6,559 houses in redevelopment areas. In 1952, a reorganisation brought all architectural and planning functions together under the new city architect, A G Jury, who proceeded to produce a report demonstrating the need for 135,000 new houses, 100,000 for the people on the waiting list and 35,000 for those displaced by redevelopment (Brennan, 1959). These would be separate houses in an open environment, not tenement flats. It was clear, particularly in view of central government restrictions on building in the green belt, that this could only be achieved by overspill and, under considerable pressure from the Scottish Office, the corporation came round, even accepting the designation of a second new town at Cumbernauld (Carter and Keating, 1986). The final version of the development plan, completed in 1954 after a public enquiry and modifications by central government, accepted the green belt philosophy and provided only for 21,000 corporation and 3,500 private houses on new sites, plus 5,138 on redeveloped sites. So over 100,000 new houses would be required elsewhere. In 1954, the corporation, to permit the development of Cumbernauld, repealed the 1946 resolution committing itself to rebuilding entirely within its boundaries, accepted that only 40% of its needs could be so met and after new legislation in 1957 it set about a vigorous overspill scheme for population and industry. By 1959, a scheme was in place to help employers who wished to move out of the city to dispose of their premises and recruit workers willing to join the overspill schemes (Glasgow, 1959). In due course, overspill arrangements were negotiated with over 60 local authorities in addition to the arrangements with East Kilbride, Cumbernauld, Glenrothes, and Livingston new towns.

So it appeared that the advocates of dispersal had won. The estimates of the extra houses which could be built within the city had been reduced from 73,000 to 30,000. Yet, by 1959, no less than 45,000 had been so provided (Brennan, 1959) and building in the periphery was still continuing. So the policy as incorporated in the development plan was not effective in preventing piecemeal erosion of the green belt. In the late 1940s, the Secretary of State had reversed his predecessor's decision and allowed a major development at Castlemilk, despite its proximity to East Kilbride new town, leaving only a mile or so of green belt and threatening to merge the new town with the city sprawl, and in the early 1950s permission was given to proceed with another scheme at Drumchapel. The reason was the sheer pressure to provide housing units irrespective of wider considerations and at the lowest cost, together with slow progress of the overspill programme. A natural growth of the region's population of 400,000 between 1951 and 1971 (Smith and Farmer, 1985) against the Clyde Valley plan's prediction of a stagnant population, offset the flow from emigration. Other factors pushing up the estimates of the numbers of new houses needed were changes in household size and the establishment of new households with the post-war 'baby boom', the growing awareness of the problem of 'sub-tolerable' property and the redevelopment of the inner city.

The 1954 development plan first confronted the problem of the renewal of the urban slums, selecting three redevelopment areas in the city. Subsequently, this was raised to 29 neighbourhoods, designated as comprehensive development areas, in which everything would be demolished and rebuilt, including the road layout. 100,000 houses, a third of the city's stock and half of all property not already owned by the corporation, would be demolished after compulsory purchase, to be replaced by municipal housing. In 1957 the first such scheme was approved for Gorbals-Hutchesonstown, at £13 million the largest such development so far in the United Kingdom. Everything was to be demolished and the population reduced from 26,000 to just 10,000. Half the new houses were to be in ten-storey blocks and the rest in four-storey blocks, to an award-winning design. Shops were to be reduced from 444 to 57 in line with corporation policy, public houses from 46 to 9 and industry was to move out altogether. The Saltire Society's citation on granting its award to the first phase of this scheme described it as 'probably the most striking of all local authority housing completed in Glasgow in 1958, both as a symbol of the new Glasgow and by contrast with its appalling surroundings. Here is new life growing out of the slums of the worst crowded city in Western Europe' (Glasgow, 1960). The subsequent disastrous history of this development is covered in chapter 5.

By the 1960 quinquennial review of the development plan, the housing waiting list was still over 100,000 and land in the city was fast running out. This was despite the fact that land on the periphery originally zoned as green belt had been built on and that recent schemes, both there and in the central redevelopment areas, had been built to much higher densities than originally envisaged. In the peripheral schemes, densities of up to 100 persons per acre, 40% higher than those recommended in the 1940s, had been attained (Smith and Farmer, 1985). This was achieved by a return to tenement flats as against cottage-type buildings.

The only parcels of land left, apart from the comprehensive development areas, were at Sumerston and Darnley, together with the fringes of the rest of the periphery and the Secretary of State's permission was to be sought to build on these. In the following ten years, some 41,000 houses were erected on these sites, at ever higher densities. With initial encouragement from central government, the corporation moved beyond tenement building to

TABLE 1.8    % OF TYPES OF MUNICIPAL HOUSE BUILT

|         | Flats | Cottages | Temporary Houses |
|---------|-------|----------|------------------|
| 1920-29 | 29.48 | 68.84    | 1.68             |
| 1930-39 | 68.24 | 31.76    | —                |
| 1940-49 | 21.42 | 63.09    | 15.49            |
| 1950-59 | 86.03 | 19.37    | —                |

Source: Corporation of Glasgow, *First Quinquennial Review of the Development Plan. Survey Report* (1960).

tower blocks, including the Red Road flats, at 36 storeys the highest in Europe. While originally, these had been intended only for city centre sites, by the late 1960s high-rise building had been extended to the peripheral schemes at densities of almost 200 per acre (Smith and Farmer, 1985). By the end of the 1970s, there were 321 tower blocks in the city (Gibb, 1983).

Yet by 1970 a housing review (Glasgow-SDD, 1970) found that there was *still* a need for 100,000 houses, though the population estimate for 1981 had now been revised down to 800,000. The overspill arrangements with other local authorities had produced disappointing results, with only 33 being implemented, for a total of 4,000 houses. The new towns had provided more, at 9,600, while the Scottish Special Housing Association had built 5,400 houses for Glasgow overspill families. Nor had the overspill programmes made a direct impact on congestion and slum-dwelling, as it had tended to be the more mobile, skilled workers, already reasonably well-housed, who had left, though in turn their vacated houses could be occupied by slum-dwellers (Smith and Farmer, 1985). Of the 100,000 houses needed, it was estimated that 25,000 could be provided in the city, mainly in the comprehensive development areas and at high density, with a further 10,000 from improving existing houses, leaving an outstanding requirement of 65,000. While private building in the region and spontaneous population movement might provide 23,000 and overspill arrangements some 25,000, that still left a shortfall of 17,000. So overspill should be stepped up. In 1973 central government responded by designating another new town at Stonehouse.

At this period, too, Glasgow turned its attention to an ambitious programme of urban highway development. The 1965 *Highway Plan for Glasgow*, owing not a little to the old Bruce plan, was one of the most ambitious in the United Kingdom and, proceeding in parallel with the CDA programme, promised a complete transformation of the city by the end of the century. Thinking was on a large scale and dominated by the problems of physical reconstruction and movement. The details of the highway schemes and the fate which befell them are covered in chapter 4.

We have traced the early post-war struggles between the advocates of dispersal and those who believed that Glasgow could solve its housing problems within its boundaries. Formal victory went to the former, with the official adoption of overspill policies and the creation of the new towns. Yet most of the proposals of the latter had in fact been implemented. All the available land within the city was developed, leaving no green belt within the city boundary, and building was to high densities. The balance between council-owned and privately-owned housing was to shift from 66% private in 1960 to 63% public in 1981. Four great housing estates, 'schemes' in the Scottish parlance, had arisen on the periphery, at Easterhouse, Drumchapel, Castlemilk and Pollok, with little except municipally-owned rental housing— shops, schools and community facilities did not come until much later and there was an acute shortage of open space. These peripheral schemes were themselves to pose some of the most severe social, economic and environmental problems faced by urban policy in the 1980s (chapter 6). Little progress had been made by the early 1970s on the 29 comprehensive development areas, though schemes had been completed at Pollokshaws, Anderston and Cowcaddens, in addition to Gorbals-Hutchestonstown. Elsewhere, large areas lay blighted by planning delays and highway schemes, to await the policy shift of the mid 1970s.

## From Regional Planning to Urban Crisis

The Clyde Valley Regional Plan of 1946 was never formally adopted as policy, largely because of Glasgow's dissent from its main recommendations. It did, nevertheless, guide many of the responses of the Scottish Office to development issues on Clydeside in the following years. In 1955, the Scottish Office planners persuaded both Glasgow and the government to agree to an additional new town at Cumbernauld (Carter and Keating, 1986) and, as we have seen, overspill was accepted as corporation policy throughout the late 1950s and 1960s. The revival of regional planning in the 1960s, however, stemmed from a growing concern about the state of the Scottish (and British) economy. The recession of 1958-9 hit Clydeside hard, providing a salutory reminder of the vulnerability of its economic base. By 1959, Glasgow's unemployment was at the (then) alarming rate of 4.5%, against 4.0% for Scotland and 1.9% for Britain as a whole. At the 1959 general election, while the Conservatives increased their majority overall, Scotland swung to Labour, which won ten of the fifteen Glasgow seats. The 1958 Industrial Finance Act and 1960 Local Employment Act marked the beginnings of what was to be an elaborate system of regional economic incentives and several major investments were steered to central Scotland. These included the Rootes car factory at Linwood near Glasgow, the BMC vehicle plant at Bathgate between Glasgow and Edinburgh, the new steel plant at Ravenscraig near Glasgow (split at the last moment between Scotland and Wales) and the Post Office Savings Bank in Glasgow. These were the years in which national government was converted to indicative planning, with the creation for Britain as a whole of the National Economic Development Council (NEDC or 'Neddy'). In 1961, the Scottish Council (Development and Industry), an industrial research and pressure group with close links to Government, published (with Scottish Office help) the Toothill Report on the Scottish economy. In 1962, the Scottish Development Department was created to bring together the major physical development functions of the Scottish Office and link these into physical and economic planning. It was responsible for the White Paper, *Central Scotland—A Programme for Development and Growth*, partly in response to the Toothill Report but also reflecting a strengthening of central attitudes to regional development, a realisation that circumstances had changed since the post-war plans, the significance of the shift of coal mining from west to east, concern about the handling of the Glasgow overspill issue and the need for coordination in local planning (Carter, n.d.). The White Paper broke new ground in bringing together economic/industrial and physical/land use planning, selecting eight 'growth areas' in which development could most profitably be encouraged. Further new towns were designated, at Livingston and Irvine and these, together with Cumbernauld and East Kilbride, featured among the growth points, so adding the task of stimulating growth and attracting outside investment to the traditional one of simply drawing population and industry out of Glasgow. In 1966, as part of the Labour Government's abortive national plan, a further paper was published, *The Scottish Economy, 1965-70*. As well as considering prospects for Scotland as a whole, this included an analysis of seven 'sub-regions' into which the SDD had divided the country.

National economic planning collapsed with the demise of Labour's national plan in 1966-7, but the idea of regional planning was kept alive in Scotland. In 1967, the Scottish Office formally designated eight planning regions and by 1970 plans had been produced for all but the west central region, which included Glasgow. The delay in producing the latter has been ascribed (Carter, n.d.) to the fact that local planning in Clydeside had adhered largely to the 1947 Plan, to the concentration in the 1963 White Paper on Glasgow and to the production of the *Greater Glasgow Transportation Study*, covering one of the key issues. There was also some difficulty in getting Glasgow to cooperate wholeheartedly in a regional approach. The delay was to be significant in policy terms, for by the time the plan was published in 1974 perceptions of the problems of Clydeside and particularly the inner city had changed dramatically.

## The Rediscovery of Poverty

The delayed *West Central Scotland Plan* was finally produced in 1974 by a consortium of local authorities with the Scottish Development Department. As this was the eve of local government reorganisation (see chapter 2), it confined itself largely to setting guidelines for the new Strathclyde regional council. The delay had a further effect, for circumstances had changed markedly from those prevailing when its predecessors elsewhere in Scotland had appeared. Nationally, attention was beginning to shift to the problems of the inner cities, with the 'rediscovery of poverty' and the analysis of the 1971 census data, which showed severe problems of urban deprivation (Keating and Boyle, 1986). In 1968, the Urban Programme had been launched, initially on a small scale, to provide grants for needy urban areas and in England a series of *Inner Area Studies* was completed in 1973. The Community Development Project (CDP) and Comprehensive Community Programme (CCP) were experiments in social intervention in small areas, initiated by central government, aimed at tackling the problem of 'multiple deprivation'. Multiple deprivation was a complex phenomenon, only partly understood by policy makers—we shall examine some of the problems of definition in chapter 6—and CDP and CCP were seen as forms of 'action research', an attempt to learn about the problem while tackling it in a small experimental area. Glasgow itself was not chosen for either of these but there was a CDP at Ferguslie Park in Paisley and a CCP in Motherwell and the philosophy of a coordinated attack on multiple deprivation on an area basis was to underlie the initiatives of Strathclyde and Glasgow councils in the 1970s and 1980s.

Glasgow corporation had begun to reappraise its planning strategy in the early 1970s, under the influence of a new generation of officials and the Scottish Office, which was reflecting the new national priorities for urban policies. The second review of the development plan in 1972, produced with the help of SDD officials, while still largely concerned with the physical aspects of policy, put considerable emphasis on the extent of multiple deprivation in the city, making it the subject of a special report (Mansley, 1972). The index of deprivation used covered household structure, unemployment, social grouping, retired persons, housing conditions, occupancy rates and house-hold size, grouped into six national score classes. On this more comprehensive index of social deprivation, no less than 13,000 acres, half the city of Glasgow, came into the worst three classes. The 1960 development plan, which had confined itself to physical conditions, had identified just 4,000 acres of con-gested and substandard property in need of comprehensive redevelopment. According to the new statistics, the problem of social deprivation extended well beyond the old slum areas and included large parts of the corporation's post-war housing schemes. In Easterhouse, no less than 34% of all households had outstanding requests for transfers, 58% of these wanting to go back to the Gallowgate area in the old east end, itself no haven of prosperity but more familiar and less isolated from the facilities of the city. Community facilities in the estates were seriously lacking and there was evidence of considerable social stress. According to the report, an end to Glasgow's overall housing shortage was now in sight purely in terms of numbers but the problem of housing quality remained acute. There was no room for new building in the periphery—indeed, selective demolition was suggested to make room there for open space and community facilities. Comprehensive redevelopment was increasingly recognised as socially and environmentally damaging, and, if pursued, could alter the character of older areas like Partickhill, Hillhead, East Pollokshields and Dennistoun, while increasing the proportion of houses in the public sector to socially undesirable levels. The emphasis in the inner areas should therefore be shifted to the rehabilitation of older property. This was a major challenge to the Glasgow orthodoxy of the post-war years, suggesting that the peripheral schemes and large-scale municipal development had been a failure, and it was not well received by sections of the Labour leadership who had been associated with these past policies. It was, however, to have a major impact on the new district council after reorganisation and amongst the younger, newer councillors and officials.

The *West Central Scotland Plan* of 1974 pointed in the same direction. Urban outmigration had turned into a flood. While the 1960 development plan had anticipated a population fall for the city from 1,055,000 to 997,000 by 1970, the actual fall had been twice that, to 908,000 and to 850,000 by 1973. 25,000 people were leaving every year, mostly among the professional and skilled working classes (WCSP, 1974). Although many of these were moving within west central Scotland, a substantial number were moving right out of the region, whose population, contrary to the assumptions of earlier plans, was falling, as was that of Scotland as a whole. Manufacturing industry was in steep decline, particularly in the immediate Glasgow conurbation, though clear reasons for this were less easy to establish. It seemed that industrial failure could be accounted for neither by Clydeside's industrial mix, the size of firms, the environment nor the location. Factors like poor industrial relations and poor, unimaginative management were less amenable to quantification but were considered important (WCSP, 1974).

Much of the blame for inner-city decline was at this time being attributed to the overspill policies, the creation of new towns and the type of redevelopment which had characterised the 1950s and 1960s. The new towns, in fact, were relatively blameless for, as we have seen, the philosophy of the 1949 Clyde Valley Regional Plan had to a considerable extent been undermined in practice. Formal overspill arrangements, including new towns, had accounted for only 6,300 annual movements out of Glasgow, against a planned 10,000 and paled against the 18,500 annual spontaneous moves. Nor could the decline of urban industry be put down to the new towns. Although, as we have seen, these had originally been intended to receive industrial as well as residential overspill from Glasgow city, most of their industry had come from outside the west central Scotland region. According to Henderson (1974), only 20.1% of jobs transferring out of Glasgow between 1958 and 1968 had gone to new towns. In 1968, only 3.4% of manufacturing employees in Cumbernauld and 7.5% in East Kilbride worked in establishments which had transferred from Glasgow. In view of the revised projections being made for population, the *West Central Scotland Plan* recommended that work on the newly-designated Stonehouse new town should be suspended until the new Strathclyde regional council had had time to reconsider the need for it. This was to herald the end of the new towns' overspill role. Increasingly, they were to be promoted as a means of bringing industry into Scotland from England and overseas.

The *West Central Scotland Plan* also drew attention to the severe environmental decay affecting the city. Progress with the comprehensive development area programme had been slow and in 1971 there were 17,000 empty dwellings in the city awaiting demolition. Conservation was becoming more fashionable and, following a report by Lord Esher, Glasgow was recognised as probably the finest Victorian city surviving. Like the 1972 Glasgow report, the *West Central Scotland Plan* called for a move to rehabilitation and improvement of older residential areas although still indicating that redevelopment would be the most common form of treatment. Noting that improvements to council-owned property had been stepped up since 1968, it pointed to the need for an expansion of improvement in the private sector, too, and for trial schemes for private house-building in central Glasgow. The *West Central Scotland Plan* also followed the changing national concerns by emphasising the extent of deprivation on Clydeside though, because it used a different set of criteria to the 1972 Glasgow report, it found deprivation to be concentrated more in the inner city than the outer estates, highlighting what was to be recognised as Glasgow's peculiar problem of having a deprived periphery as well as a deprived core.

To regenerate the region's economy, the *Plan* proposed a new type of agency, the Strathclyde economic development corporation (SEDCOR) which would concentrate on indigenous industry, administering government grants, advising on industrial relations and encouraging industrial development generally. While the *Plan* is short on specifics as to exactly what the SEDCOR would do, it can be recognised as the forerunner of the Scottish Development Agency proposal incorporated in the 1974 Labour Party manifesto and set up in 1975.

In its proposals and priorities, the *West Central Scotland Plan* set the tone for the new authorities which came into existence soon after. The themes were: the regeneration of the city, with an end to overspill and a concentration of resources on the inner core; a limitation of comprehensive redevelopment in favour of piecemeal change, rehabilitation and conservation; policies to tackle urban deprivation; and policies to tackle economic decline and unemployment. None of this was accepted overnight, in Glasgow or in other British cities; but in due course, as we shall see, the policy changes were considerably more radical in practice than was anticipated in the *Plan*.

# 2   The Government of Glasgow

## Urban Government and the Search for Integration

The remaining chapters of this book examine the ways in which solutions to the problems of urban decay which we have traced have been forged and carried out, focusing on the period since the reorganisation of local government in 1975. The mid 1970s have an added significance as a starting point, for in these years there was a sharp change in the direction of British urban policy, against dispersal and overspill and in favour of regenerating the inner cities. Before examining policies and policy-making in Glasgow, though, we must trace the institutions of urban government and assess the capacity of each to formulate policy choices and moblise resources for their realisation.

The government of any city is a complex matter but the British tradition has a number of features marking it off from systems of urban government both in the United States and in continental Europe. British urban government consists of three broad categories, central government departments, local authorities (elected councils) and *ad hoc* agencies of various types, appointed by and responsible to the central government but with a degree of operational independence. Each has a separate status, is responsible to a different constituency and has its own allocated functions. We must ask what is the power of each and how this power is exercised in the making of public policy for the city.

There is a strong tradition in Britain favouring the public planning of urban growth and change, in contrast to the tradition of privatism which prevails in the United States (Heidenheimer *et al.*, 1983). Related to this is a belief in the desirability of comprehensive approaches to the problems of the city, with urban problems seen 'in the round' and a coordination of public and private effort behind agreed goals, an approach which contrasts with the pluralism of the American city. On the other hand, Britain is marked off from a country like France with its strong conception of the unitary state of which local government is an integral part. Indeed, from the perspective of France, Britain has certain affinities with the United States, with its tradition of local self-government based on the liberal principle that communities have different needs and wants and that each should be allowed to administer its own affairs up to the point at which its own activities affect other communities. Just why local government exists in Britain has been the subject of numerous scholarly works, from J S Mill onwards. All have encountered great difficulty in distinguishing, descriptively or normatively, separate roles or spheres of action for central and local government within the urban arena, given a major paradox. Britain is a unitary state with no constitutional guarantee for local government and whose only real constitutional principle, that of parliamentary sovereignty, allows the centre theoretically unlimited powers. Yet, at the same time, there is a tradition of local self-government which, until recently, aroused considerable admiration in European nations whose urban government was based on centralising napoleonic principles. Heidenheimer *et al.* (1983, p.278) go so far as to claim that:

> Historically, local government in Britain was not a creation of national government. In fact, many municipal corporations predated the formation of the central government but were later integrated into the national system.

One could go further in the case of Scotland and note that the Act of Union, the nearest Britain has come to a written constitution, specifically guarantees the position of the royal burghs. The suggestion here is that local government exists because it has always existed, part of the unquestioned inheritance of British constitutional practice. Yet this has not prevented the development of the doctrine of parliamentary sovereignty or the assumption of unlimited powers over territorial government by the centre. This belief in the desirability of local self-government, however, is only weakly rooted in pluralist principles. Local government has rarely been seen as a counterweight to the central state, rather as a complement to it, undertaking tasks handed down by central decision-makers. Indeed, contemporary local government, with its lack of constitutional guarantees and the constant changes made in its status over recent years, must be seen as the creature of statute.

Local government has, in fact, to be seen in two guises, as part of the administrative system of the unitary state, subject to central control and guidance and as a series of local political systems, subject to local electoral control and the influence of interest groups. In the nineteenth century, the 'local political system' model might have had some validity, with what Bulpitt (1983) calls the 'dual polity' allowing municipal councils a considerable degree of autonomy, albeit on the centre's terms and within tightly defined spheres of action, while central government confined itself to the 'high politics' of foreign affairs and finance. In the years since the second world war, however, three factors have undermined the distinction between central and local roles, in Britain as elsewhere.

Firstly, there is the acceptance by central government of responsibility for economic management. For much of the post-war period, this was confined to Keynesian manipulation of the macro-economic variables but, from the early 1960s, as we have already seen in the Glasgow case, it involved more detailed intervention and spatial planning to secure economic growth and control its effects. This in turn brought central government into the details of physical planning and urban development, breaking down the old distinctions. Secondly, there is the growth of the welfare state which, in Britain as elsewhere, has had a centralising effect (Heidenheimer *et al.*, 1983) as governments have sought equity both for social and for economic reasons. The promotion of uniform standards has had an obvious effect on local distinctiveness, while the means by which governments have sought to develop welfare services, through financial transfers, have also reduced the scope for independent local action. Thirdly, there is the 'nationalisation of democracy', the process whereby local elections are seen simply as a referendum on the performance of the government in power, making it very difficult for local politicians to build up political support in case of conflict with the centre. So there is an intermingling of local and central roles similar to that found in other western liberal democracies and policy making has come to be increasingly complex.

Returning to the theme with which we started this discussion, this does create problems for the comprehensive and integrated solutions to urban problems to which so much lip service has been paid in Britain as elsewere. The essential problem is how to attain a unified approach to urban regeneration in a context of institutional diversity and interest group conflict. It is this search for integration which underlay much of the institutional reformism of the 1960s and 1970s, with central decision-makers searching for some sort of reconstituted dual polity adapted to the needs of the modern interventionist welfare state in which broad goals would be laid down for an essentially co-operative local government to follow, allowing the centre to withdraw from the concern with detail which had been thrust upon them. Local political conditions, together with fiscal crisis and the confusion of their own strategic aims, though, seems to have frustrated this strategy and, instead, urban government has become ever more complex.

The structure of urban government in Scotland is quite different from that in England, with a separate department in charge of central government's input to a distinctive structure of local government, and a different pattern of *ad hoc* agencies. We must examine the power and resources of each (Rhodes, 1981) in making policy for the city.

## Central Government

Most urban policy functions in Scotland are the responsibility of the Scottish Office, a central government department under its own Cabinet Minister, the Secretary of State for Scotland. Founded in 1885 to coordinate the untidy array of boards and burghs which undertook most administration in Scotland, it gradually extended its functions and in 1939 moved from London to Edinburgh. With the gradual disappearance of the old board system, the Scottish Office took over important administrative responsibilities in areas such as education, agriculture, police and the local government system, to which were added, after the Second World War, the National Health Service, town and country planning and the expanding social services (though social security was centralised in London). In the 1960s, it gained further responsibilities of a 'promotional' nature in the field of economic development and since then there has been a progressive increase in the Scottish Office's economic functions. There are now five departments as follows:

> *Scottish Development Department*, responsible for local government, housing, planning and transport;
> *Scottish Education Department*, responsible for education outside the universities and social work services;
> *Department of Agriculture and Fisheries for Scotland*;
> *Scottish Home and Health* Department, responsible for the National Health Service, police, fire and prisons;
> *Industry Department for Scotland*, responsible for disbursing regional industrial assistance under national guidelines, new towns, electricity, supervision of the Scottish Development Agency and the Highlands and Islands Development Board and, more generally, advising the Secretary of State on the Scottish economy.

In addition, a sixth unit, Central Services, is in charge of personnel and finance, including local government finance. So the whole range of local government functions in Scotland comes under a single central department, in contrast to the position in England where responsibility is shared between the Department of the Environment and a number of functional departments. We must ask, therefore, whether this makes any practical difference in terms of the interests which find expression, the policies which are formulated and the resources which can be mobilised.

The role of the Scottish Office in British government has been described by Keating and Midwinter (1983) as threefold:

> —to administer those functions which, because of Scottish institutional features, notably the distinctive Scottish legal system, need separate administration;
> —to provide for some distinctiveness in policy-making for Scotland and for a Scottish input into UK policy-making;
> —to lobby for Scotland within the central decision-making instances of British government, notably the Cabinet and its committees.

In administrative terms, the Scottish Office is structured like other departments of British central government, though the wide range of its responsibilities means that the Secretary of State can rarely give his full attention to all the issues of the day. Even his junior ministers, numbering between three and five, have wider responsibilities than their Whitehall counterparts— combining, for example, agriculture and housing or education and industry— and this, together with the added problem of the 400 miles between Edinburgh, where nearly all the civil servants are located and London, where ministers sit in Parliament, may create difficulties of control. It has been suggested that, as a result, ministerial leadership in the Scottish Office may often be weak, with more initiatives left in the hands of the permanent civil service (Keating and Midwinter, 1983a).

The Scottish Office's role in policy-making has been described in terms of two modes (Keating and Midwinter, 1983a), *policy autonomy* and *policy leadership*. Policy autonomy occurs when the Scottish Office is permitted by Cabinet or the appropriate Cabinet committee to proceed on its own with a policy initiative, merely keeping other departments informed as to what it is doing. This occurs occasionally where the Scottish Office has the entire administrative responsibility for a matter, where there are few cross-border spillovers to England and Wales, where the Treasury is satisfied as to the financial implications and where the issue is not central to party politics, so allowing a party government to adopt different positions on either side of the border. Examples in recent years include the Social Work (Scotland) Act, 1968 and the reform of local government in 1973-5. Even where the Scottish Office does design its own policy and frame the legislation, though, it is often the institutional form rather than the substance of policy which differs so that Scotland gets 'concurrent policies' (Rose, 1982), achieving the same result in different ways. Sometimes, Scotland is allowed to go ahead to test out policies subsequently extended to England, as has happened with legislation on local government finance in the 1980s. The more common mode of policy making, though, is policy leadership, in which policy is made jointly by the Scottish Office and the corresponding Whitehall department, with one department assuming the lead role. In these cases, the Scottish Office's aim is to maximise its input to the process and, specifically, to ensure that Scotland's distinctive needs and conditions are taken into account.

The lobbying role has two aspects. The Secretary of State must try and ensure that his own departmental budget is maximised and, more generally, he must seek to intervene where other departments or Cabinet as a whole are taking decisions with a Scottish impact. Historically, Secretaries of State have been quite successful in budgetary terms, protecting Scotland's share of UK expenditure even when Scotland's relative population was falling and intervening to make a special case for Scotland wherever possible. As a result, Scottish per capita expenditure by the mid 1970s was running some 20% ahead of English levels. Then a formula was introduced, providing that Scottish Office expenditure should be related to English decisions such that, for the relevant programmes, increases or decreases should be distributed among England, Scotland and Wales in the proportions 85:10:5, that is, roughly, according to population. The effect is to freeze Scotland's base expenditure relative to England's while apportioning changes at the margin by reference to population (Heald, 1980). The formula is applied to a range of cash-limited services accounting for some two-thirds of the Secretary of State's budget. Within the block thus determined, the Secretary of State is then theoretically free to allocate moneys at his discretion. So for example, he may have received an increase in his budget because of an increase in English health service expenditure but in principle he need not apply this to health in Scotland; he could choose instead to increase spending on education or housing. In practice, his discretion in this respect appears tightly constrained (Keating, 1985c) by Cabinet policy and Treasury influences and there is no evidence of the Secretary of State using this freedom to strike out on his own in policy terms. On the other hand, it does give him a small room for manoeuvre at the margin when faced with political pressures within Scotland.

The second aspect of the Secretary of State's lobbying role is most apparent in the field of economic and industrial policy. In the 1960s, interventions by Secretaries of State were crucial in bringing to Scotland a number of major industrial investments, including the Rootes car plant at Linwood, the BMC vehicle plant at Bathgate, the Ravenscraig steel complex (split at the last minute between Scotland and Wales) and the aluminium smelter at Invergordon, mentioned in the previous chapter. More recently, his task has been to fight against closures, often of these same industrial plants. In this, he is usually able to count upon the support of a fairly cohesive territorial lobby, unique in the United Kingdom, in which party differences are temporarily sunk in the defence of Scottish industry. For a large part of the 1980s, the major issue preoccupying the Scottish lobby was the defence of Ravenscraig, though there was also a notable battle to defend the last Scottish-owned bank, the Royal Bank of Scotland, against external takeover.

In summary, we can say that the Scottish Office is distinctive not so much in what it does as in how it does it (Ross, 1981). Its control of the instruments of policy implementation can, however, be quite significant in its effects. It controls the Rate Support Grant and can determine whether preference should be given to urban or rural areas; it sponsors the Scottish Development Agency and can influence its priorities; it can determine health service priorities and the pace at which some items of legislation should be implemented. It has also been suggested that, with its control of nearly all the urban policy functions, it can give a greater coherence to central government activity than is achieved in England. Although Page (1978) has cast some doubt on the Scottish Office's ability to act in a 'corporate' manner, it is clear that the departmental divisions within it are less marked than those between English departments and that a more coherent view of spatial problems and priorities is possible from Edinburgh than is available in Whitehall. It is significant that it was the Scottish Office which pioneered regional planning in the 1960s and 1970s though, with the demise of planning, the capacity to take a coherent view of the problems of areas has been fatally weakened. The Scottish Development Department, established in 1962, continues to look after local government but the Scottish Economic Planning Department, founded by the Heath Government in 1973, was renamed Industry Department for Scotland in 1983, to emphasise the Thatcher Government's rejection of planning.

# Local Government

## Local Government Reform

Although local government in Britain has deep historic roots and, in Scotland, the royal burghs, often created in the middle ages, owed their status to charters predating the institution of Parliament, in the modern age it must be considered the creature of statute. A series of acts of Parliament in the nineteenth century laid down the status of local government as a subordinate part of the state, its powers restricted to those specifically devolved by legislation. In time, the scope of local administrative activity came to be considerable as much of the regulatory and welfare activity of the modern state was handed down to local government to administer and it was the need to cope with this administrative load which led central governments to successive reorganisations of the system in the course of the nineteenth and twentieth centuries, following the 'dual polity' theme in which the centre avoided burdening itself with the details of local administration. The latest reorganisation, in the mid 1970s, was part of a movement across western democracies, in which governments sought to consolidate local jurisdictions in the interests of efficiency and resource equalisation (Heidenheimer *et al.*, 1983). In many countries, this process was effectively defeated by the weight of entrenched local interests—this happened in France in the 1970s—or was severely attenuated by these pressures. In England, the path of reform was drastically altered by the arrival of a new government which saw its partisan interests as lying in the abandonment of its predecessor's proposals. What is striking in the Scottish case is the relative ease with which reform was effected despite the radical nature of the changes. The explanation appears to lie in the leadership assumed in the whole process by Scottish Office civil servants, with a correspondingly weak political input and, specifically, in the weakness of the Conservative presence in Scottish local government, which meant that one powerful vested interest which may have been influential on the ruling party was largely absent.

The process of reorganisation in Scotland started with the report of the Wheatley (1969) Commission, itself the culmination of years of dissatisfaction with the previous arrangements. Prior to reorganisation, the principal units of local government in Scotland outside the cities were the county councils. Below the counties were large burghs, with most powers except education, small burghs with very limited powers, and districts with no powers as of right but in receipt of delegated powers from the counties. In the four cities of Glasgow, Edinburgh, Aberdeen and Dundee, there were all-purpose city councils known as corporations. By the 1960s, the system was widely agreed to be in need of reform. Many authorities, particularly the small burghs, were too small effectively to undertake their responsibilities, producing a fragmentation of services. Boundaries were outmoded, taking little account of the facts of contemporary economic and social geography. Low turnout at elections was taken as a sign of public apathy and it was said to be difficult to attract the right 'calibre' of person to serve as elected councillor or official. One problem which particularly exercised the Scottish Office was the inability of the fragmented local authorities to play their part in planning for economic and industrial development. Problems increasingly cut across local authority boundaries and conflicts of interest among councils made solutions difficult. Most of the difficulties in practice had occurred in the Glasgow area which, as the only conurbation in Scotland, occupied a great deal of the Scottish Office's attention. When the car plant was established at Linwood in Renfrewshire, for example, Scottish Office civil servants encountered great difficulty in getting councils to cooperate in providing infrastructure and other necessities, forcing them to intervene constantly, getting involved in precisely that degree of involvement in local detail which central government has traditionally sought to avoid. This they found extremely irksome and unrewarding. The implementation of the *Greater Glasgow Transportation Study* was also likely to be held up by inter-authority arguments.

Larger authorities were also being advocated in the 1960s in the name of efficiency in service provision. The evidence here was much less clear than in the case of physical and economic planning and has since been subjected to harsh criticism (Dearlove, 1979). It was widely accepted that the small burghs and smaller counties might have to go. There was less consensus on the proposition that the city of Glasgow was unable to run its own social work and education services.

At the same time, the Scottish Office was engaged in the series of regional planning exercises for the eight 'sub-regions' of Scotland. In central and eastern Scotland, these were based on the major urban centres, taking in the rural hinterland and, in the case of Glasgow, Edinburgh and Dundee, on the major river estuaries, following current planning practice. Except for the *West-Central Scotland Plan* (1974) all the sub-regional plans appeared between 1968 and 1970; for the Glasgow region, we have noted the earlier precedent of the 1946 Clyde Valley Plan. As a result of this experience, officials in the Scottish Development Department were convinced that the way forward for Scottish local government was the establishment of a regional tier which would have both planning responsibilities and the powers and resources to implement their plans. These could engage in a dialogue with central government on priorities and programmes but then be left to get on with the implementation themselves, freeing the centre from the irksome business of detailed intervention. Local government's role, too, would change from a purely administrative and regulatory one to that of an active promoter of development and change. So the Scottish Office joined in the fashionable cry for 'stronger' local government, obscuring the two very different meanings which that phrase could have. As a former senior Scottish Office official has indiscreetly revealed (Ross, 1980), what the Scottish Office wanted was local authorities better able to carry out central policy, not local authorities which could pursue their own line in defiance of the centre. In other words, the centre was seeking a reformulation of the 'dual polity' (Bulpitt, 1983), allowing it to concentrate on broad policy matters while local collaborators took on the burden of implementation. In a period of consensus, with general agreement on the priority of development, of bringing industry to Scotland, of planning for the expansion of public services, it was easy to overlook this ambiguity of meaning. In the years since, as we shall see, it was to become more apparent.

After a false start in 1963, local government reform commenced in earnest with the appointment of the Wheatley commission by the Labour Government in 1966 and its report in 1969. Wheatley identified four weaknesses in the existing system:

*Structure.* There were too many authorities and the fragmentation of the
system inhibited coherent planning or the solution to the problems of
a city like Glasgow, which could not confine its concerns to its own
boundaries;

*Functions.* Small authorities were inefficient and resources could not
always be applied where need was greatest;

*Finance.* An equitable spreading of burdens was needed and, with larger
authorities, equalisation could be undertaken within local government,
eliminating the need for such a high level of central intervention;

*Membership and organisation.* Councils were unable to attract the right
sorts of people and their organisation encouraged an excessive concentration on administrative detail at the expense of policy.

*Relationships with central government.* Functions had been removed
from local government to *ad hoc* agencies and central government was
forced to intervene in the details of local affairs with constant guidance
and advice.It was a set of themes being stated across western Europe
at the time as governments grappled with the problem of territorial
administration in the interventionist state. The requirements of a new
system as identified by Wheatley also have a familiar ring about them,
being stated succinctly as power, effectiveness, local democracy and
local involvement.

In practice, Wheatley was heavily influenced by the Scottish Development
Department (SDD) in the Scottish Office and its preference for a solution
based on the planning sub-regions. Other Scottish Office departments, including the Scottish Education Department (SED), were less keen, worrying
about the excessive size of the regions and the problems of managing services
on such a large scale, but it was the planning imperative which prevailed.
Scotland should be divided into seven regions—based on the planning sub-
regions—which should have control of all the important local government
responsibilities, including housing. Because of the size of the regions and the
problems of remoteness and the loss of a sense of community, however, there
should be a second tier of local government, the districts, underneath the
regions. Here the commission fell into some confusion. If districts were to
be established, they argued, they would need to have important functions,
otherwise the best people would be unwilling to serve on or work for them.
This, in turn, meant that they would have to be quite large. The problem here
is that large districts, particularly when based on large historic cities, could
come to see themselves as rivals to the regions, whatever their formal status
and could lose their role as essentially local bodies. In a well-argued note of
dissent, two members of the commission took on this problem and argued
for small, local districts without powers of their own but with a 'general
competence' role, able to supplement or fill in regional services across the
board (Harvie Anderson and Johnston, 1969). There would thus be a clear
distinction in status between regions and districts while avoiding the problem
of dividing up functions.

The problem was particularly acute in the Glasgow area. The Wheatley commission recommended that the whole area of west-central Scotland should comprise a single region, based on the Clyde estuary and that Glasgow should form a single district within it. While the region was admitted to be very large, encompassing half the population of Scotland, the commission, calling on evidence back to the 1946 *Clyde Valley Plan*, insisted that it was an economic unit and should not be divided. The lack of a unified administration was 'one of the greatest impediments to the economic and social regeneration of the West of Scotland today' (Wheatley, 1969, p.186). As for the city of Glasgow, it was recognised that it had outgrown its 1939 boundaries, with the development of owner-occupied suburbs to the north and south. An area like Bearsden, a middle-class dormitory suburb with its own burgh council, should be considered functionally as part of the city, given that 71% of its working population worked in Glasgow and shopping and leisure patterns were similarly focused on the city. So the boundaries should be extended to take in these suburbs, while excluding established towns like Paisley, Motherwell and Dumbarton, which were themselves centres of employment. Whatever the functional logic of this, it was seen as 'the city' extending its boundaries at the same time as it was losing functions on demotion to second-tier district status. It would also produce a district accounting for nearly half the region's population, making it not only by far the largest district in Scotland but larger than any region except the west central region itself. Whether such an entity would be content with the status of a mere district council was doubtful from the start.

The Wheatley recommendations were accepted by the Labour Government in 1969 but, before they could be implemented, the Conservatives returned to power. In England, the new administration largely abandoned the work of the corresponding Redcliffe-Maud Commission but in Scotland they stuck with Wheatley. It is clear that the Conservatives at this time had few fixed views on Scottish local government structure. They were only just beginning to organise seriously in local government in Scotland and there was no council lobby within the party to push for a particular solution. So ministers took their lead from the civil servants and pressed ahead with Wheatley. Some changes were in fact made. In response to pressure from the Borders (the areas south of Edinburgh adjoining England), where local Conservatives hoped to unseat the Liberal MP, a separate Borders region was created. Separate all-purpose authorities were created for the island areas of Orkney, Shetland and the Western Isles, which the majority of the Wheatley commission had wanted to incorporate in the Highland Region. This in itself was a modest step but the concession of all-purpose status to areas of as little as 17,000 population drove a coach and horses through the argument that economies of scale required such large authorities on the mainland. Highland region was further reduced in size by transferring Argyll to the proposed west central region (later called Strathclyde) centred on Glasgow, so giving the new region a highland periphery radically different in character from its urban core.

Finally, the government decided that housing should be allocated to the districts. This was ostensibly in order to give the districts a major function to perform but political considerations were clearly visible. Housing is (or was until recent legislative changes) one of the few areas in which local government has an effective capacity to redistribute income, by subsidising council rents from the rates. Subsidies to owner-occupiers are paid nationally (see chapter 5). If housing were allocated to the regional tier, then Labour-controlled regions would have enhanced scope to use the revenues generated in rural and suburban areas of owner occupation (and Conservative electoral support) to subsidise urban council tenants (overwhelmingly Labour voters). By allocating housing to the districts, the government also gave suburban areas an added incentive to resist incorporation into city districts.

It is unusual in the British Parliament for substantial changes to be made to a government's legislative proposals. Most changes are the result of lobbying by interest groups directly on government departments before the legislation reaches Parliament. Even changes made in Parliament are usually the result of pressure brought on ministers who themselves propose amendments (Griffith, 1974). This was something of an exception. Lacking real understanding or conviction about the proposals, ministers lost control of the Bill implementing the reform in the Scottish standing committee (Keating, 1975). This could have led to the unraveling of the whole scheme were it not for the sense of purpose maintained by the civil service and most of the opposition Labour Party who kept the bill largely intact. Two significant changes were made, though. After a determined campaign, the county of Fife succeeded in gaining regional status for itself, so upsetting the Wheatley logic in the east of Scotland. Instead of a region based on Aberdeen and two estuarial regions based on the Tay and the Forth, there were five regions, with the estuaries reverting to their historic role as boundaries rather than unifying features. The proposals for the west central region (Strathclyde) faced a strong attack from Members who thought that the region would be too large and unbalance the system for Scotland as well as from members from constituencies, particularly in Ayrshire, where there were fears of Glasgow dominance. In the event, though, these proposals won through.

The plan for an expanded Glasgow district was not so successful. The Bill, following Wheatley, proposed taking into the city the middle-class suburbs of Bearsden and Milngavie and Bishopbriggs to the North and Newton Mearns and Giffnock to the south, together with the strongly working-class burgh of Clydebank to the west and the ancient burgh of Rutherglen to the east. The patchy extension of the city boundary before the Second World War and the building of the peripheral housing schemes after it, had created a marked pattern of residential social segregation around the urban periphery. All the land within the boundary had been taken for council house building while private building had boomed on the land outside it. The unplanned effect, of the city boundary snaking out to take in the council estates and in again to exclude the owner-occupied suburbs, was to the liking of residents of the suburbs, who could take advantage of city centre services while avoiding rate contributions to them or to Glasgow's housing programme. This is a familiar problem in metropolitan consolidation in Europe and North America. In Britain, the regressive distributional effects of this are mitigated in practice by the equalising effects of the Rate Support Grant system, while the creation of the regional council as the main spending authority for local services would serve as a further equaliser, but there was still an advantage for the suburbs in staying out of the Glasgow district, with its large public housing programme. There was also a widespread fear that Glasgow, with its historic problem of land shortage, would seek sites for council housing in the middle-class areas. In the case of Clydebank and Rutherglen, the class issues were less salient but there was a strong sense of injured municipal pride in being forced into the city.

The suburban authorities gained much sympathy among Conservative MPs, though the issue was not resolved without some extraordinary confusion. Areas were taken in and out of Glasgow at all stages of the Bill's passage until finally, after defeats in both the Lords and the Commons, the government conceded the case for excluding Bearsden and Milngavie, Bishopbriggs, Newton Mearns and Giffnock (the middle class suburbs) together with Clydebank, but Rutherglen was brought into the city. As a result, the city boundary remained largely unchanged, with profound effects on the social and political composition and balance of housing tenure of the new district (see Figures 1.2 and 1.3).

Despite the preference of the SDD for a system in which the regions were clearly predominant, the Local Government (Scotland) Act, 1973 makes it clear that each tier is quite independent of the other, exercising separate responsibilities. The region is responsible for education except for the universities and some higher educational institutions run directly by the SED. It is responsible for social work, for the police service which, in contrast to England, is not run at one remove through a special authority and for the fire service. It runs public transport services through the passenger transport executive and is the highway authority except for some trunk (national) roads. It is also responsible for water and sewerage. The district is responsible for council housing and for improvement grants for private housing, as well as for libraries, cleansing, leisure and recreation and a range of licensing functions. Planning, such an important theme in the reorganisation debate, is split. The region has responsibility for the structure plan laying down the basic principles of development policy, while the district is responsible for producing local plans to give this detailed effect and for development control, that is, the issuing of permission to build or change the use of a building. To ensure that its strategic priorities are safeguarded, the region has a 'call-in' power, allowing it to take development control decisons itself.

With the truncation of the proposed regions in the east of Scotland and the timid reorganisation of local government in England, Strathclyde emerged from the reform as the only truly regional authority in Britain, covering the whole conurbation and with a hinterland ranging as far as the Highland periphery of Argyll. The result was a system in which the region was the more powerful force in local government, responsible for the great bulk of revenue spending (notably in education, police and social work). It was not, however, the predominant force anticipated by Wheatley as the district accounts for around two-thirds of local authority capital spending in the city (notably on housing). Despite the insistence of both Wheatley and the Scottish Office on the separate nature of the two tiers and the absence of a hierarchy between them, it is clear that their responsibilities were highly interdependent. Here we have an example of the confusion about the status and role of local government which was alluded to earlier. The debate on reorganisation was powerfully influenced by the need for integration and coordination in the framing and implementation of urban policies. An accompanying theme to structural reform was a reform of the decision-making system which, under the heading of 'corporate management', sought to achieve comprehensive solutions to urban problems (see chapter 3). Yet the very existence of a two-tier system of local government, especially in a city which historically has had one-tier local government, could be seen as a move away from integration. The problem was particularly acute in the field of planning, the policy field which had been so influential in shaping the reform. In the debate on the reform Bill, the responsible minister, after insisting that powers should be exercised independently 'to resist a hier-archical situation in which the second tier was subservient to the first tier', went on to recognise an effective functional hierarchy because 'regional plan-ning authorities have the general responsibility for planning in their area' and 'their proposals . . . cannot be effective if they are not reflected accurately and in good time in local plans, which are the main means through which development control will be exercised' (First Scottish Standing Committee, 8.5.73, cols. 2249-2293). The uncertainty over which level has the ultimate responsibility for planning and urban development priorities was to give rise to a series of conflicts in the following years. The roots of this contradiction are the insistence by central government on maintaining direct links with all local authorities for all their functions, avoiding the creation of an inter-mediate tier of government which might become a power in its own right, an insistence shared by politicians looking for political careers at the district level who valued their direct access to central government. The result, though, was to create two local governments in the cities, each with its own statutory functions and of equal legal status. The resulting conflicts are traced below (see Table 2.1).

A major criticism of the reform was the failure to give new powers and responsibilities to local government. The Wheatley commission's brief had been to examine the system in relation to its existing functions. Certainly, these included the recently-reformed planning system which was intended to give local government a greater strategic role but no additional powers were conceded to make this a reality. In particular, the planning role remained a purely indicative one, attempting to encourage and steer development but without strong powers of intervention to bring that development about. The establishment of the Scottish Development Agency was to fill this gap to some degree in the years ahead but the Agency's relationship to the new local government system was to pose a problem. The other great weakness of the reform was the failure to consider local government finance, which was to prove the major issue of contention and the pretext for a drastic weakening of local government in the following decade.

TABLE 2.1    RESPONSIBILITIES OF SCOTTISH LOCAL COUNCILS

| Region | District |
| --- | --- |
| Strategic planning, structure plan. | Local plans and development control. Building control. |
| Industrial development. | Housing. |
| Highways. | Leisure and recreation. |
| Transport. | Libraries. |
| Water and sewerage. | Environmental health. |
| Education. | Licensing. |
| Social Work. | |
| Police. | |
| Fire. | |
| Registration of births, deaths and marriages. | |
| Registration of electors. | |
| Consumer protection. | |

## Reaching the grassroots. The role of community councils

In its advocacy of large and powerful regions and districts, the Wheatley commission was conscious of the criticism that local government was becoming too 'remote'. It therefore proposed the creation of community councils as a sounding board for local opinion and to undertake tasks of local improvement in their areas. To some extent, this was to replace what had gone before. In the rural areas, the small burghs had provided a focus for local patriotism, the provost (mayor) being a well-known figure in the community. In Glasgow, a system of 'ward committees' sought to involve local residents in civic affairs. Wheatley's proposal was not greeted with universal enthusiasm. Some councillors were suspicious of bodies which might rival them as representatives of local opinion within their own electoral districts while some activists in voluntary organisations, residents' associations and tenants' groups feared that the enthusiasm and spontaneity so essential to grassroots activism would be dashed by an 'official' system. Others questioned whether any body could properly claim to 'speak' for all the residents of an area, who might be very divided on issues of local politics and policy.

Nevertheless, under the reform legislation it was laid down that district councils have a duty to draw up a scheme, including boundaries, for community councils in their areas. While the scheme is produced by the district council, within the limits set by the legislation, the details still have to be approved by the Scottish Office. If 20 electors in any area so requested, elections would then have to be held and a council established. Most districts responded early though in Edinburgh both main parties regarded community councils as unnecessary and dragged their feet on implementation so that it was not until 1980 that a scheme was put in hand. For the rest of Scotland,

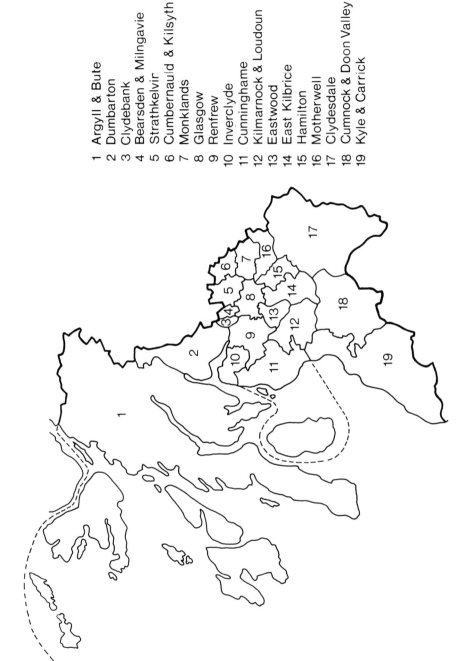

1 Argyll & Bute
2 Dumbarton
3 Clydebank
4 Bearsden & Milngavie
5 Strathkelvir
6 Cumbernauld & Kilsyth
7 Monklands
8 Glasgow
9 Renfrew
10 Inverclyde
11 Cunninghame
12 Kilmarnock & Loudoun
13 Eastwood
14 East Kilbrice
15 Hamilton
16 Motherwell
17 Clydesdale
18 Cumnock & Doon Valley
19 Kyle & Carrick

FIGURE 2.1  Strathclyde Region and its districts. *Source*: Strathclyde Regional Council.

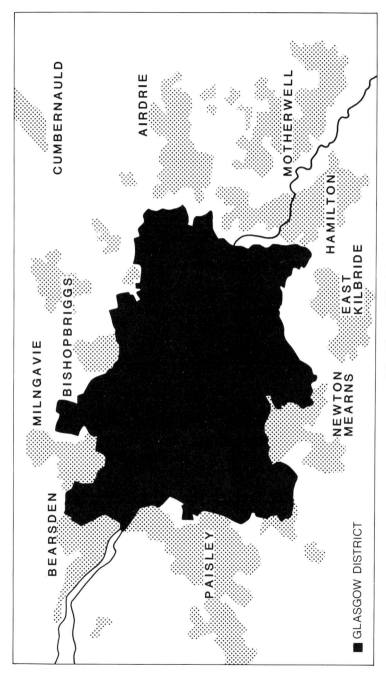

FIGURE 2.2   Glasgow District.

over 1,100 community councils had been established by 1978, including some 100 in Glasgow. By 1983, a Scottish Office research team found that there were 1,131 community councils in Scotland, including 83% of those originally established and covering some 80% of the population. While Aberdeen and Edinburgh still had relatively few councils, Glasgow, along with Dundee, stood out as having a very high coverage (SOCRU, 1986). They have certainly increased involvement in local affairs. While the effect of reorganisation was to reduce the number of councillors in Scotland from 5,400 to just 1,600, community councils have some 10,000 elected members, in addition to people coopted from voluntary organisations. The procedure for electing community councillors varies from one district to another according to the district council's scheme, but in Glasgow there is an 'at large' election within each community council area, with additional members being nominated by voluntary organisations. It is in fact extremely rare for there to be sufficient candidates to make a contested election necessary and, indeed, there could be severe technical problems if one were to occur, since the Glasgow system allows voting for community councils at the age of 16, as opposed to 18 for other elections. This would require the production of a special electoral roll. There is, in fact, a shortage of candidates, with just a third of Scottish councils managing to fill all their vacancies. The provision for adding non-elected members from local voluntary organisations did cause some controversy in the early days since it appeared to violate democratic principles, but was defended on the ground that community councils do not have spending or service responsibilities but are essentially sounding-boards for local opinion. The organisations represented include churches, sporting and social clubs and residents' associations.

Glasgow's high rate of community council formation undoubtedly owes a great deal to the supportive attitude of the district council which provides funding and a community council resource centre which helps with advice as well as practical matters such as photocopying and publicity. In addition, some support in kind is available from the region. Community councils are consulted on planning matters and other items of local interest and there are usually district and/or regional councillors in attendance at meetings. On the other hand, a third of the councillors in the all-Scotland sample surveyed by the Scottish Office study on community councils did not see the community council as an appropriate body to consult on local issues, some because they had never seen the need for a community council, others because they doubted its representativeness (SOCRU, 1985).

When it came to providing for community councils, central government was extremely wary of giving them statutory powers or even the right to run services on behalf of regions and districts. So, although they may have a limited role in running community halls or organising local fetes, they are essentially consultative bodies. Matters raised by them are diverse but with a concentration on roads and transport and planning matters. The allocation of housing, including the question of 'anti-social' tenants and licensing matters also feature. With the end of the old veto poll system of local prohibition, it appears that many community councils are exercising their right to object to applications for liquor licenses to the same effect. Other matters raised include policing, environmental health and cleansing, leisure and recreation and education while a range of matters is pursued with public utilities, including British Telecom, British Rail, the Post Office and the Electricity and Gas Boards.

The health of community councils varies enormously from one part of the city to another. In an area like Corkerhill, where there is a stable community dating from the nineteenth century, a vigorous community council has established itself, consolidating its position as the representative of local opinion in a series of battles over the closure of the Kilmacolm railway line and the threat of the Ayr motorway. In other parts of the city, councils are moribund or have been taken over by vociferous and defensive minorities. They are a modest contribution to grassroots democracy in the city but, given their lack of resources, powers and political 'clout', their influence on public policy is, overall, minimal and they will feature very little in our studies of policy-making in the city. They lack legal powers and financial resources, they are incapable of the political mobilisation of their communities. Their political resources are further reduced by the questions about their representativeness, and their consent is not required by other agencies before proceeding with policy changes.

## The Scottish Development Agency

An important factor in the urban policy field, created around the same time as the new local authorities, is the Scottish Development Agency (SDA). The idea of a Scottish Development Agency had been around since the 1930s but gained increasing support in the 1960s, when the Scottish Trades Union Congress suggested an agency to revitalise the Scottish economy. In 1974, as we have seen, the *West Central Scotland Plan* had proposed a Strathclyde development corporation, an idea which gained considerable support in various quarters. In the same year, the Scottish Council Research Institute— attached to the Scottish Council (Development and Industry)—proposed a Scottish development corporation. Shortly before this, the Labour Party's Scottish Council had proposed a Scottish national enterprise board as a subsidiary of the national enterprise board to which the party was committed, but with considerable operational independence (Labour Party, 1973). Its role would be to intervene to create and preserve industrial employment and reorganise industry in Scotland. There was no suggestion at this time that it should have a specifically urban focus or be concerned with environmental matters.

It was the political pressure on the Labour Party from the advance of the Scottish National Party (SNP), however, which finally brought the SDA into being. In its October 1974 manifesto, Labour promised a Scottish Development Agency to be 'the main instrument for the regeneration of the Scottish

economy', with responsibilities for tackling industrial decay and unemployment as well as environmental dereliction, paying special attention to
those areas which had suffered the worst effects of decline. In 1975, the
Agency was duly established, taking over the Scottish Industrial Estates
Corporation, the Small Industries Council for the Rural Areas of Scotland
and the section of the Scottish Development Department responsible for
administering grants to local authorities for derelict land clearance. In
addition, new responsibilities were created, marking an expansion in the role
of government in Scotland, and were given to the Agency. These were the
power to invest in Scottish private industry in the form of money and management services; the promotion of private investment in Scottish industry,
particularly from overseas; and the coordination of major comprehensive
urban development schemes. This last, thrust upon a reluctant Agency virtually from the moment of its creation, meant in practice the Glasgow Eastern
Area Renewal (GEAR) project. Some of the Agency's tasks are financed by
grants from central government. Investment is financed by borrowing, within
a limit set by Parliament. Sponsorship of the Agency rests with the Secretary
of State for Scotland, through the Industry Department for Scotland. He
issues guidelines, agreed with other relevant government departments, and
can issue instructions of a specific or general character. In practice, policy-
making in the Agency is a more subtle affair, influenced by appointments to
the Board, by discussions with Scottish Office officials and by the reading by
the Agency's senior officials of the political climate of the time. They know
that they are dependent on the Scottish Office both for their finance and for
protection against the Treasury and jealous Whitehall departments. The
Scottish Office, in turn, appreciates that a degree of operational independence
is desirable and useful, particularly in the Agency's dealings with firms and
local authorities. The SDA is also the respository of much knowledge and
experience on economic development matters. The Scottish Office could, no
doubt, take this all 'in house' by absorbing the Agency but, as long as it does
not do so, the latter will possess a reserve of 'informational resources' in its
dealings with central government departments. Its main power resources in
its relationships with local councils are this same degree of knowledge and
experience, on which councils are anxious to draw, together with its financial
resources and the ability to place these where it chooses.

It was born into a difficult political environment and for some years its
survival was at issue. Conservatives criticised it as an agent of 'backdoor
nationalisation' and predicted that it would merely prop up 'lame duck'
industries. The Labour government replied by pointing to the requirement
for a specified return on the Agency's investments, which were to be limited
to firms with prospects for moving into profit. The argument came to hinge
on the question of whether there was an 'equity gap', an area of business
finance in which potentially viable firms were unable to get investment capital
because of lack of access to financial markets or the time-scale of their plans.
In a gesture of support before the 1979 general election, Labour increased
the Agency's borrowing limit to £800 million; the new Conservative administration promptly reversed the decision. Both gestures were entirely symbolic

as; given the strict guidelines on investment, there was no prospect of the Agency being able to spend anything approaching this sum. Further restrictions were placed on investment activity, with a lowering of the limit above which investments required the specific approval of the Secretary of State. An attempt to hive off the investment function altogether, however, failed, when the banks declared, in effect, that they did not believe in the equity gap. Instead, a new body, Scottish Development Finance Ltd., was set up within the Agency to involve private businessmen in investment decisions. New guidelines were issued removing the requirement to create jobs and substituting that of providing 'stable and productive employment.'

Generally, then, the SDA survived the change of government little scathed, though its investment function continued to be regarded with some suspicion. A more serious battle was to be fought over the inward investment function, that is the task of attracting private investment into Scotland from overseas, in competition not only with other European locations but also with England and Wales. After the task of attracting overseas investment to Scotland was transferred from the Scottish Council (Development and Industry) to the Agency in 1976, offices were opened in New York, San Francisco and Tokyo, to the intense chagrin of the Department of Trade's Invest in Britain Bureau and the Foreign and Commonwealth Office. At the same time, regional and district councils and new town development corporations began to mount their own inward investment efforts. Further confusion was added after 1979 with a series of trips organised by the Scottish Office minister for industry. The conflicts thus engendered came to a head in 1980 with an investigation by the parliamentary select committee on Scottish affairs. Amid intensive lobbying, the committee divided on party lines, with the Conservative majority, still basically hostile to the SDA, voting to close the offices. The government's decision compromised with the creation of a new body, Locate in Scotland, jointly run by the Agency and the Scottish Office. They ensured that the effort was still in Scottish hands but with more influence held by the civil servants in the Scottish Office who, as part of the unified British civil service, are more closely linked into the central government machinery than the more free-wheeling officials of the SDA. In the Local Government and Planning (Scotland) Act of 1982, restrictions were placed on local authorities' investment promotion activity, bringing their overseas visits under the control of LIS. This delicate institutional compromise was soon itself under attack, with a renewed assault by the Department of Trade and Industry in 1984. By this time, Scottish interests were more united, with Conservative and Labour MPs defending the separate Scottish effort. Indeed, the Conservative Secretary of State was making political capital out of the fact that he had created Locate in Scotland (ignoring the fact that it had replaced the more independent SDA effort). So the separate inward investment effort was now firmly within the embrace of the cross-party Scottish lobby.

Apart from ensuring its own survival, the SDA had over its early years to develop a positive strategy. It had been given only the vaguest idea of what its task should be, apart from the series of inherited commitments in environmental renewal and industrial estates. Almost immediately it had been established, it was pushed by the Scottish Office into taking the lead role in the GEAR project for the east end of Glasgow. There was a danger that its efforts and resources might be swallowed up, on the one hand, in responding to appeals from firms and local authorities and, on the other, in 'fire brigade' operations undertaken at the behest of the Scottish Office. So a more purposive strategy was needed, to allow the Agency to set its own priorities and seek out opportunities for promising developments. 'Opportunities' soon became the Agency's watchword, with an insistence that it was not in business to deal with the 'problems' of firms or areas. It is in business to encourage internationally competitive industry in Scotland and to exploit the potential of sectors and areas which can contribute to this. Such a hard-nosed approach helped the Agency to survive in the changed political climate after 1979 but inevitably led to a downgrading of the wider social objectives, including employment creation, envisaged in 1975.

SDA strategy, as developed over the years, has now come to focus on three concerns, major firms, sectoral initiatives and area development. Sectoral initiatives, focused on the needs of industrial sectors across Scotland, have been undertaken in electronics, health care industries and energy-related industries, including North Sea oil (Hood and Young, 1984). Area development focuses on the regeneration of specific locations. Priorities for this were worked out in the early 1980s, following projects in the Garnock Valley (Ayrshire) and Clydebank, on the borders of Glasgow, into which the Agency had been directed by the Scottish Office following major industrial closures. There followed a project in Leith (Edinburgh) and area projects in several Strathclyde districts. These were joint economic and environmental renewal schemes, agreed between the SDA and regional and district councils. The agency made available funds for environmental improvement, factory building and investment, while the regional and district councils agreed to provide infrastructure and other facilities for industrial regeneration. At their best, these coordinated projects represented positive planning of the sort for which critics of traditional planning policies based on development control had long called (Keating and Boyle, 1986). There were, however, several problems, which we will explore in the Glasgow context in chapter 7. One of these is the relationship between the area and the sectoral approaches, with major projects arising from the Agency's concern with individual industrial sectors often being unsuitable for location in urban priority areas. The same problem arises in relation to the clash between 'opportunities' and 'problems'. In its task of developing internationally competitive industry in Scotland, the Agency will seek out the most promising locations. These may not be the urban areas suffering the most severe problems of unemployment, environmental decay and poverty—indeed, the record shows that they rarely are. In its early days, the Agency was encouraged to take a comprehensive view of urban renewal. This was the philosophy of the GEAR project (chapter 4). Since then, however, it has taken a more hard-headed view of its role as an economic development agency, reducing its concern with purely social problems. We shall see later that this has led to something of a disintegration of the various strands of urban regeneration policy in Glasgow, disappointing the hopes raised in the 1970s of a comprehensive approach. Another development in recent years has been the pressure from central government to provide more private sector involvement in urban regeneration and, where possible, to hand the leadership of urban renewal projects over to the private sector, a factor which has created problems over priorities and strategies for economic regeneration in Glasgow (chapter 7).

## Other Agencies

Two other types of agency, of some importance in implementing public policies in Glasgow deserve a brief mention. The national health service is run by the Greater Glasgow health board, one of fifteen Scottish boards appointed by, funded by and responsible to the Secretary of State for Scotland. Board members are drawn from local authorities, the health professions and other organisations and are officially in charge of policy issues and resource allocation within the limits of national government policy, while day to day management is in the hands of the area executive group of senior officers. Under the board are districts to which much operational authority is devolved. There are also professional advisory committees at each level and local health councils, whose role is to represent community and consumer interests. At the time of local government reorganisation, it was widely suggested that the new regional councils could assume responsibility for the health service but because of central government's timid approach to decentralising power and, perhaps more importantly, because of strong opposition from the medical profession, the separate agency structure was maintained. Given the common interests of the health service and local authority social work, education, housing and other departments, there is a need for liaison and, as we shall see, the main integrated approaches to social problems (GEAR, area initiatives) have involved the health board as a participant. Power and control in the health services is still an under-researched topic but there is strong evidence that the medical profession comprise the 'dominant coalition' at board level, while the Scottish Home and Health Department has an important directive role. The influence of the community health councils, on the other hand, is slight, given their lack of formal powers and the technical way in which policy decisions are approached. Nor do the district and regional councils have a major influence over health board decisions, though much of their work, in housing and social work particularly, is closely related to, and affected by, health policies.

The Manpower Services Commission was set up in the early 1970s to take over the Department of Employment's employment and training services and the Government's special employment creation programmes. The commission itself consists of nominated members representing government, employers, trade unions and other interests and is responsible for broad policy. There are separate lines of management for three divisions, employment services, training services and special programmes, reaching down to the local level. Cutting across these is a regional structure, with Scotland comprising one region. The Scottish director has line responsibility for the special programmes division but, for the other two divisions, has only a coordinating role. There is also an MSC advisory committee for Scotland and a manpower research unit. Although the MSC is sponsored by the Department of Employment (DE) and its employees are officially part of the DE group of the civil service, the Secretary of State for Scotland does have a role here in guiding its activities. He is consulted by the Secretary of State for Employment before the MSC's corporate plan is approved and, within the framework of this plan, a plan for Scotland is drawn up. This is in turn subject to approval by the Secretary of State for Scotland in consultation with the national chairman of the MSC and, where appropriate, the Secretary of State for Employment. Most of the work of the MSC in Scotland is funded through the Scottish Office vote, though this is not part of the expenditure block over which the Secretary of State has unlimited powers of virement— in other words, he cannot reallocate MSC moneys to his other functions or to other agencies. So MSC initiatives in England will be reproduced in more or less identical form in Scotland.

Power and influence within the MSC are a subject of some mystery but in the 1980s the government has seen it and its programmes as a valuable way of 'massaging' the unemployment figures through job creation programmes for which resources have been found even during the severest expenditure squeezes. Government has also seen the Commission, coming directly under its control, as a vehicle for channelling resources into areas while by-passing the local authorities. This has been important in job creation, in training and, in the mid 1980s, in education, with the Commission seeking to wrest from local government and the education profession parts of the education service in order to press more vocational and less liberal programmes. The main power resource which it has at its disposal is money. The MSC has been extremely generously funded in recent years, because of government's concern to 'massage' the unemployment problem and because of the Commission's enthusiastic pursuit of policies in accordance with the prevailing ideology. As a result, it has been able to induce local councils to bend their own policies and priorities to its preferences. Chapter 6 examines one example of this, the Technical and Vocational Education Initiative.

# 3 Politics in the City

## Electoral Politics

We have referred earlier to Britain's tradition of local self-government, an essential element of which is the ability of communities freely to elect their own councils. This implies a need for elections in which the issues are debated and an electorate sophisticated and informed enough to make choices on the basis of these issues and the perceived competence of the competing candidates. In practice, local government in Britain's cities has long fallen short of this ideal. Turnout is low, varying typically from 30% to 50% of the registered electorate. Voters are ill-informed about the responsibilities of local councils and the identities of local political leaders. Certainly, party politics, which prevails in all British cities, serves to simplify choices and guide voters, but at the expense of reducing local elections to mere referendums on the popularity of the party in power in central government. In our earlier look at Glasgow politics before local government reorganisation, we noted the decrease in political competition, the existence of machine politics, the focus of local political attention on a narrow range of issues, particularly council house rents and the problems of political recruitment in the city for both local and parliamentary office. One of the stated objectives of local government reform was to improve the quality of local democracy by encouraging higher turnout at elections, the clear presentation of issues and a wider choice of candidates. The results, in terms of these objectives, have been disappointing.

Regional and district councils in Scotland are elected for four-year terms, with elections for one or other tier every two years, though to phase in the system, the first two district councils were elected for three year terms. The first elections, held for both levels on the same day in 1974, did seem to increase interest, for turnout was relatively high by British local government standards, at 51.7%. Thereafter, there has been a falling-off of interest, with just a slight recovery at the regional elections of 1986. In American terms, of course, these figures look quite impressive, especially bearing in mind that in Britain voter registration is largely automatic, so that turnout figures are a good approximation of participation by the whole eligible electorate. By west European standards, on the other hand, the turnout figures are extremely low. The Glasgow figures are somewhat depressed, especially up to the late 1970s, by the large number of movements around the city by people rehoused under the renewal programmes who have either to return to their old neighbourhood to vote or apply for a postal vote—most do not bother to do either. Despite this, Glasgow's voting figures are higher than those of most British cities. On the other hand, turnout levels of barely half the electorate fall far short of the hopes held at the time of the 1975 reform.

For both Strathclyde regional and Glasgow district council elections, contests have been the norm, with no uncontested seats in the city at either set of elections and only isolated examples in the rural areas at regional elections (in contrast to the rural district councils within Strathclyde, where unopposed returns are common). With an increased number of candidates there appears to have been an increase in political competition. Labour contests all seats apart from some rural and island areas, the Conservatives continue to stand widely, the Scottish National Party (SNP) has adopted a policy of trying to present candidates everywhere and the Liberal/SDP Alliance have greatly increased their numbers of candidates. In addition, the Communists manage to present a surprising number of candidates (given their electoral weakness) and the Greens have entered the field. So the local elections remain an occasion for the parties to flex their muscles, keeping up the morale of activists and maintaining the machinery in readiness for parliamentary elections—but there is an air of unreality about most of the contests, given that so few seats are marginal between the parties. Leaflets are usually distributed but there is little door-to-door canvassing these days, little activity on the streets and little airing of the local issues in the media. The parties have often had difficulty in recruiting candidates, in the early years, to 'fly the flag' in unwinnable seats, but in recent years they have sometimes had trouble finding candidates for winnable seats as well. It has become increasingly common for there to be only one contender for the Labour Party nomination even in safe Labour seats in the city where the Labour Party nomination is tantamount to election. This clearly has a great deal to do with the unattractiveness of local council service. The demands on a councillor's time are considerable, in the case of the region, because of the range of its responsibilities and the size of its administrative machine, in the case of the district because of the heavy case-load of constituency business, especially in housing

TABLE 3.1    % OF REGISTERED ELECTORATE VOTING AT LOCAL ELECTIONS

|      | Glasgow | Strathclyde |
|------|---------|-------------|
| 1974 | 52.0    | 51.7        |
| 1977 | 46.6    |             |
| 1978 |         | 47.2        |
| 1980 | 42.6    |             |
| 1982 |         | 42.4        |
| 1984 | 40.2    |             |
| 1985 |         | 45.3        |

Source: J Bochel, University of Dundee.

TABLE 3.2   % SHARE OF VOTE, STRATHCLYDE REGION

|                  | 1974 | 1978 | 1982 | 1986 |
|------------------|------|------|------|------|
| Labour           | 44.0 | 43.0 | 45.8 | 54.6 |
| Conservative     | 28.4 | 30.0 | 22.5 | 12.0 |
| Liberal/Alliance | 4.5  | 1.8  | 18.1 | 14.4 |
| SNP              | 15.1 | 22.6 | 12.5 | 17.1 |
| Independent      | 4.9  | 0.7  | 1.6  |      |
| Other            | 3.1  | 1.8  | 0.5  | 1.8  |

Source: Bochel and Denver (1974; 1983); *Glasgow Herald.*

in a city where nearly two-thirds of households are tenants of the district council. In the case of the SNP and other minor parties, it is likely that their ability to mobilise such a large number of candidates is related to the very low risk of actually being elected! The election results at the regional level have marked a steady consolidation of the Labour dominance which we have already traced in the post-war period. Labour has consistently controlled Strathclyde with a large majority, drawing on its strength not only in the city but in the industrial and mining areas of Ayrshire, Lanarkshire, Dunbartonshire and Renfrewshire. Conservative support is isolated in shrinking pockets of south and west Glasgow, together with the suburbs and some seaside and rural outposts. In the elections of 1986 the party won no seats at all in the city, hanging on only in the suburbs; nor, for that matter, did they win any seats in Argyll and the islands (Strathclyde's Highland periphery), where the seats were shared by the SNP, Alliance, Labour and an independent. The uneven pattern of contests makes judgement on the basis of overall percentages of the poll difficult but the share of the vote in the region since reorganisation clearly illustrates Labour's predominance.

The workings of the first-past-the-post (single member district plurality) electoral system, with a weak and divided opposition, have exaggerated Labour's advantage to create almost the impression of a one-party system.

TABLE 3.3   SEATS WON BY PARTIES, STRATHCLYDE REGION

|                  | 1974 | 1978 | 1982 | 1986 |
|------------------|------|------|------|------|
| Labour           | 71   | 72   | 79   | 87   |
| Conservative     | 20   | 25   | 15   | 6    |
| Liberal/Alliance | 2    | 2    | 4    | 5    |
| SNP              | 5    | 2    | 3    | 1    |
| Independent      | 5    | 1    | 2    | 1    |
| Other            | 0    | 0    | 0    | 0    |

Source: Bochel and Denver (1974; 1983).

TABLE 3.4    % SHARE OF VOTE, GLASGOW DISTRICT

|                 | 1974 | 1977 | 1980 | 1984 | 1988 |
|-----------------|------|------|------|------|------|
| Labour          | 47.7 | 35.1 | 54.3 | 60.8 | 58.0 |
| Conservative    | 28.8 | 28.7 | 22.0 | 17.2 | 14.3 |
| Liberal/Alliance| 2.2  | 1.9  | 5.5  | 11.7 | 6.5  |
| SNP             | 19.2 | 32.7 | 16.0 | 9.7  | 21.0 |
| Independent     | 0.7  | —    | —    | —    | —    |
| Other           | 2.4  | 1.7  | 2.2  | 0.6  | 0.3  |

Source: Bochel and Denver (1977); *Scotsman.*

Labour's performance at the district level has been less consistent. While Labour won a comfortable majority of seats at the 1974 election, the 1977 election was held at a time when, nationally, the Labour Government was at the nadir of its popularity and the SNP at the height of theirs. In addition, local factors may have played a limited part, adding to disenchantment with the Labour Party in the peripheral housing estates (see chapter 6). The result was a 'hung' council, with the SNP holding the balance. By 1980, Labour's fortunes had recovered locally and, in contrast to its fortunes nationally, it continued to strengthen its position in the early 1980s, gaining, in 1984, a majority as impressive as that which it held in the regional council.

A definitive explanation of Labour's increasing success in the west of Scotland is impossible for both empirical and theoretical reasons—the absence of survey data with a large enough sample for the region, and the lack of academic consensus about the factors making for electoral change in Britain in the 1980s. One explanation of the above results which can be eliminated is that voters were guided in local elections primarily by local government issues and a perception of the performance of the regional and district councils, as parliamentary election results in Glasgow reflected the same trends, also diverging from the national patters so that by 1981 there

TABLE 3.5    SEATS WON BY PARTIES, GLASGOW DISTRICT

|                 | 1974 | 1977 | 1980 | 1984[1] | 1988 |
|-----------------|------|------|------|---------|------|
| Labour          | 55   | 30   | 58   | 58      | 60   |
| Conservative    | 17   | 25   | 11   | 5       | 4    |
| Liberal/Alliance| 0    | 1    | 3    | 3       | 2    |
| SNP             | 0    | 16   | 0    | 0       | 0    |
| Independent     | 0    | —    | —    | —       | 0    |
| Other           | 0    | 0    | 0    | 0       | 0    |

[1] In 1984 the number of seats was reduced.
Source: *Glasgow Herald.*

were no Conservative members of parliament at all in the city. Certainly, the Glasgow results reflect a north-south divide upon which observers of British politics have frequently commented, with Scotland seen as an increasingly Labour country. Indeed, Labour's dominance is often taken as a natural fact of life in need of no explanation, an attitude which forgets the Conservatives' absolute majority of the Scottish vote in 1955. The facts are more complex for it is only in the central industrial belt that Labour is strengthening its position, while elsewhere the decline of the Conservative vote has been to the benefit of the Alliance and the SNP (Keating, 1986); though admittedly the central belt is where the bulk of the population live.

At a rather superficial level, Glasgow's electoral behaviour fits most of the correlates of Labour voting which have been identified in the literature. It is predominantly working class, it has a large proportion of council housing, its traditional industries and public services are largely unionised, it is economically depressed and it is situated in the periphery of the United Kingdom. The problem lies in isolating and quantifying these effects and constructing a theory which would give them explanatory power. One major theme in the literature on electoral change is the decline in class-based voting (Franklin, 1985) as a result of social and economic change in British society. Class as identified with occupation is becoming less salient as a mark of social identity while the relationship between class and voting behaviour is also weakening. It is possible that in Glasgow this change has been slower to take effect. In the past in Glasgow, religion has been a factor, especially among Catholic voters (chapter 1) and the decline in this does seem to have made class attachments relatively more important, if not more deeply rooted (Butler and Stokes, 1969). This, however, is not a sufficient explanation. McAllister and Rose (1984) in their categorisation of British parliamentary constituencies, take a wider definition of socio-economic status, embracing occupational characteristics, housing tenure (council or owner-occupied) and unemployment. They still find that in industrial Strathclyde (i.e. excluding Argyll), Labour in the 1983 General Election polled some 8% better than would be predicted from the social structure of the region. In a year when Labour lost votes everywhere, this meant that the party lost significantly less here than in other regions with similar socio-economic characteristics. One possible explanation is the 'milieu' effect, by which electors are said to adopt the predominant voting behaviour of their neighbours and workmates; so in a city where Labour was dominant, even those groups who might otherwise have been expected to vote Conservative would lean to Labour. This fits the Glasgow case, but is empirically untested (and probably untestable).

Other authors (Dunleavy, 1980a; 1980b) have postulated a radically different type of explanation for voting behaviour in the urban context, based on the notion of consumption cleavages. This grew out of dissatisfaction among Marxist scholars (Castells, 1978) with the assumption that all social conflict could be reduced to class struggles over the means of production. There were also conflicts over the 'collective consumption' represented by the provision of state services in education, health, housing, transport and so on. Dunleavy's analysis seeks to explain voting behaviour by reference to people's consumption needs and preferences, for example whether they are dependent on the state or the private sector for their housing or transport. This is, in fact, a variant of the 'rational voter' model in which the elector chooses the party which offers him the ideal combination of services and taxes, but expressed in class rather than individualistic terms. Labour will appeal to those dependent on state services while the Conservatives will gain amongst those able and willing to make private provision. This does appear to open up new possibilities in the analysis of urban politics, for we have seen (chapter 1) and shall note again the importance both of the collectivisation of consumption (in transport and housing) and of the control of the collectivised resources in the politics of Glasgow. Dunleavy has, however, been criticised in turn (Franklin and Page, 1984; Franklin, 1985) both on empirical grounds and on the more general ground that people's consumption functions are not additive (they could take their housing from the state but their transport from the market) and that people do not in any case accurately perceive their own consumption functions. Another problem is that housing tenure is also used by supporters of the political socialisation model of voting behaviour as an indicator of social status (we have seen that McAllister and Rose do this) so that to discover that council tenants are disproportionately likely to vote Labour does not tell us whether this is because their tenure maintains and reinforces their working-class identity or because instrumentally they believe that Labour will give them low rents. Glasgow would be a good place to test out this argument. Consumption functions are probably more additive than elsewhere in a city where just 30% of the housing is in owner occupation, 8% of the school population is in private schools (one must presume that these are all children of owner-occupiers) and there are just 0.35 cars per household (largely confined to the owner-occupiers?), leaving the great bulk of the population dependent on public services. Moreover, politicians have consciously behaved as though the theory were true, notably in the vital field of housing. Labour councils have sought to expand council housing and councillors and MPs would lobby hard in the 1960s and 1970s to get new council developments sited within their constituencies, while the Conservatives have consciously striven to break the pattern of collective provision, for electoral as much as ideological reasons. Indeed, Conservative politicians frequently attack council housing on the ground that it represents a kind of feudal hold by the Labour Party over urban Scotland.

At a more general level, there is a plausible argument to be made that the 'Thatcherite' Conservative values of individualism and self-help have less appeal in practically all social categories in the west of Scotland, where collectivist values still prevail, than in the south of England. The Scottish Conservative Party, unable to articulate a distinctive message, has lost all political initiative. Teddy Taylor, the last exponent of a Tory urban populism which was once an essential ingredient in Scottish Conservatism, lost his parliamentary seat at Glasgow, Cathcart in the 1979 General Election. Other populist figures have left the party or drifted out of politics. In 1986, for example, the Government's alleged neglect of Scottish industry epitomised by the refusal to reprieve the Gartcosh steel mill led to the resignation from the party of Ian Lawson, another urban populist and Conservative candidate, to join the SNP. The failure of the Scottish Tories to develop a political style distinguishable from the high-class tones of the English Home Counties has created a cultural gap between them and large sections of west of Scotland society which is an intangible but real element in the politics of the region. The modern Conservative Party is seen as increasingly based on the prosperous areas of southern England and as rejecting the Britain of the old heavy industries. Organisationally, too, Scottish Conservatives have long been weak. The demise of independent capitalism in Scotland, and particularly in Glasgow, removed much of the base of indigenous Conservatism; the problems resulting are well-illustrated by a little-remarked incident in the 1970s. Then, at the height of Scottish nationalist fervour, the Scottish Conservatives were obliged to merge their organisation with its English counterpart because, with the demise of Scottish-based industry, financial contributions were drying up. In the 1980s, in Strathclyde and Glasgow, the Conservative Party often gave the impression of having simply given up; without prospects of office, many of its ablest members drifted out of politics and took up other activities.

These explanations are not mutually exclusive, though the advocates of the contending theories sometimes appear to claim so. All point to a consolidation and growth of the Labour vote in Glasgow. Labour's resulting hegemony, though, must be fragile, the product of ineffectual opposition as much as Labour's own efforts. If the party were to continue in opposition, the instrumental value of voting Labour could be called in question, while if it were to form a government, disillusion would no doubt set in, as in the 1960s and 1970s. The beneficiaries, in that case, could be the Alliance or the SNP.


## Politics in the Councils


The power relationships and patterns of political conflict which have developed within Strathclyde regional council and Glasgow district council since 1975 are quite complex. Party competition electorally and within the councils has been, as we have noted, relatively unimportant. Instead, most of the political conflict occurs within the Labour Party, an organisation notorious in Britain for its internal divisions. There are several dimensions to this conflict. One, effecting the region, is territorial, with Glasgow politicians resenting the loss of all-purpose status for the city council and regional councillors from outside the city fearing that regionalisation would represent a takeover of the old county areas by city interests. There is the ever-present conflict between right and left within the Labour Party, a conflict ostensibly based on ideology but with ideology often used as a pretext for personal and factional rivalry. Within the Labour groups (the caucuses of Labour Party councillors) on the regional and district councils, there is a permanent tension between the group leadership and the rank-and-file councillors (called 'backbenchers' by analogy with non-ministerial members of Parliament). There is a constant tension between elected councillors and the mass party organisation, which itself has a bewilderingly complex structure. There is a balance of power and influence to be struck within the councils between the elected members, especially the leadership of the ruling group, and the permanent paid officials. Finally, we must consider the relationship between the regional and district councils themselves, bearing in mind the confusion over their proper relationships at the time of reorganisation.

Strathclyde region's first political task was to establish its position in the face of the hostility we have noted both from Glasgow politicians and from the old counties. In the event, the fear of a Glasgow takeover proved ill-founded. Although the first convener (chairman) of the region was from Glasgow, the leader of the Labour group was a Lanarkshire man. Since then, the principal positions (convener, leader, deputy leader) have tended to be held by non-Glasgow people. Indeed, a judicious balance is maintained to prevent any of the constituent parts of the region appearing to have the upper hand. Separatist feeling was nevertheless strong in the early years and continues to have an emotional appeal, particularly in Ayrshire, whose deep-rooted Labour traditions based in the small towns and mining areas are quite distinct from those of the city. Partly because of the fear of separatism, the ruling Labour group from the beginning was organised in a tightly disciplined and centralised manner, a style which in any case came naturally to the politicians from the old county Labour parties. Labour politics in the city, by contrast, has always been more fragmented and open and, with the break-up of the old communities and the political machines which they sustained, has become increasingly so. In the early years of the council, leadership was shared by the convener, Geoff Shaw, who had come into local politics quite late and acquired immense respect for his integrity and idealism, and the Labour leader, Dick Stewart, a tough Lanarkshire politician of the old school. With Shaw's premature death in 1978, the convenorship became more of a symbolic position, the public face of the council, while effective political power shifted to the leader of the Labour group. Organised on the basis of tight discipline, with the right of public dissent strictly limited, the Labour group is the effective centre of power in the council and its leader has enjoyed an influence probably greater than any other local authority figure in Britain. In Labour Party terms, the group was well to the right, at least in the early days and this, together with the traditions of solidarity and loyalism of Labour on Clydeside—especially outside the city—have enabled the leadership to maintain its position without difficulty although from the early 1980s a small left-wing caucus did emerge, calling for a relaxation of group discipline and a more radical approach to policy. The 1986 elections saw something of a move to the left and, by rapid organisation, the left-wing caucus was able to secure the support of a number of the younger newcomers in the elections to the group executive. More importantly, Stewart was replaced as leader by the less authoritarian Charles Gray and the younger, newer councillors in the swollen majority were not content with the traditional passive role of the backbencher. So debate began to open up within the group and support grew for a less centralised, disciplined style of operation.

In Glasgow district, by contrast, the early emergence of a strong centralised leadership was inhibited by the city's differing traditions and by the electoral setback of 1977, which swept away much of the old leadership and deprived Labour of its overall majority. So devastated was the Labour group in this year that, although it remained the largest single group on the council, it was unable to form an administration. Instead, a minority Conservative administration, dependent on the SNP, was formed and a period of considerable confusion in municipal affairs ensued, with no-one knowing from one day to the next who was really in charge of the council and with none of the parties really enthusiastic about forming a minority administration—in one notorious incident, two Conservative councillors were hidden up a chimney to prevent a quorum for an important vote! Later on, a minority Labour administration was formed under Jean McFadden, who had taken over the leadership in 1977 and, with the elections of 1980, a secure majority was obtained. The group continued to be divided on personality and ideological grounds, however, and the position of the leadership was altogether more precarious than that of its counterpart in the regional council. Nevertheless, a strong leadership pattern emerged after 1980, with key decisions taken largely by the triumvirate of leader, treasurer and housing chairman, in consultation with officials; this coincided with the introduction of corporate management (see below) with its strengthening of the position of the chief executive and central management team against the departmental officials. There was, however, a constant battle between factions within the Labour group. At the 1984 elections, the housing committee chairman, John Kernaghan, a member of Labour's right-wing and a key figure in the Labour leadership, left the council and a substantial number of left-wingers were elected, including five members of the trotskyist Militant Tendency. Jean McFadden's leadership was repeatedly challenged, partly on ideological grounds, to capitalise on left-wing discontent about housing policies (see chapter 5) and the failure to confront central government, but also because of backbench discontent with a centralised political leadership style which downgraded both backbench councillors and the main council committees. After the 1984 elections, a truce appeared to have been reached, with the appointment of the left-winger David Wiseman as deputy leader and Pat Lally as treasurer. Lally, an ambitious politician of the old school who had previously been deputy leader and had lost his seat in the rout of 1977, nevertheless emerged as the champion of the neglected backbenchers and challenged McFadden in 1985 and 1986 on a platform mildly to the left but, more importantly, promising more power for the ordinary councillor and less for the corporate system. In 1986, winning by a margin of three votes, Lally became leader, just at the time when Strathclyde region was also experiencing the backlash against centralised political and official control.

Glasgow and Strathclyde reflect a common, if paradoxical, tendency in British local government of strong political leaders but an absence of personalised political leadership. Few people in the city could name the leader of either council and there is no suggestion that personalities swing votes in elections. The leader serves at the discretion of the party caucus which, as we have seen, can easily remove him or her. The power of leaders owes a great deal to Labour Party traditions of solidarity and discipline and is undoubtedly maintained by the very burdens of office. Leading councillors must be full-time or almost full-time in order to keep track of the complexity of council business and most backbenchers are content to let them carry the load. The personality of individual leaders also plays its part. With a few exceptions, Glasgow has not produced flamboyant characters in positions of municipal leadership. Nor does the structure of local government encourage per-sonalised leadership, as the 'dignified' offices of Lord Provost of Glasgow and Convenor of the Regional Council are separated from the powerful political offices of leader of the ruling group on the council. One figure in recent years who did make a major public impact was Glasgow's Lord Provost Michael Kelly (1980-84). Kelly had been chosen as Lord Provost by the Labour group because, being young and politically ambitious, he was considered unlikely to drift in the direction of his immediate predecessors, who saw the post as the culmination of their careers and an opportunity to rise above the fray as the representative of the city as a whole. In 1979, the Lord Provost had given great offence to the party by meeting the South African ambassador. Kelly's efforts did not, however, bring political rewards, and the office of Lord Provost, for all its civic dignity, remains a political cul-de-sac.

A survey of Glasgow councillors (the full results of which will be published in 1988-9) indicated that the Glasgow Labour councillor is a more traditional figure than in some English cities where the 'new urban left' (Gyford, 1985; Boddy and Fudge, 1984) has brought in more radical policies, a campaigning style including confrontation with central government, decentralisation and a break with the bureaucratic style of municipal labourism as well as issues such as opportunities for women and minorities, often neglected by Labour in the past. Its rise has reflected the growing influence within local parties of middle class professionals, often employed by the public sector, with a more ideological outlook than the traditional working class councillor. In Glasgow, we found that 59% of councillors were currently in non-manual occupations, a figure consistent with the findings in a sample of English cities in a 1975 survey (Gordon and Whiteley, 1979) but lower than might be expected in the late 1980s. Fully 63% had started their careers in manual work and 76% came from working class families. The finding that no less than 78% described themselves as 'working class', including many of those in middle class occu-pations may be a reflection of their family background or part of the 'workerist' posturing common in the Labour Party. The same phenomenon was found my Gordon and Whiteley (1979). There is some evidence that in Glasgow, as in other cities, the Labour Party is dominated by people employed in the public sector. Just 22% were employed in the private sector, while 42% were employed by public authorities, 18% of these in education, 22% were unemployed or retired and the remainder worked for trade unions or voluntary organisations. On the other hand, there was a tendency for the most left-wing councillors to be not the new service professionals as might be expected on the 'new urban left' argument but those with working class occupations. The Glasgow left while, as we have noted, it was strengthened in the 1980s, is more of a traditional 'tribunite' left than the new left orientation common in England. Significantly, the Glasgow Labour group declined in 1986 to include a clause about welcoming applicants of any sexual orientation for posts in the city administration, a key 'new left' issue. The prominence of Catholics in the Glasgow Labour Party is illustrated by the fact that 50% of councillors described themselves as Catholics, with another 11% having been brought up as Catholics but lapsed. Over a third of councillors attend church at least once a week. The religiously practising (both Catholic and Protestant) are markedly less left-wing than the others, suggesting that the religious influence continues to moderate attitudes among Labour leaders in the west of Scotland, compared to English cities. Just over half of Glasgow Labour councillors are owner-occupiers, a figure larger than for the city as a whole, but a substantial proportion, 40%, rent from the council. The picture of a traditional Labour Party is reinforced by the finding that just 11% of councillors are women and less than 20% were under 40 years of age. While a distinct 'hard left' group does emerge, it is a minority. The Militant Tendency has full-time organisers in the city but only 5 of its members had been elected to the district council and one to the region by 1986. These are preliminary findings but it does appear that Labour councillors in Glasgow have succeeded by sticking to traditional Labour values in a city less affected by social change than some of its English counterparts.

Relations between the Labour groups on the regional and district councils and the membership organisations outside have been strained at times, reflecting developments in the party at large as well as local issues. From the late 1970s, the Labour Party was engulfed in a debate about 'party democracy', an attempt by forces on the left to render members of Parliament and local councillors more accountable to the party and, generally, shift the locus of power from the elected representatives to the party activists. At the local level, the principal demands were that local manifestos should be prepared by the party organs and not by the councillors, that Labour groups on councils should be bound by the manifesto and that any decision to depart from the manifesto or, indeed, any matter not anticipated in the manifesto, should be subject to the local party gathering. In addition, it was being demanded that council leaders and chairmen of council committees should be selected jointly by councillors and party committees and not by councillors alone. The left's programme has been criticised (Geekie and Keating, 1983) as a means to shift power from one set of élites to another, given the unrepresentative nature of party gatherings, and as concerned more with shifting the substance of policy to the left (given the leftward bias of activists) rather than democratising decision-making. There are also legal problems involved, as councillors are subject to heavy legal sanctions including personal surcharging for exceeding their powers, while the activists are immune. So the whole area was, and remains, highly contentious. The party organs most concerned in our case are the Glasgow district Labour Party, with representatives from constituency parties and trade unions, and the Strathclyde regional Labour Party, which includes only constituency representatives, although a number of places are reserved for members who have come onto their constituency management committees as trade union delegates. The constituency parties, in turn, are composed of delegates from branches, trade unions and affiliated bodies like the Fabian Society or the Cooperative Party. Branches consist of all card-carrying party members and are usually based on local government electoral districts. The complexities of the structure and the distortions of representation are comparable to those found in the Democratic Party in the United States. It is possible, for example, for an individual to have several votes in selecting delegates to a constituency party, by being a card-carrying member, a trade unionist and a member of a socialist society or women's section. For the district party, though not for the regional party, unions have direct representation in addition to their representation through constituency parties. The whole structure is a complex and confused mixture of individual and corporate representation ill-adapted to the taking of decisions. Indeed, the very cumbersomeness of the arrangements was a factor in sustaining the power of the group leadership, at the regional level at least, in making policy. The regional Labour Party meets about every two months and the District Labour Party monthly. In addition, each body has an executive committee, which also meets regularly.

Of the two party bodies, it is the district Labour Party which has proved the more influential. It attracts more interest from constituency activists, who feel more able to identify with the city than the region, notwithstanding the fact that it is the region which is the more important tier of local government. It also meets more frequently, allowing factions to develop and organise and is more left-wing than its regional counterpart and more willing to assert itself against the Labour group on the council. It has long claimed extensive rights in policy-making and decision-making and, while neither the Labour group in Glasgow nor the party nationally has conceded these claims, in practice it has gained considerable power. The activists in the district Labour Party are the same activists who, at branch level, select candidates for elections and it is open to local parties to refuse their endorsement for a councillor who has failed to toe the party line. Given the tendency of the city electorate to vote for the party and not the individual, the withdrawal of the party label is almost invariably the end of an individual's political career. The divisions within the Labour group have also strengthened the district Party, with left-wing councillors conceding the party's claims to power and generally agreeing with it on substantive issues.

On the other hand, the district party is not invariably to the left of the group. Given the strong trade union representation, its preoccupations are often related to industrial relations problems within the council; indeed it is often criticised as an extension of collective bargaining by other means. While, during the late 1970s and early 1980s, there was a fairly stable alliance between the unions and the left, their views do not always coincide. In particular, the unions have been less willing than middle-class ideologues to support a confrontation with central government which could put their members' jobs at risk. On the crucial rents decision, too, since the trade-off has been estab-lished between rents subsidies and capital spending on housing (see chapter

5), the unions have tended to go for maintaining the capital programme (and thus building jobs) rather than keeping rents down. In any case, the complexities of governing are such that it has often proved possible for the group leadership to outmanoeuvre the party (as on disposals of land to developers—see chapter 5) or demonstrate the impracticality of its demands. In time, too, some of the party activists have come onto the council (the shortage of candidates makes this easy to do) while others, confronted with the hard choices involved in governing, have moderated their demands. The potential for conflict is also reduced by the partial nature of the party's interests. The annual decision on rents and spending levels attracts great interest, as do symbolic issues such as the Hutchesonstown E affair (see chapter 5) but other issues pass it by. The peak of the party's influence was probably the early 1980s, paralleling the ascendancy of Labour Party conference and national executive over the parliamentary party. By 1986, it had swung so far to the centre that, despite the years of conflict, it backed Jean McFadden to retain the group leadership. Again, this was more than a local move and reflected the national mood of consolidating under the existing leadership after the disputes of the past. On this occasion, its advice was ignored and Pat Lally was elected leader.

The regional Labour Party, by contrast, attracts less interest. Attendance is poor and members, coming from the various parts of the region, are less likely to know each other or to share common interests. Some of the Ayrshire and Lanarkshire delegates resent having to come to Glasgow for meetings, take little interest in Glasgow issues and, sometimes, continue to question the very existence of the region itself. Regional affairs are often complex and do not include housing, a major focus of Labour Party interest. So the Regional Party has exercised little influence over policy. Major developments are planned within council departments and committees and even the more political elements of Strathclyde's programme, such as the social strategy, have been initiated by leading councillors and committed officers, being endorsed later by the regional party for insertion into the next manifesto. As in the district, the left has sought from time to time to make the party a power base, but divisions within the region are as much territorial as ideological, inhibiting the emergence of a left-wing caucus.

## Managing the Authorities

One of the purposes of local government reform was to improve the quality of management and instil a greater concern with policy development and planning. This was part of the push for integration and coordination of urban government which we have already noted. One obstacle to this which was widely identified in the literature was the structure of local councils themselves. They have traditionally carried out their business through committees on which all parties were represented. Corresponding to these were departments headed by permanent, full-time chief officials which undertook the administration of the committees' decisions. The full council adopted the annual budget and received reports from committees but often had few opportunities to confront broad policy questions. Of course, there were variations from one council to another. Where there was partisan political control, as in the large cities, then the party caucus and its leadership were the real focus of power, with an organised caucus on each committee as well as on the council as a whole. Even here, though, there was often a lack of integration and a tendency to react to issues coming up through individual committees rather than setting policy guidelines for the council as a whole.

In the approach to local government reform, the Paterson (1973) Committee was set up to consider management arrangements for the new authorities and councils were urged by the Scottish Office to adopt its recommendations. These centred on the need for 'corporate management', a decision-making structure in which the whole range of the authority's activities could be coordinated and resources placed behind the achievement of clearly defined policy goals. Councils in the past, it was argued, had been fragmented, concerned with the administration of individual services rather than the overall impact of local government on the community, while committees of councillors had proliferated and were poorly integrated with one another. The era of big local government, of planning and social and economic change, demanded reform. To this end, Paterson recommended the reduction in the number of committees, the creation of a post of chief executive in charge of the council's administration, a management team of the principal officers and, for the elected members, a policy and resources committee to guide the policies of the council, and a range of management techniques, including position statements and new budgetary procedures. Midwinter's (1982) analysis divided Scottish local authorities into three categories; those, mainly rural and non-partisan councils which had largely persisted with traditional management forms; those, often mixed urban/rural councils or medium-sized districts, where improved management techniques had been introduced for major spending programmes without a comprehensive system of corporate management; and those large, urban, party-controlled councils which had introduced the full corporate system.

Corporate management has been criticised on the left (Dearlove, 1979) as a device to reduce democratic and working-class input in favour of the interests of the dominant classes. Others have criticised it as a technocratic device to depoliticise decision-making and strengthen the power of permanent paid officials who are familiar with the management jargon and procedures used, against elected councillors. Its defenders, on the other hand (Stewart, 1974; 1985) have insisted that, by setting clear priorities and procedures for carrying them through, it can strengthen political control. What is clear, however, is that, if it is to have an impact, corporate management must involve a change in power relationships within the authority, with a downgrading of the traditional service committees and, possibly, an increase in centralisation. Indeed, some of the early advocates of corporate management wanted to restructure local councils on the model of British central government, with a 'Cabinet' of leading councillors in charge of policy and its implementation and the rest of the elected members reduced to the role of the Westminster backbencher. If corporate management is not to develop on these lines but is to involve all councillors, then it involves a change in the role of the councillor, away from the traditional concern with the details of administration and constituency work, towards a concern with broader policy issues. Not all councillors welcome this; indeed, many find dealing with administrative details, especially in their own wards, more satisfying than reading lengthy briefing papers and debating abstract policy issues. There is also a belief that concentrating on case-work for individual constituents is the best way to win votes, despite all the evidence that what really matters is the party label.

At the same time, the need for research, support and advice means that the permanent officials, too, must be more concerned with policy. This can cause great resentment among councillors who, if they are not 'policy-minded' themselves, still deny the propriety of officials engaging in policy-making. When pressed, these councillors tend to see policy as coming from the political parties. As we shall see in subsequent chapters, the parties have not been the principal policy initiators in Glasgow and Strathclyde. Policy has in practice come from central government stimulus, force of circumstances, official initiatives or the work of leading councillors. Inevitably, then, the introduction of corporate management is associated with tension within the authority.

## Management in Strathclyde Region

Strathclyde region emerged as one of the authorities which had gone furthest towards corporate management. The political circumstances were favourable, with stable political control and a centralised, disciplined Labour group. A policy and resources committee was established on which, until 1986, only the ruling party was represented and policy priorities were developed to guide the main planning exercises, including the regional report, the structure plan, the transport policies and programmes and the region's economic and social strategies. These corporate priorities, to combat unemployment and multiple deprivation, were also intended to inform the work of the main service committees. On the permanent officials' side, a policy planning department was initially established to work on corporate policy priorities and, later on, incorporated in a powerful chief executive's department. The latter now includes five depute chief executives whose responsibilities cover central administration, corporate planning and services on a programme-area basis. So the chief executive's department is able not only to help formulate corporate priorities but to follow their implementation. This applied not only to matters which are 'corporate' in the sense of involving more than one department; the chief executive's officials have a research role in relation to all policy areas, applying demographic and other data and scrutinising budget proposals. The combination of strong political leadership with strong official leadership through the chief executive and the close working relationships between the two which marks Strathclyde out among British local authorities encouraged corporate approaches to policy making. Policy innovations have often come from committed officials working closely with leading councillors in a way which might not be possible where control of the council was liable to change from one election to the next.

The shift in power involved in the corporate system has produced some resentment about the powerful role of the central institutions, especially the chief executive's department. No-one advocates a return to the old days of local government but there is a widespread feeling that the policy and resources committee and the chief executive's department go too far into the implementation phase and should confine themselves to broad policy issues, a concern which came out strongly in the new council elected in 1986. Among officials in service departments there is also some resentment at relatively junior officials on the chief executive's staff 'telling them how to do their job'. This is not the way matters are seen from the centre. There the concern is that most of the day-to-day administration and the individual spending decisions come not from the chief executive's department or the policy and resources committee but from the individual service departments and committees and here professional perspectives and service-bound considerations sometimes triumph over the corporate approach. So the education service will tend to perceive problems differently from the social work department, while the highway engineers may work to a set of technical criteria in conflict with the corporate priorities of the authority. So a degree of conflict is always present. Yet another perspective sees both the chief executive's department and the service departments as too strong and wishes to increase the political input to policy-making.

One device with which Strathclyde has experimented to overcome this problem is the 'officer-member groups' which bring together officials and councillors to examine specific issues cutting across departmental and committee boundaries. These are set up by the policy and resources committee, to which they report and are serviced, with research back-up, by the chief executive's department. Their membership goes beyond the traditional policy-making 'inner circle' to include more junior officials, including those working in the field, and 'backbench' councillors. Although this membership gives them less political weight than the mainstream committees and departments, provision is made for their findings to be fed into the policy process and the early groups, operating in the area of social policy, appear to have been quite influential in setting the direction of council policy (Martlew, 1986). The social work department was sympathetic to their viewpoint and both councillors and officials found the experience of the groups satisfying, with less inhibition on both sides than in the conventional committee format and a willingness to criticise existing practice. Officials saw the groups as a way of getting members to address the issues seriously rather than react to proposals in the more customary superficial way (Martlew, 1986). Critics might see this in itself as suspicious, suggesting that the groups are no more than a way of conditioning councillors to accept the officials' line. However, in the case of Strathclyde, many of the officers involved were themselves committed politically to the council's strategy, making for an alliance between them and some of the backbench councillors against the mainstream departments and, indeed, some of the committee chairmen. So the groups do seem to have potential as a mechanism for policy innovation, the proof of this lying in the opposition which their proposals have encountered. While social work, as a relatively new profession, has few fixed boundaries, education guards its prerogatives very jealously. So in 1981 we find the director of education casting doubt on the officer-member groups' usefulness (Martlew, 1986), while junior officials involved in the groups risk upsetting their own chief officers (and thus their career prospects) by moving out of line with departmental policy.

Another device widely adopted to improve management and, particularly, the responsiveness of local government, is decentralisation of administration and 'area management'. This takes a variety of forms. In some cases, there is a desire to push responsibility for decision-making down to neighbourhood committees of various sorts. In other cases, the aim is to coordinate the authority's own services on the ground at neighbourhood level, but without necessarily devolving decision-making powers. While other councils were experimenting with area management and decentralisation, Strathclyde was inhibited in its early days by the fear that the region's *raison d'etre* might be called into question. In particular, there was no question of establishing machinery at a political level corresponding to the six divisions in which the administration was organised, since these corresponded to the old pre-reorganisation counties and city and could encourage the separatist tendencies referred to above. Officials in the chief executive's department, too, were unenthusiastic about area management and decentralisation, fearing that it might create vested interests and put at risk something which they saw as the region's major asset, its ability to redistribute resources spatially across half of Scotland. The implementation of the area-based anti-deprivation strategy itself (discussed fully in chapter 6), however, required some area structures, though in the early years these were small scale and *ad hoc*. The experience of the small-scale area initiatives showed serious problems of coordination and support for the strategy at divisional level and this led in the third council to the divisional deprivation groups. Finally, in the fourth council, community development committees were established at divisional level, consisting of all the councillors for the division and with, it was hoped, real power over the administration of their divisions. While these were initially related to the social strategy, there were those in the council who wished to see them develop into the basis of a comprehensive system of area management and control, taking in all the regional departments, though this continued to be opposed both by mainline committees and departments and the corporate political and administrative leadership. That these committees were established and supported by the leadership is a reflection of a greater feeling of security about the future of the region, a lessening of the earlier fears of disintegration. It also reflects the less centralised style of the fourth council, not to mention a shrewd calculation by the new leadership that 87 councillors kept busy with the affairs of their localities might be less difficult to handle. Suggestions were also being made that responsibility for some of the less ingratiating tasks, such as deciding which schools should be closed in their areas, might be devolved to the committees. The area-based deprivation strategy is discussed more fully in chapter 6.

## Management in Glasgow District

In Glasgow district council, the circumstances were initally less favourable to corporate management. Without a firm political leadership for three important years, officials lacked the backing which their regional colleagues enjoyed in introducing corporate control. Internal Labour politics and the need to distribute chairmanships and committee opportunities, indeed, led at first to the creation of no less than three housing committees, in contradiction to the corporate push for simplification and coordination. Later, after a single housing committee had been set up, the problem of membership of this key committee was solved by including all the councillors on it! Nor does corporate management have the same compelling logic in a district council, with its smaller and rather disparate range of services. Indeed, one of the key linkages if corporate planning is to work is between housing, a district service and a range of regional services (including social work and strategic planning); it was this consideration which had led Wheatley to recommend that housing be assigned to the regional level.

With the appointment of a new chief executive who had been a member of the Paterson committee and the restoration of clear political control in 1980, however, a corporate approach was adopted, with, at official level, a central policy core group and four programme-area teams in housing, environment, leisure and recreation and economic development. These were headed by existing directors of departments appointed for their personal qualities, though the boundaries of the programme areas do not always correspond to those of departments. In contrast to Strathclyde region, there is no powerful chief executive's department. Instead, the chief executive was advised by a group of policy and research staff located in the planning department, though some of these were later transferred to come directly under the chief executive. On the elected members' side, there is a policy and resources committee and, reporting to it, a number of programme area working groups. The evidence from Glasgow confirms the general picture of tension between the institutions of corporate management and the traditional structures. While some directors of departments have learnt to use the programme area structure effectively, others have resisted the new ways of working. Among councillors, there is little interest in the programme area working parties whose deliberations are seen as too abstract; service on traditional committees taking concrete decisions on cases is still seen as more attractive. So, while a corporate plan was produced in the early days, it was not an integral part of the decision-making process but an 'add-on' and was not repeated. Nor has it always proved possible to integrate the budget-process into the corporate system, given the need to respond to short term pressures and centrally-imposed cutbacks. Capital spending priorities can be identified through the programme area teams, the area committees and the service committees, with the policy core group (of directors of area programme teams) and the Leader of the council producing a final list. The revenue budget has been put together by the leader, deputy leader, treasurer and deputy treasurer (the gang of four) sitting with the chief executive and director of finance. As in the region, the system is regarded as not sufficiently corporate by those at the centre and as too centralised by those on the periphery. There is no doubt that resentment at the centralising elements of the new system (policy and resources committee, gang of four, policy core group) was an important factor in the fall of Jean McFadden as leader in 1986, with her successor, Pat Lally, promising to restore power to backbench councillors and service committees.

Another Glasgow innovation was the establishment of area management, widely advocated in local government as we have noted, as a means of improving service delivery, coordinating the work of administration on the ground and tailoring services to the needs of individual areas. In Glasgow, the initial objectives were ill-defined but were related to the general feeling, when Labour came back to office in 1980, that in the past it had not been sufficiently sensitive to the needs of local communities, particularly in the management of housing. So area coordinators were appointed, initially from the housing department, though later the task was taken on by specially appointed officials answerable to the chief executive. On the elected members' side, area committees were set up, consisting of all the district councillors plus the local regional councillors and the member of Parliament. Some of the leading councillors at the time had high hopes for the system, envisaging that in due course the area committees could assume executive powers and rival, if not replace, the traditional service committees, but at the outset their role was to advise the council and to manage modest area budgets for things like local environmental improvements. In their advisory role, they have occasionally intervened to some effect in major decisions but, like the corporate devices at the centre, they have sometimes fallen foul of the traditional structures. With the change in leadership in 1986 heralding a consolidation of the traditional system, it is likely that the area committees will remain as consultative bodies only.

## Region-District Relations

The Local Government (Scotland) Act of 1973 followed Wheatley and the advice of the SDD to Wheatley that a two-tier system of local government was possible and desirable for mainland Scotland. In accordance with the British tradition, each tier was given its own functions, with no element of hierarchy between them. As Wheatley (1969) put it: 'Like the region, the district exercises important functions; but the overall range of functions is quite different, and so is the place of the region in the scheme of local government.' In practice, however, functional differentiation is virtually impossible in the modern world and, in any case, goes against the logic of corporate management, which tries to bring local government functions together. The separation of housing from strategic planning and social work, against Wheatley's advice, broke an important corporate link, while the division of planning itself has caused a number of problems. These took on a particular importance in Glasgow because district councillors and officials tend to regard their authority as a continuation of the old corporation which has 'lost' functions to the upstart region. As the district is larger in population than any Scottish region apart from Strathclyde itself, it has never accepted that it should be treated like the other eighteen second tier councils in the region and there is some hankering, particularly among the older councillors and permanent officials, for a restoration of lost powers. Certainly, civic pride is maintained by the possession of the old city chambers, the office of Lord Provost and the pomp and dignity inherited from the corporation, which contrasts with Strathclyde's more workaday image but this may make the loss of real power more acutely felt.

Specifically, problems of inter-authority working have arisen in the field of planning and development policies and over a range of day-to-day matters (Keating and Midwinter, 1983b). In planning, the legislation lays down that the region should be responsible for strategic matters, including the structure plan and the 'call in' of individual developments with strategic implications. The difficulty has arisen over the definition of what constitutes a strategic issue and what criteria should be applied. The district's position has been, essentially, to deny the regional role altogether when considering development applications, focusing purely on the needs of the city. So it has tended to welcome applications for more shopping provision to bring business into Glasgow, while the region has tried to control these in order to safeguard other shopping centres in the region. As we shall see, (chapter 4) the district has even interpreted its planning responsibilities sufficiently widely to refuse planning permission for the region's highway plans! Other difficulties have arisen over spatial priorities for urban renewal and anti-deprivation policies, with GEAR, the peripheral estates, the Maryhill corridor and area initiatives outside the city receiving differing amounts of attention from the two tiers from time to time. There are managerial problems about programming joint works; for example the Citizens' Theatre was to have been refurbished jointly, with the district looking after the interior, the region the facade and the Scottish Development Agency the landscaping. For years, the refurbished interior and landscaping have contrasted with the crumbling facade as the region's share of work has been delayed. Other managerial problems arise from the differing area management systems of the regional and district departments, each tailored to specific functional requirements. At times, these problems have been compounded by differing professional perspectives of the type which corporate management was supposed to transcend within the individual authority. So community activism is often regarded by housing officials of the district as a source of opposition and trouble, while to social workers it is a sign of life in the community, to be encouraged. Political differences, too, have emerged between the two levels, even when both have been controlled by the same political party. The District came out at an early stage against the region's ambitious highway plans and among activists in the district Labour Party and some councillors the region has been viewed as 'right wing' (in Labour Party terms).

In the years since reorganisation, region-district conflict has tended to decrease. Officials whose formative years were spent in the old corporation have in many cases retired and their younger replacements do not feel the same sense of grievance over 'lost powers'; on the other hand, some of the old corporation officials who had worked together in the past did provide a network of contacts within and between the new authorities to smooth over difficulties. The same applies to councillors with the added factor that many regional and district councillors work for local government themselves and, in the event of a restoration of the old system, would be ineligible for election. There is still a good deal of suspicion and some overt conflict between region and district but, generally, the reformed system has gained acceptance and, while some district councillors and officials may hanker for all-purpose status, there is a realisation that this is not currently on the political agenda and will not be unless a Scottish assembly is established at some time in the future. On the other hand, it would not be true to say that relationships between the tiers are characterised by harmony and collaboration. Rather, each has settled into its own sphere of activity, with only isolated joint initiatives such as the proposals for coordinated programmes of regeneration for the peripheral estates of Easterhouse and Drumchapel (chapter 6). The division of city government between two councils has probably helped the Scottish Office to 'divide and rule' in the city, as well as enhancing the influence of the Scottish Development Agency since there is no one elected body able to speak authoritatively for Glasgow. On the other hand, it provides for an element of political competition in proposing and debating policy issues which, given the one-party electoral dominance, might not otherwise occur. The implications of these points will be followed up in subsequent chapters.

## Organised Complexity or Chaos?

This review of government and politics in Glasgow has confirmed the picture of complexity, with power resources distributed among and within the various organisations of urban government and intricate patterns of relationships developing among them (Rhodes, 1981). In turn, the actors within these organisations are subject to a variety of social, political and economic influences which both mould their policy goals and affect the way in which they can be pursued. No one agency has the responsibility for managing the process of urban change or the resources to achieve its own goals unaided so that effective policy-making must involve collaboration and cooperation. This, however, has proved increasingly difficult to achieve in the economic and political climate of the 1980s, as the studies of policy-making in later chapters will show. In particular, relationships between central and local government have been subjected to great strain.

## Central Local Relations and Finance

Local government reform was, as we have seen, conceived in a period of relative consensus, both on substantive issues of policy and on the machinery of local government. Partnership was the key theme, with central and local government collaborating in the pursuit of agreed goals in physical, social and economic regeneration, the whole structured through a series of planning systems. Partnership, though, was always an ambiguous notion for all depends on the terms upon which the partnership is launched, especially the relative power of the parties and the resources available to each in the process of negotiating agreed goals. In the immediate aftermath of reorganisation, this was not yet apparent, for there was no clash of objectives between central and local government in Glasgow. Clydeside continued to be a major preoccupation of the Scottish Office, with the GEAR project and encouragement from the centre for the Region's social priorities. From the late 1970s the climate began to change with the increased fiscal squeeze, especially after the intervention of the International Monetary Fund in Britain's affairs and the consequent search for cuts in public spending programmes. From 1979, with the advent of the Conservative government of Margaret Thatcher, the old collaborative style of central-local relations began to give way in many parts of the country to overt confrontation.

The new government's determination to attack the post-war collectivist consensus was bound to bring it into conflict with local authorities which, in their range of activities, were its foremost representatives (Ranson, Jones and Walsh, 1985). There was an assault on municipal housing through controls on capital spending and sales of houses (chapter 5), on municipal transport (chapter 4), and on council's direct labour organisations while the parents' charter gave parents greater powers in relation to education authorities and the assisted places scheme restored a form of direct subsidy to private schools. At the same time, there was ever-tighter central control over local finance accompanied by diminished central interest in the details of services. So local authorities, with their budgets squeezed, were told to manage their social problems on their own and not to come appealing to the centre for help. This was more than a simple exercise in centralisation—it was a combination of financial centralisation, privatisation and central disengagement from responsibility for service levels which boded ill for the future of local government as an institution.

The response to this has revealed the weakness of local government in Britain. A central government with a working parliamentary majority has in its hands unlimited legal powers. If local council breaches the law, individual councillors are liable to be disqualified from office, fined and personally surcharged to the amount which has been lost by the council or the ratepayers by their action. If a central government minister breaches the law, he can get it changed retrospectively and faces no penalty—this has happened on several occasions in recent years. Nor does local government possess a great deal by way of political resources, the ability to mobilise political opposition and cause political damage to central government. This is because voters are largely indifferent to local government and, even where local politicians 'win' a political battle with the centre, in terms of convincing public opinion, as happened in the 1980s over the abolition of the Greater London Council and the English metropolitan counties, the political penalty to be paid by the centre is never large. The main instrument which councils have at their disposal lies in the bureaucratic and informational resources which they must possess in order to carry out their role as policy executors. They can delay implementing central government's wishes and they can seek to subvert central policies in the process of implementation. Even this, however, is becoming increasingly difficult as central government imposes more detailed controls. Above all, though, local councils have in recent years lost the financial independence which in the past allowed them a degree of discretion in deciding policies and service levels.

Local government expenditure is divided into two rigid categories, legally separate, capital and revenue, which are treated differently for the purposes of management and control. Capital expenditure, on the creation of fixed assets, is subject to control by central government in the form of 'capital allocations' for each major service. These are determined on the submission of the local authority's financial plan (or Transport Policies and Programmes or Housing Plans in the case of those services) and consitute permission to spend on capital account up to the amount allocated, the money being found mainly by borrowing. Interest payments and the repayment of capital borrowed are met from annual revenue expenditure. In addition, local authorities are allowed to spend on capital projects a proportion of their 'capital receipts' from asset sales, notably the sale of council houses; lest this seem a generous loophole, it should be noted that, in determining the capital allocations, central government includes a figure for the expected capital receipts, so that a major effort of asset disposal, over and above the target figure is required to generate scope for extra capital spending from that source.

Revenue expenditure is spending on consumables such as salaries of staff and purchase of materials. This is financed from three main sources: rates; rate support grant; and charges for the use of services. Rates are a property tax levied by both district and regional councils, based on the notional rental value of domestic, industrial and commercial property. The use of notional rental value as the basis of rates is an archaic relic of the days when most property was rented from private landlords. With nearly all domestic property now in owner occupation or rented from public authorities, the rental value figure is something of a fiction but no government has got around to changing the system because all governments in recent years have, in principle, wanted to reform the whole of the local taxation system. In practice, until recently, none have had the political will to undertake such a reform, so the old system has lingered on. Valuation of property is undertaken at the behest of central government by valuers who, though employed by the regional councils, are independent in the performance of their duties. Because of changes in relative property values, revaluations always shift the rates burden, producing outrage from those who lose but little gratitude from those who gain and, because of this, governments have put off revaluations in England since the early 1970s. In Scotland, they are still held regularly and, while a pretext was found to delay the last one until the 1983 general election was over, its implementation in 1985 resulted in a transfer of the burden from industrial to domestic ratepayers. The subsequent political row was the key factor in determining the Scottish Office to get Cabinet approval for a scheme to replace rates with a poll tax—in the innocent belief that this will prove politically more popular!

Rate support grant (RSG) is the main form of central support and accounts for something over half of local government revenue spending in Scotland (excluding housing). It has three components, needs, resources and domestic. The needs element, by far the largest, is intended to compensate local authorities for the differential cost of providing the same level of service in all parts of Scotland and has in recent years been calculated according to the 'client group' method, which calculates the clientele and cost for each service. The resources element is to compensate for the differing product of the rate poundage in different localities and is intended to benefit poorer areas but in recent years it has been cut back considerably. The domestic element was introduced in the 1960s to defuse the political impact of rates increases by providing a subsidy to domestic ratepayers. It was increased again in the mid 1980s for the same reason, following the row over revaluation. While the RSG formula is apparently a matter of objective calculation, there is in practice considerable scope for manipulation. Increasing the needs element at the expense of the resources element penalises high-spending councils as the resources element is distributed in relation to expenditure levels. By altering the variables used in the regression or their weighting, the Scottish Office can skew the distribution of the needs element. While in England the large number of authorities makes it difficult to predict the results of this, in Scotland things are rather simpler, especially in the case of Strathclyde region and Glasgow district, with half and a sixth of Scotland's population respectively and with well defined socio-economic characteristics. The RSG formula is a constant source of political contention.

Housing expenditure is treated rather differently. The cost of maintaining council houses is met from rents, a contribution from the rates and a housing support grant paid by central government to a small (and diminishing) number of councils. In this case, there is a link between capital and revenue as central government has in recent years set a limit on the contribution from the rates to the housing account and councils exceeding this have had their capital allocations for council housing reduced pound for pound. From 1985, control on this was further tightened when these limits were given the force of law, so effectively removing the need for the capital penalty.

Central government's motives in their determined campaign of recent years to cut back local spending are often obscure and, to say the least, confused. Under the Labour government, from 1976, the emphasis was on the priority for the 'industrial strategy' and the release of resources for investment. It was never clear just how resources would be transferred from local government spending to industrial investment and in fact the main impetus to spending cuts appears to have come from the International Monetary Fund as part of its conditions for the loan of 1976. From 1979, the Conservative government has placed the accent on reducing total public spending, of which local government spending is a part, in order to control the public sector borrowing requirement (budget deficit). The problem with this is that, apart from capital expenditure, which is already tightly controlled by central government and has fallen substantially, local government spending does not contribute to the public sector borrowing requirement as local authorities are not legally permitted to budget for a deficit on revenue expenditure. Ministers have also argued that rates pose an intolerable burden on households and commercial businesses. This is debatable, for rates comprise only a small proportion of expenditure in each case and, in any case, the main cause of rates increases in recent years has been the withdrawal of central grant. In fact, between 1978 and 1986, while Scottish local government revenue spending increased in real terms by just 2.6%, domestic rates in real terms doubled, as the result of the withdrawal of grant and the controversial property revaluation which transferred the burden from industrial to commercial ratepayers (Keating, 1985a).

It has also suggested from time to time that local expenditure is 'crowding out' private investment by pre-empting limited resources. This is a complex issue. Two 'crowding out' mechanisms have been identified in the literature (Heald, 1983). One is physical, where public expenditure pre-empts too large a share of physical resources, depriving the market sector. This is really only plausible in conditions of full employment and where public and private resources are mutually substitutable. The other mechanism is financial, where excessive public expenditure financed by borrowing drives up interest rates or inflationary expectations, depriving industry and commerce of finance. This mechanism cannot apply to local government revenue spending, in so far as it is financed by rates and charges. It can apply only to that part of local government spending which contributes to the public sector borrowing requirement, that is spending financed by central grant and capital spending financed by borrowing, both of which are already controlled by central government, not by local authorities.

Finding a coherent strategy behind all this is consequently difficult but what does seem to impel the Scottish Office in its search for cuts are three considerations. First, there is the pressure of the Treasury, which traditionally seeks to maintain a ceiling on all public expenditure by whatever agency; it regards local government spending for planning and control purposes as part of the Secretary of State's budget, so that any overspend in relation to the planning totals in the annual public expenditure White Paper will count as a black mark against the Secretary of State. Secondly, there was, at least in the late 1970s and early 1980s, considerable pressure from ratepayers' groups, particularly in Edinburgh, for the government to intervene to curb rate increases. Rates as a form of taxation are peculiarly liable to this type of revolt as, though they are not unduly burdensome in comparison with most forms of central taxation, they are highly visible, not deducted at source or hidden in the price of purchases and, given the infrequency of property revaluations, are non-bouyant, requiring annual increases in the rate merely to keep pace with inflation. In Glasgow there has been a remarkable absence of ratepayers' revolts, despite the city's having the highest rate poundages in Scotland, a reflection of differing political attitudes and perhaps a higher valuation of public services in a poorer city. Central government's third concern is the belief that rates increases are damaging the health of industry and commerce.

The effect of spending levels on the local economy is, indeed, controversial. Revenue spending on salaries of local government employees does, of course, contribute to effective demand in the local economy, with favourable multiplier effects. However, in so far as it is financed from rates, the disposable income and hence the ability to spend on privately-provided goods and services is reduced by an equivalent amount. If increased local spending is financed by increased central goverment grants, on the other hand, there may be an increase in aggregate demand though, local economies being inherently open, the multiplier may be small, much of the increased spending by council employees seeping out in purchases elsewhere in the UK or abroad. Given that local councils are not able to borrow to cover their revenue expenditure and that central government grant and capital spending are tightly controlled, it it not in fact possible for councils to pursue 'local Keynesianism', reflating the local economy by increased expenditure. Cuts in central government grants, on the other hand, will have a deflationary effect, forcing local authorities to reduce their employment or increase rates, reducing the disposable income of households. This may be offset by whatever compensating increases in national government spending or reductions in national taxation filter down to the locality but, in recent years reductions in central grants to local government have been aimed at reducing the public sector borrowing requirement and have not resulted in net reductions of central taxation.

Capital spending has different implications for local economies. Most of it goes directly to the private sector in the form of contract work, so creating private sector jobs. As it is financed largely by borrowing, there is no necessary offsetting reduction in private disposable income in the locality, though there is a long-term revenue cost in the form of loan charges for interest and debt repayment. Of course, it is not necessarily the case that capital spending projects will result in contracts for local businesses but in many cases, particularly for housing, they will do so; this is a vital issue in Glasgow given the historic importance of housing and housing renewal.

The new Conservative government in 1979 inherited a number of devices to influence local spending levels. It could cut capital allocations. This had already been done by the Labour government from 1976 and by 1979 capital spending in Scotland was at about half its level at the time of reorganisation. Not all of this reduction should be attributed to the search for public spending cuts in the wake of the IMF intervention; the end of the school building programme counted for a substantial part of the reduction, as did the end of the more generous allocations allowed to cope with the immediate effects of reorganisation. Figure 3.1 shows the reductions in capital expenditure for Scotland during the years of stringency.

Controls on revenue expenditure were more indirect and applied at the

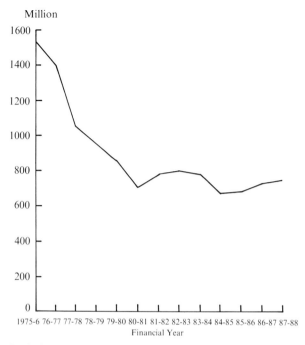

FIGURE 3.1    Capital Spending Estimates, Scotland, 1982-3 prices. *Source*: CIPFA.

level of Scotland as a whole. The Secretary of State could reduce the amount of spending allowed for in the rate support grant settlement and could reduce the proportion of spending financed by grant which, under successive Secretaries of State, has gone down from 75% in 1976-7 to 56.1% in 1986-7. Figure 3.2 shows rate support grant for Scotland in constant price terms. After an increase at the time of reorganisation, it was brought down to its old levels then, in the early years of the Conservative government, drifted up again (along with public expenditure generally) before being brought down in the mid 1980s under pre-reorganisation levels.

Another instrument of control was the abatement procedure popularly known as 'clawback' whereby RSG was reduced across the board where expenditure levels for Scotland as a whole were considered excessive. Finally, advisory guidelines on revenue spending were issued to each council. These had been introduced at the request of the Convention of Scottish Local Authorities (COSLA) in the balmy days of post-reorganisation consensus, to help councils plan their expenditure levels but, as they came increasingly to be used as an instrument of control, COSLA turned against them.

In the early years of the Conservative government, the running in the battle against central control was made not by Glasgow or Strathclyde but by the more left-wing councils in Lothian region, Dundee and Stirling districts and,

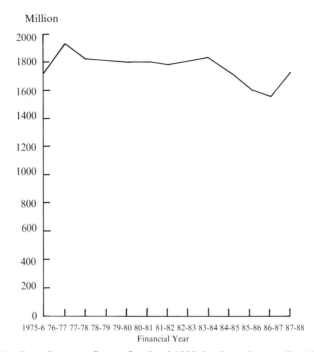

Million

FIGURE 3.2    Rate Support Grant, Scotland 1982-3 prices. *Source*: Scottish Office.

after 1984, Edinburgh district. There ensued a complicated series of legislative changes, progressively tightening central control. The first came in 1981 when Secretary of State George Younger introduced the innocuously named Local Government (Miscellaneous Provisions) (Scotland) Act, giving him power to withdraw rate support grant at budget stage from any council which in his view was planning 'excessive and unreasonable' expenditure. In making his judgement, he was to have regard to:

a)  the expenditure or estimated expenses in that or the preceding year, of other local authorities which are, in the opinion of the Secretary of State, closely comparable (or as closely comparable as is practicable) with the local authority concerned;
b)  general economic conditions;
c)   such other criteria as he considers appropriate.

These criteria pose immense problems for a city like Glasgow. As it is the only conurbation in Scotland, there are no authorities which could be considered remotely comparable. General economic conditions would have very different implications for Keynesians and monetarists; and, as critics did not fail to point out, criterion (c) is so wide as to make (a) and (b) redundant. The power was nevertheless used against seven councils chosen in a manner apparently

owing rather more to political considerations than objective analysis of all
Scottish budgets (Midwinter, Keating and Taylor, 1983). Neither Glasgow
nor Strathclyde featured on this 'hit list'. The following year, the law was
changed again, to give the Secretary of State power to force local authorities
to make refunds to ratepayers and to strike a lower rate. This time, four
councils, including Glasgow were caught in the net. In 1984, the law was
changed yet again, allowing the Secretary of State to make the abatement of
rate support grant proportional to each council's spending over its guideline
figure. The abatement was then calculated on a progressive scale such that,
while councils just over their guideline would lose pound for pound on rate
support grant, those more than 3% over would lose up to £1.70 in grant for
every £1 over guideline. A council in this position could either make cuts in
the course of the year and, by coming in under the guideline at the end of the
year, get back the withheld grant or, if it failed to do this, find itself with a
deficit at the end of the year which, legally, would be the first charge on
the following year's rates. The corresponding rates hike could then provide
grounds for the Secretary of State to intervene to force a rates cut; the council
would then be obliged to cut its expenditure. This abatement procedure has
been used regularly since.

We can now consider how all this has affected Glasgow and Strathclyde.
Figures 3.3 and 3.4 show capital allocations for general services and housing

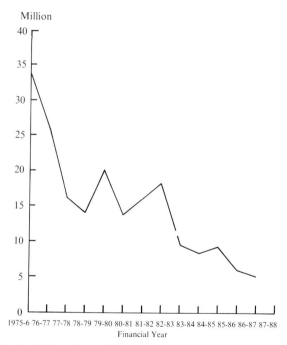

FIGURE 3.3   Capital Allocations, Glasgow District General Services 1982-3 prices.
*Source*: Glasgow District Council.

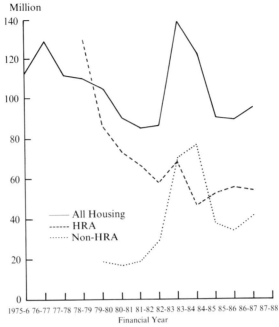

FIGURE 3.4    Capital Allocations for Housing, Glasgow District, 1982-3 prices. *Source*:
Glasgow District Council.

respectively for the district council in constant price terms. The cut in the
general services allocation has been particularly severe, with few major projects proceeding—the earlier years included major works such as the Burrell
Gallery and the Mitchell Library extension. In housing, expenditure has been
cut over the period, though in the early 1980s there was a steep increase in
the amount allowed in the non-HRA allocation, that is, for grants to private
housing. Council housing investment (the HRA account) has been cut back
sharply; in the early years, these two accounts are not distinguished. The
meaning and significance of these trends in housing expenditure is discussed
more fully in chapter 5.

Figure 3.5 shows Glasgow district's rate support grant, along with the
housing support grant. The most striking trend is the cut in housing support
grant, a phenomenon common to the whole of Scotland and which was
intended by the Conservative government to force councils to increase their
rents. If they chose, instead, to put the burden on the rates by increasing the
rate fund contribution, they would fall foul of the penalty system described
above. In Glasgow, this was a particularly traumatic issue, given the importance of the low rents policy in Labour tradition and the new Labour majority
in 1980 initially took a a fairly hard line, opting to keep the rents down. The
result was penalties on the HRA capital account of £10.71 million in 1981/2

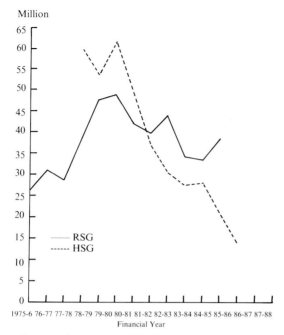

FIGURE 3.5    Rate Support Grant (RSG) and Housing Support Grant (HSG) Glasgow
1982-3 prices. *Source*: Glasgow District Council.

and £17.1 million in 1982/3. With a squeeze on RSG at the same time, rate
levels were increased from 35p in the pound to 48p in 1981/2 and then 58p
in 1982/3. Thereafter, the district's tactics changed, partly because of a more
flexible line in the Glasgow district Labour party, where union interests were
worried about the cuts in the capital programme and the penalty for 1984/5
was just £5.5 million. Since then, the legal limitation on the rate fund contribution has removed the whole agonising choice from the council.

Glasgow's rate support grant shows a fairly steady increase to 1980 and a
decline thereafter, a watershed coinciding with the change in government.
Under the Labour Secretary of State (the only Glasgow MP to have sat in
the Cabinet since the war) the city had a sympathetic ear and was able to get
the RSG formula changed to allow a larger *per capita* allocation for large
urban areas experiencing rapid population loss—a rule which, in the Scottish
context, would apply only to Glasgow, though there is international evidence
to sustain the view that older cities losing population do face higher *per capita*
spending needs. So there were steep rises in RSG until 1979-80. Thereafter,
the Conservatives changed the formula, gradually introducing the 'client
group method' under which the city has suffered severely. Glasgow's complaint is that the Scottish Office formula fails to take into account its metropolitan status and the increased costs imposed by the large numbers of people

who visit Glasgow to work, to use the cultural and leisure facilities or as tourists. Perhaps if Glasgow were politically more marginal and subject to political competition in national as well as local elections, these arguments would carry greater force.

Figure 3.6 plots changes in guidelines and the corresponding expenditure levels (that is, those expenditure items which are considered for guideline). It will be noted that expenditure has consistently been over guideline, notably in 1983/4, when expenditure went up while the guideline figure was cut. With the council 36.5% over guideline, the Secretary of State intervened to cut the city's rate levels. Midwinter (1984) has described the considerable confusion surrounding all this, with the Scottish Office admitting to a £4 million error in its calculations and choosing to compare Glasgow not just with Edinburgh but with Clydebank (population 53,000) and Cumbernauld (a new town with 63,000 population) districts. He suggests that a critical factor was the government's determination to punish councils making high Rate Fund Contributions to their housing accounts, though this was already the subject of a separate penalty procedure.

Glasgow was not subjected to the selective penalty procedures in the years immediately following, as both central and local government were engaged in a learning process. For central government, there was some embarrassment

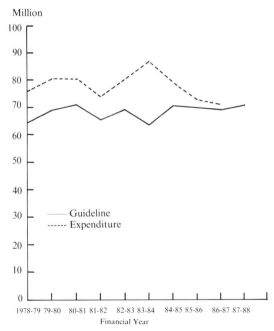

FIGURE 3.6   Current Expenditure Guidelines and Expenditure against Guideline, Glasgow District 1982-3 prices. *Source*: Glasgow District Council.

when the rebates to ratepayers following the forced reduction came out at an average of just 19p per week while in the district council those seeking confrontation came to lose influence as the leadership and officials increased their skill in playing the system. So the Secretary of State imposed the statutory limit on the rate fund contribution to housing and relied increasingly on the automatic clawback system with the threat that any council piling the cost of the clawback on the next year's rate could still be subject to selective action. In the council, budget discussions were still conducted in a highly charged atmosphere with threats of breaking the law floating about but the officials busied themselves with ever more elaborate forms of 'creative accounting'. It is this latter factor which makes the figures for expenditure out-turns in recent years increasingly unreliable. With the percentage claw-back rate varying from year to year, the council can choose to load expen-diture into a relatively lenient year; within the statutory limits, it can capitalise revenue spending or *vice versa*; other devices are legion. It can also exploit the existence of underspending or delayed spending in programmes, keeping more tight central control over departments to ensure that these fortuitous savings accrue to the authority as a whole and are not diverted into new projects. So, in practice, it can produce its books at the end of the year showing an out-turn close to the guideline figure. The figures (Figure 3.6) show spending just below the levels of 1978-9 though creative accounting means that this should be treated with great caution. For internal Labour Party purposes, the council leadership must set a budget above government guidelines, as a gesture of defiance to the centre. As far as possible, however, the out-turn figures, that is the actual expenditure, will be brought within the guideline in the course of the year. The large cuts since 1983/4 are mainly due to the forced reductions in the rate fund contribution to subsidise council housing (see chapter 5 for the effects on rents).

For the region, the position is quite similar, albeit on a bigger scale. Strathclyde is Britain's largest-spending local authority, with a revenue budget of some £1.4 billion, though without the large capital programmes in housing which are so important for the district. Figure 3.7 shows the sharp reductions in capital allocations in the late 1970s, the biggest cuts falling jon education, with the end of the school building programme.

The trend in rate support grant, shown in Figure 3.8 is not dissimilar to that for Glasgow district, with a small increase following reorganisation disappearing in 1976 but steady increases for the remainder of the Labour government, up to 1979. Therefter, the change in the formula, with the introduction of the client group method and the reduction in the resources element, has hit Strathclyde hard, with a steady loss of grant during the mid 1980s.

The region's response to the pressure for cuts has been even more low-key than that of the district, reflecting its political style. Central government, too, has tended to shy away from a confrontation with Scotland's largest local authority. The region has, nevertheless, suffered grant reductions under the automatic penalty procedure and has come under pressure not only to reduce its expenditure but to shift its priorities. This is because central government's

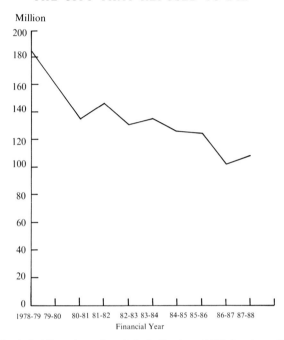

FIGURE 3.7    Capital Allocations Strathclyde Region, 1982-3 prices. *Source*: Strathclyde Regional Council.

planning assumptions, as reflected in the national public expenditure white
paper have anticipated a reduction in education spending in line with the
falling school-age population, but some increase in social work spending to
cope with the effects of unemployment and an ageing population and in
police as a matter of national Conservative policy. Shifting resources out of
education, however, has proved difficult because the teachers' unions and
Strathclyde's own policy have ruled out compulsory redundancy while there
is intense local opposition to any proposal for school closures. So spending
on education has not fallen in line with the reduction in the client group.
Instead, the fiscal squeeze has become tighter every year, exacerbated by the
penalties for exceeding guidelines. Creative accounting and underspend on
programmes, of course, serves to reduce the gap between guideline and out-
turn at the end of the year but each year the deficit which has to be rated for
in the new financial year increases.

   Both tiers of local government in the city have suffered real cuts in central
support in recent years as a result of political decisions to reduce local
government spending overall and to change the formula for calculating the
rate support grant. Yet the response has been to work within the rules of the
game to try and beat the system. There has been none of the brinkmanship
seen in Liverpool or, on a lesser scale, in Edinburgh, in spite of some rum-

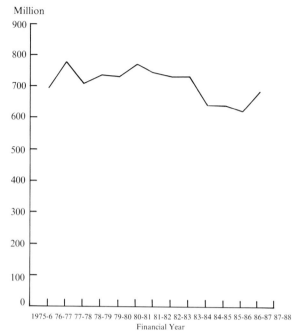

FIGURE 3.8    Rate Support Grant, Strathclyde Region 1982-3. *Source*: Strathclyde Regional Council.


blings from the activists. The district have engaged in some public displays, such as placing large signs on derelict sites informing the public that development has been halted by government capital cuts or halting the stone-cleaning of the city chambers half way as a highly visible reproach to the Scottish Office; but, by and large the effects of cuts are less visible and less dramatic. They have, nevertheless, had consequences, which we shall be examining in later chapters (5 and 6).

The repeated changes in the system of local finance have not come to an end at the time of writing. Following the property revaluation of 1983, Conservative ministers came under renewed pressure from ratepayers' groups in the east of Scotland, who found a sympathetic ear from the Prime Minister, and turned back to the old manifesto pledge to abolish the system of domestic rates altogether. This was not an issue which the Scottish Office could decide on its own and the issue went to Cabinet. As usual, the Treasury proved reluctant to concede any bouyant taxes to local government and there was, in any case, a strong assumption within the government against a local income tax, given the Conservative antipathy to income taxes and their determination to reduce them at the national level. Sales taxes were ruled out because of administrative difficulties and European Community regulations, leaving a poll tax as the only feasible alternative to the existing property-based tax.

Under severe political pressure from Scottish Conservatives and needing some sort of political initiative to try and shore up the party's dwindling fortunes in Scotland, the then Secretary of State, George Younger, went for the poll tax solution. The Department of the Environment, responsible for local government in England, went along with the idea of abolishing domestic rates on a Britain-wide basis but, sensitive to the political damage which the new tax could bring, postponed the English legislation until safely after the next General Election. As has happened on a number of issues, they were content to use Scotland as a testing ground for the new policy.

All adults in Scotland will be liable for a 'community charge' levied at a flat rate by each district, regional and islands council. Business rates will, as an interim measure, be linked to the inflation rate as measured by the Retail Price Index and, in the longer run, a uniform national business rate will be introduced for the whole of Scotland, set by central government and with the proceeds distributed among councils.

The Government's defence of the flat-rate charge is essentially to the effect that, as rates fall on householders alone, a minority of the population pays them. The majority thus have an incentive to vote irresponsibly for high-spending councillors, safe in the knowledge that someone else will pay. This majority includes other members of households in which the head of the household pays rates and those who receive rate rebates through the social security system. No-one has ever produced a single piece of evidence to the effect that voters behave in this way; indeed, it goes against everything that is known about British voting behaviour. It also includes the spouses of ratepayers amongst those who have an interest in irresponsibly high levels of local taxation, on the cynical calculation that they will not have to pay, though in most households these expenses are pooled. At the same time, the government insists that the rating system is unfair, citing the example of the widowed pensioner living in the large house who has to pay more than the family with grown-up children all in work crammed into a smaller house next door. Against this, of course, one can cite the example of the millionaire living alone in a large house who henceforth will have to pay a single community charge, while the large poor family in a run-down property elsewhere in the city will have to pay several times as much.

In the words of the Secretary of State, Malcolm Rifkind, the new community charges will bring fairness, simplicity and accountability. Michael Ancram, Minister for Local Government, amplified the point about fairness in these terms: 'The new community charges will be fairer because they will mean that many more of those who benefit from local authority services will contribute to the cost of providing them. And this in turn will be good for the local democratic process because everyone will in future have a personal interest in the cost of policies they vote for.' This certainly did not satisfy critics of the proposals who continued to accuse the Government of confused thinking. In particular, there was confusion over whether 'fairness' meant that local taxation and service provision was to be redistributive or not. If fairness means that people are to be charged according to their usage of services, that is, there should be no redistributive element, then extra charges should be levied on large families, old people and others who use services most. If, on the other hand, 'fairness' is related to ability to pay, that is, there is a redistributive element, then a local tax should be devised which is related to ability to pay, local income tax being the obvious example. A flat rate tax bears no relation to any recognised criterion of fairness.

Despite the government's denials, the implication that people who vote should bear the taxes remained clear. It was sensitivity to the charge that they were taxing the right to vote which led Ministers to coin the euphemism 'community charge' to replace the term 'poll tax', in the erroneous belief that the latter referred to polls as in voting. Later, they stood somewhat corrected, conceding that: 'A poll tax is a tax payable by all adults. In that sense the community charge can be considered a poll tax. But many people take the term "poll tax" to mean a tax on the right to vote. It will not be a poll tax in that sense because there will be no direct connection with people's right to vote.' This does not get around the fact that the justification for the tax put forward by ministers is that those who vote for services should pay the cost; in other words, there should be no representation without taxation. It is, in any case, questionable how far this will increase accountability to voters, since, with the national capping of the business rate, the proportion of local spending over which the voter will have control will fall.

The impact of the community charge was calculated by the Scottish Office for all Scottish districts. On the basis of 1986-7 expenditure, it would vary from £161 per adult in Gordon to £261 in Glasgow, with 3.85 million people liable to the charge, against 1.5 million ratepayers at present. About half the population would be better off and half worse off. These figures, however, assume a 100% collection rate. In practice, critics claimed that the administrative complexities of the scheme would allow a substantial number of people to escape the net, imposing an added burden on those who are duly registered to pay. It is not difficult, then, to envisage more than half the population being worse off, with important political repercussions. Calculations by Glasgow District Council showed most areas of the city as suffering increases in local taxation, with the gains confined to a few well-off areas.

One of the most vexed questions concerns the system of rebates and here the Government was caught between conflicting objectives. On the one hand, it insisted on everyone paying towards local services. On the other, it claimed that its new system would be fair to all, including the poor. The result is a compromise, with rebates of up to 80% of the community charge on a tapering scale. A Glaswegian household on the minimum subsistence income would have to pay £1 a week extra for each adult member. Further cuts in central government grant leading to increases in community charges, could well push this up before the starting date.

What proved most striking as the proposals were elaborated, however, was the administrative difficulties involved. Identifying those liable for the charge is the first problem and here the Government was uncharacteristically coy. The task was to fall on the Community Charges Registration Officer, who is to be the present valuation assessor (for the rates). Being currently responsible for preparing the valuation roll and the electoral register, 'he will therefore already have a great deal of information to hand about residents in his area.' This implied that he would be able to use the electoral register for compiling the community charge register, reawakening all the fears about a tax on voting.

Further administrative difficulties involve people moving house, who will be obliged to inform the Registration Officer in their new area. If they do not do so, after the abolition of valuation rolls, one assumes that he will again have recourse to the electoral register. Tracing the transient population of a city the size of Glasgow, though, could well prove impossible. For lodging houses or houses in multi-occupation, the Registration Officer will have the right to impose a collective community charge payable by the landlord—a rate by any other name! Similarly, 'housing bodies' such as District Councils, New Towns and the Scottish Special Housing Association, will collect the charges from people living in the houses they let. As it is well known that most of these tenants do not at present distinguish between rates and rents, it is difficult to see them distinguishing between community charges and rents, so destroying the government's accountability objective—unless, of course, the agencies go to the expense of establishing quite separate collection systems.

Full-time students will be registered to pay the charge at their place of study, a provision obviously dictated by administrative convenience more than logic, but which will give a boost to the incomes of councils in cities such as Glasgow and Edinburgh with student populations well into four figures. The students' home councils will be less lucky. It is intended that the average cost of community charges will added to students' grants. If we take the Government's cynical view of the local elector, voting for higher spending as long as others are paying for it, we would predict that students would register to vote in their home towns, there to demand higher spending. In practice, of course, such speculation merely serves to highlight the dubious behavioural assumptions on which the whole scheme is based.

The additional cost of collection of the new charges was estimated by the Government at £16-22 million per year, with an additional cost of about £9 million for setting up the billing and collection procedures in 1988-9. This, at a time of retrenchment and constant exhortation from the Scottish Office to cut back on spending, aroused particular resentment among councils.

In proceding with their version of rates reform, the Government were taking a big political gamble and, though implementation of the scheme was not due until after a General Election it appears to have been a factor in the Conservative rout in Scotland in 1987. There is also a clear calculation that, as a modestly regressive redistribution of the fiscal burden, the new system will appeal to middle-class Conservative voters. This certainly helped to maintain the impetus for reform with the Conservative Party, though there was a danger that, in appealing to its own diminished band of supporters, the party would fail to attract new support away from its competitors. The effect of the new system of central-local relations will be profound. With the nationally-set business rate, the community charge will be the only element of local taxation which councils will be free to determine, amounting to just 15% of local government expenditure in Scotland. So increases in spending, or merely attempts to make up for future cuts in central support, will require disproportionately large, and unpopular, increases in the community charge. This, too, is certainly behind the government's calculations, allowing it to tighten the fiscal squeeze on councils and removing almost all their remaining freedom to set their own spending levels. Just in case this should prove ineffective and electors be prepared to pay much higher levels of community charge, the selective penalty procedures are being retained, together with a power to intervene to set the community charge for any council.

Central-local relations in Britain have been going through a period of extreme turbulence with, as we have, seen a marked reduction in the financial independence of local councils. This has sharply reduced the capacity of both Strathclyde Region and Glasgow District to frame strategies for urban renewal and service development. With their commitments and statutory duties overwhelming their limited resources, the margins for innovation have been whittled away. They have consequently been forced to look for new resources wherever these may be available, entering into partnerships with public agencies such as the SDA and MSC into which central funds have been diverted, and with the private sector. In the process, they have lost much of the leadership role which they might have been expected to assume after reorganisation. This, too, appears part of the overall design of the Conservative government in the 1980s, a design in which the leading role in urban change and development would be taken by the private sector, with local government in a subordinate role, providing services on demand, following closely central government guidelines, but not engaging in policy innovation itself. Some of the effects of this in practice will be examined in the remaining chapters.

# 4   Planning the New City

## Planning for Regeneration

The previous chapter showed how one of the main impulses behind local government reform and the creation of the new regional council was the need for physical, social and economic planning. To this end a series of 'planning systems' was established as a framework for local government's own activities and a mechanism for central-local dialogue, in the spirit of the new partnership. In the event, the experience of planning was to prove something of a disappointment and many of the major developments in the regeneration of the city have effectively by-passed the planning system. The main planning instruments were to be regional reports, structure plans (for the region), local plans (for the district), financial plans (for both tiers), transport policies and programmes (for the region) and housing plans (for the district).

The regional report was conceived by the Scottish Office as an inducement to corporate management in the regional councils, a focus for planning going beyond the traditional land-use concerns. It had to set out strategic policies of the regional council and how they were to be achieved. It was anticipated that, with the regional report in place, Scottish regional councils would not necessarily have to produce structure plans for the whole area of their respective regions. This contrasts with the position in England where structure plans must eventually be produced to cover the whole country. The first regional reports were called for immediately after reorganisation, to be submitted to the Scottish Office within a year. Strathclyde's regional report was based on the *West Central Scotland Plan* (which had never been officially adopted) and set out the council's priorities as combating urban deprivation and unemployment. These were to remain Strathclyde's strategic objectives, to inform its other planning instruments and give rise to the social and economic strategies which we shall be examining in subsequent chapters. As with its predecessor, the *West Central Scotland Plan*, the regional report put the emphasis on the regeneration of the older urban and industrial areas, with an end to overspill and new town development. On its recommendation, the Secretary of State in 1976 cancelled the new town at Stonehouse which had barely started work and announced that the resources and staff would be transferred to a major inner-city regeneration scheme, the Glasgow Eastern Area Renewal (GEAR) project (discussed below). Despite its importance in setting the strategic direction for the new authority, the regional report exercise has not been repeated. The Scottish Office feared that councils were merely using the system as a means to bid for extra resources from central government at a time when it was trying to cut back on local spending. Later, they were overtaken by the anti-planning philosophy of the post-1979 Conservative Government which saw them as a time-consuming exercise for which staff could not be spared. Nor did Strathclyde Region itself update the document, concentrating, instead, on developing the specific policies which stemmed from it.

The structure plan is intended to consider strategic questions of land use and provide the basis for the local plans of district councils and the infrastructure development of the region itself. As a strategic document it should not be concerned with detailed questions of planning and, rather than a map, consists of a written statement and a key diagram. It is subject to a process of public consultation and examination in public and must be approved by the Secretary of State. Once the structure plan has been approved, the districts' local plans must conform to it and development applications which breach it can be 'called in' by the regional council (subject to appeal to the Secretary of State). Otherwise, development control is in the hands of the district council.

Strathclyde's structure plan was produced between 1976 and 1979 con-centrating, on the advice of the Scottish Office, on the problems of the conurbation and pursuing the themes of the regional report on the need to combat unemployment and deprivation. Apart from the transport proposals (see below) the other main theme of the structure plan was the implications of the end of the absolute housing shortage in Glasgow and the need to turn attention to improving the quality of housing and diversifying housing tenure. 30% of the region's housing stock was said to have a poor environment, with 62% of this defective stock in the city. Here, the regional council anticipated some of the policy changes of the 1980s and the break with the municipal monopoly. To improve the stock and stem population decline it recommended more encouragement for owner-occupation, for housing association projects and for new types of council tenure, including tenant cooperatives. We can also see in the plan the beginnings of the new area approaches to renewal. In its advice, the Scottish Office had recommended that:

> where appropriate, the Structure Plan should indicate and describe proposed Action Areas, thus highlighting both the Regional and the District planning authorities' priorities in terms of action and investment and identifying those areas in which comprehensive treatment either by public or private agencies will be concentrated . . . it should indicate what actions are to be taken by public or private agencies, the effects of such action and the public investment implications of the scheme as far as these can be foreseen.

The action which was to be taken was not clearly specified but the emphasis here is on physical development, on housing and environmental improvement, as befits a document whose focus was on land-use. Initially, the regional council's reaction was to turn the question around and, in the first draft of the structure plan, to recommend that the Secretary of State designate a series of areas, including the four peripheral estates, the GEAR area and older areas such as Maryhill, Springburn, Partick and Possil as action areas. Predictably, in approving the plan, the Secretary of State turned the recommendation around yet again, and put the onus for preparing action programmes on the local authorities. The list of areas, though, was largely unchanged, with a small number being designated as 'early action areas'.

For industrial development, the plan put the emphasis on the needs of the older industrial areas, while recognising the potential of the new towns for attracting outside investment and pinpointing key sites for major industrial uses. The transport and highway plans of the council were incorporated in it though these were to prove more controversial.

Like the old development plan before it and structure plans in other parts of the country, Strathclyde's plan was to suffer from a time-slippage in its preparation which fatally weakened its impact. Submitted in 1979, the plan was eventually approved by the Secretary of State with effect from 1981—it had originally been intended to cover the period 1978-83. Even then, the Secretary of State attached some reservations, on housing, transport and shopping, to his approval and, rather than tackle these separately, the region incorporated them in its update, due in 1981.

Already, by this time, doubts were beginning to be expressed on how far the new local government system was achieving a real integration of the various strands of urban policy. In particular, there was doubt as to whether the physical development proposals and priorities, as identified in the structure plan, were consistent with the priorities for social regeneration (examined in chapter 6) and economic regeneration (examined in chapter 7) identified by other departments of the regional council and by the other agencies. For example, the regional council was being criticised by Glasgow District for failing to relate the areas for priority treatment (APTs) identified in the region's own social strategy (see chapter 6) to the action areas identified in the structure plan. The SDA had also displayed some reluctance to take up the region's priority areas as laid down in the plan and in due course the joint economic initiatives were to take their own course. The 1981 version of the structure plan, however, denied all this, claiming that there was a 'close relationship between the deprivation and economic strategies and the contribution which the urban renewal priority areas make to both strategies (is demonstrated).' In the APTs, particularly the priority APTs, land renewal would complement local industrial initiatives and housing action. In the joint economic initiative areas, land renewal would support industrial site preparation, factory building, business development and industrial promotion activities. In spatial terms, there was a 'strong correlation between the Council's APTs, the prospective joint economic initiative areas and the urban renewal priorities identified in the approved Structure Plan.' Only 20 out of 75 APTs were not included in the action areas for physical renewal and 7 of the 11 joint economic initiative areas were included in the physical renewal list. The fact was, however, that the fit between the various types of priority area was better in the inner city than in the peripheral estates. The latter were recognised as social priority areas but not as priority areas for physical or economic regeneration. The implications of this are pursued later (chapters 6 and 8). The lack of fit is apparent in the 1981 list of priority areas of various types (see Table 4.1).

It is clear from this that the economic initiatives were focused largely on the inner city and old industrial areas, with the periphery left to be taken care of largely by social policy measures—a reflection of the 'dual city' model, considered later (chapter 8). By the time of the 1984 revision of the structure plan, it was clear that it had ceased to be the major force guiding the urban renewal strategy. Certainly, renewal was under way in most of the renewal

TABLE 4.1   STRATHCLYDE REGIONAL COUNCIL'S REGENERATION PRIORITIES, 1981

| Physical Renewal Areas | (Those marked for Early Action) | APTs | Proposed Joint Economic Initiative | Existing Economic Initiative |
|---|---|---|---|---|
| Drumchapel | — | Drumchapel | — | — |
| Partick | Inner Docks | part | Finnieston | — |
| Possil | — | Greater Possil | — | — |
| Maryhill | Maryhill Corridor S. | Maryhill Corridor | — | Garscube Science Pk. |
| City centre | — | City centre | | |
| Springburn | — | Springburn Barmulloch Balornock Blackhill Germiston | | |
| Inner East End | Parkhead/ Shettleston | W. Carntyne GEAR Haghill | — | GEAR |
| Easterhouse | — | Barlanark Cranhill Easterhouse Garthamlock Queenslie Ruchazie | — | — |
| Hallside | Hallside | Cambuslang | — | — |
| Castlemilk | — | Castlemilk | — | — |
| Pollok | — | Darnley N. Pollok Priesthill/ Nitshill Carnwadric/ Arden | — | — |
| Govan/ Kinning Park/ Kingston | Inner Docks | Govan | Govan/Ibrox | |
| — | — | Govanhill | — | — |
| — | — | Gorbals | — | — |

Source: *Strathclyde Regional Council. Structure Plan, 1981. Written Statement.*

areas but this stemmed from a variety of forces at work at the same time. The structure plan was focused more and more on land-use issues rather than development strategy generally, but, when it looked at the sites available around the city for various purposes, it could conclude only that they were already being developed or that they were, for one reason or another, unsuitable for development. A proposal from Glasgow District that the Easterhouse estate be added to the list of early action areas was turned down on the ground that 'the vacant land is concentrated on the periphery which presents problems associated more with agricultural practice than urban renewal.' It is unlikely that this delphic observation will have much impact on renewal policies undertaken in Easterhouse.

There are several reasons why the structure plan should have had relatively little impact. The system was conceived in the 1960s when development pressure was buoyant and industry was expanding. Even in those days, the structure plan system could have been criticised as more suitable for areas in England where there was strong development pressure than for west-central Scotland where the emphasis had to be on encouraging rather than controlling development. The system lacked 'teeth' and had never been related to central government's regional development policies, as had been anticipated in the past. Even in relation to local government itself, the structure plan was weak. There was no clear link with financial planning within the regional council and no control over district council activities including housing, except through the cumbersome method of call-in. Not surprisingly, many planners were more interested in trying to make things happen than in drawing up plans and moved into the policy planning department and then the chief executive's department, where they could have an influence on the implementation of the corporate strategy in its social and economic dimensions. The structure plan has also been by-passed by central government and SDA initiatives such as enterprise zones, task forces and area projects and has come under attack within the region for its irrelevance and also its apparently dogmatic insistence on the protection of retail interests within the city centre, to the disadvantage of the periphery (chapter 6).

Local plans are prepared by the district council and give more detailed information on what types of development will be permitted in which locations as well as the district's own propoals for housing and other development. There are 47 local plan areas in the city and by July 1985 18 local plans had been adopted (they do not need approval from central government), 18 were at the stage of the written statement (for consultation), 8 were at the survey stage and 2 were proposed. In addition, there is a special subject plan prepared jointly by region and district for the Forth and Clyde Canal. At a more general level, arising out of its corporate planning exercise, the District declared six priority areas for renewal. These are the GEAR area in the old east end, the Maryhill corridor and the four peripheral estates. These in turn have been the subject of specific initiatives in housing and other fields. While the district's six priority areas do not conflict with the region's priorities, there is not always a direct correspondence at the operational level.

One comment made in the late 1970s was that, with the region having a structure plan for the conurbation and the district having plans for small areas, there was no real perspective on the *city*. Consequently, in 1979 the Scottish Office called for a city plan, to be prepared by the district. This duly appeared, bringing together the council's policies and priorities but, inevitably, making a bid for extra resources. It was filed away in the Scottish Office whence its reappearance has been awaited for several years.

## Comprehensive Renewal—the GEAR Project

One of the earliest fruits of the shift in attention to the inner city in the mid 1970s was the Glasgow Eastern Area Renewal (GEAR) project. The origins of GEAR have been attributed (Leclerc and Draffan, 1984) to impatience within the Scottish Office at the pace of urban renewal in Glasgow under the auspices of the old corporation. It is important, though, not to see Glasgow in isolation. The early 1970s had seen the English inner area studies originally commissioned by Peter Walker at the Department of the Environment, which were eventually to feed into significant policy changes under his Labour successor, Peter Shore. In a parallel development, the Urban Renewal Unit was established in the Scottish Office in 1975 to formulate general policies for urban regeneration, encompassing action on the social, environmental and economic fronts, in line with contemporary thinking on the nature of the urban problem. Not surprisingly, its chief preoccupation was Glasgow and the possibilities of mounting a major integrated renewal operation, to make an immediate impact and to derive lessons for the rest of Scotland, were soon under consideration. One possibility canvassed—which returns to the British urban policy agenda regularly every year or so—was to establish a new agency on the lines of the new town development corporations to displace the local authorities and undertake the task of redevelopment itself. This would have represented a gigantic vote of no confidence in the new local government system which was only just coming into being and was rejected in favour of working through the existing bodies, with the task co-ordinated by the Scottish Development Agency. With the SDA's powers in industrial development and land renewal and local authority powers in housing, education, transport and social services, the potential would exist for a co-ordinated attack on all aspects of urban decline simultaneously. This was very much in accordance with the thinking of the Scottish Office and the first Chairman of the SDA, a former Labour Lord Provost of Glasgow, was keen to be involved but it appears that some of the Agency's senior staff had a more narrowly 'economic' view of its role and resented the involvement in social and planning policies. As we have already noted (chapter 2), the 'economic' orientation of the SDA was to increase significantly from the 1980s, marking a major shift in the nature of its involvement in urban renewal but in GEAR it was not only involved in a comprehensive renewal operation, it had the task of coordinating the whole project.

The SDA was not, however, to undertake the project on its own; rather it would work with the local authorities and other agencies, which would be responsible for their own shares of the programme. Early in 1976, Strathclyde region, Glasgow district and the Scottish Special Housing Association were brought into the negotiations and were later joined by the Housing Corporation, the Manpower Services Commission and the Greater Glasgow health board. With the abandonment of Stonehouse New Town in 1976, there was political pressure for a statement of the alternative urban strategy—the Labour Government was under intense pressure from the SNP and a breakaway Scottish Labour Party (Keating and Bleiman, 1980)—and in May the GEAR project was unveiled. The choice of location had not been without its difficulties. Indicators of deprivation showed the worst problems to be concentrated in the inner city and the peripheral estates but the time was not yet ripe for an admission that the estates, built within the last few years, were already in need of a major regeneration programme. It was also felt that, given the economic dimension of the project, it should be located in an area with an economic and industrial base, albeit a declining one. This indicated one of the inner comprehensive development areas, with the new project carrying through the redevelopment in a more imaginative and expeditious way while paying attention to social and economic as well as purely physical considerations. The choice narrowed down to four areas; Govan, Maryhill, Springburn and the East End (Leclerc and Draffan, 1984) with the latter emerging as the final choice.

The GEAR area covered 1,600 hectares, 8% of the area of the city, with a population of 45,000, having shrunk from 145,000 in 1951. Stretching from the city boundary to the heart of the old city at Glasgow Cross, it included seven comprehensive development areas and in 1976 presented a picture of urban devastation as bad as any in Europe. It was typical of the areas which had been said to suffer from the overspill policies and spontaneous migration, with an ageing population, a large proportion of long-established residents, low incomes and high unemployment. At the same time, though declining, it continued to play an important role in the Glasgow economy, with 42,000 jobs, of which 55% were in manufacturing, 37% in service industries and 6% in construction. Housing conditions were very poor, with a predominance of unimproved nineteenth century tenement buildings.

Such was the political urgency to announce the GEAR project that, although it was unveiled in 1976 as the largest integrated urban renewal project in Europe, aimed at the 'comprehensive social, economic and environmental regeneration of the East End and the creation of conditions for the development of a balanced and thriving community', there was at that stage no operational plan or strategy and no clear indication of what resources would be available and from where. Indeed, it took several years for the GEAR strategy to emerge from the machinery established in 1976. The principle of the organisation was that each agency would remain responsible for its own budget and programmes within the context of the coordinated scheme as a whole. A governing committee was established, chaired by a Scottish Office minister and serviced by the Scottish Development Department, and consisting of senior local councillors and board members of the participating agencies. A consultative group of senior officials, including the chief executives of the regional and district councils, was chaired by the secretary of the SDD. From 1980, a management group of officials with operational responsibility for GEAR within their own agencies was created (Leclerc and Draffan, 1984). Within the SDA, the urban renewal directorate, largely composed of staff transferred from the abandoned Stonehouse development, had responsibility for the Agency's contribution, though later they were subsumed under the new directorate of area development, as the SDA expanded its area projects (Keating and Boyle, 1986).

The delay in producing the overall plan for GEAR was partly the result of the three main agents (region, district and SDA) being so new and having other concerns, partly the result of the method adopted. An early attempt at a highly rationalistic procedure for policy-making, area planning and implementation proved impossible given the differing procedures and priorities of the agencies as well as the weight of existing commitments. Instead, almost in a reversal of administrative theory, an implementation programme, the *Project Programme* was put in train, followed by the preparation of the *Overall Proposals*. The justification was that work was proceding in any case and could not wait until the elaboration of an overall scheme; in practice the *Project Programme* related to the coordination of existing schemes and an *Early Action Programme* of extra work by participants designed to show that GEAR was making an immediate impact. Following the *Overall Proposals*, a rolling programme of works could be developed.

The *Overall Proposals* were produced by a series of working groups of officials from the participating agencies, on population, employment, education, environment, transport, community care, leisure and recreation, shopping, housing and health. These were to identify problems and policy options and involve local residents in their elaboration. The resulting document, *The Future for GEAR*, was produced in 1978 and, after further consultation, the SDA produced the *Overall Proposals* in 1979. At this point, the Scottish Office, now under the Conservatives, appears to have become a little worried about the implications of GEAR in terms of public expenditure commitments and, in its consideration of the *Overall Proposals*, the SDA was instructed to exclude proposals which related to central government matters and those with large future resource implications (Leclerc and Draffan, 1984). As a result, the *GEAR Strategy and Programme* which finally emerged in May 1980 consisted of a statement of extremely broad objectives together with the rolling programme of works developed by the participating authorities. This immediately raised the question of whether GEAR was anything more than a fancy dressing up of existing programmes by the various agencies, with a series of vacuous objectives. The overall objectives were certainly vague, being:

1.  to increase residents' competitiveness in securing employment;
2.  to arrest economic decline and realise the potential of GEAR as a major employment centre;
3.  to overcome the social disadvantage experienced by residents;

4.  to improve and maintain the environment;
5.  to stem population decline and engender a better balanced age and social structure;
6.  to foster residents' commitment and confidence.

The production of the overall programme some four years into the project certainly caused some scepticism and some commentators (Booth *et al.*, 1982) have claimed that GEAR has achieved nothing which would not have happened in its absence. Others maintain that the identification of the area as a priority by the participating agencies has had an effect in shifting resources. The problem, as always, is in knowing what would have happened in the absence of the programme, which coincided with large cuts in public expenditure on a wide range of capital programmes and the onset of recession. Figures produced by the district council do seem to show strong discrimination in favour of GEAR in capital spending. In the period 1979-80 to 1983-4, capital investment per head by all agencies (including the private sector)in GEAR was £2,415, against a city average of £937. As we shall see (chapter 6), it was the peripheral estates which had some cause for complaint, with just 26.6% of all capital investment for priority areas between them, not the GEAR area which alone accounted for 44.1%. For the district council's own expenditure, the GEAR figure per head was exceeded only in the Maryhill Corridor, designated as a priority area in 1977. Figures for 1984-5, produced on a slightly different basis showed the same picture, with GEAR gaining £1,433 investment per head from all sources, against a city average of £492 and £911 in the next most favoured location, Maryhill. GEAR also featured among the region's areas for priority treatment, eligible for special treatment in revenue as well as capital budgets though identifying the area impact of revenue spending is notoriously difficult (chapter 6). It is argued by Booth *et al.* (1982) that GEAR has not brought extra resources into the east end, given that much of the work was programmed by the participating agencies in any case. This largely misses the point since we shall be noting in the chapters to come many examples of major investment programmes in the city which have come to nought. The figures just presented indicate that GEAR may have succeeded in maintaining the momentum of programmes for the east end at a time of general retrenchment, albeit at the expense of other areas.

This conclusion is supported by the work of Nairn (1983) who analysed the expenditure for the period 1977-82, finding that some £48.6 million, or 31% of the expenditure in GEAR could be considered 'extra'; in addition, some £19 million of private housing investment could be attributed to the project. The £48.6 million includes £26.9 million expenditure by the SDA, and £11 million for capital expenditure on roads and traffic management by the region. He points out that Glasgow district had been reducing its housing commitment to GEAR since 1978—but this reflects cutbacks in housing expenditure generally and, as Nairn notes, the district cutback in GEAR was taken up by the Scottish Special Housing Association (SSHA). In fact, for the 1979-85 period, GEAR, with some 6% of the city's population, accounted for 53.2% of public sector housing expenditure (district council, SSHA, Housing Corporation) in priority areas.

We can conclude, then, that GEAR has established itself as a capital expenditure priority at a time of cutback, a fact which is visible to anyone familiar with the area in the early 1970s and visiting it in the late 1980s. This is not to say, of course, that it has worked out as envisaged at the outset. The idea of a single comprehensive programme has given way to a series of projects by the participating agencies, albeit loosely coordinated by the SDA. The climate of the 1980s has rendered this inevitable. When the project came up for review in 1983, neither the region nor the district felt able to make long-term commitments to investment, as neither of them knows what their capital allocation from the Scottish Office is going to be from one year to the next. It was nevertheless decided to carry on the project until 1987, though with the most tentative commitments to specific programmes.

Measuring the effectiveness of the project is extremely difficult, given not only the uncontrollable variables of national economic trends but also the vagueness of the the objectives. Certainly, a great deal has been done in housing and GEAR is one area where the district council's policies of bringing back private housing (chapter 5) have borne fruit. There has also been a substantial amount of business and economic development, though this has had to work against national and local economic trends, with unemployment in the area steadily increasing (chapter 8). Nor can the project's achievements be said to be truly integrated, for there is evidence that a substantial number of the jobs created in GEAR have not gone to east end residents but to commuters—including some 'reverse commuters' coming in from the new towns.

GEAR was intended partly as a learning exercise, to test out policies which could be applied elsewhere but by the early 1980s there was no great push to do another 'GEAR'. The Scottish Office had lost the intense interest in the problems of Glasgow which had informed so many of its policies since the war and the SDA, during the course of GEAR, had narrowed its concerns, regarding the social role as the responsibility of the local authorities. Of the other sites considered in 1976 for the integrated initiative which became GEAR, the Maryhill Corridor initiative was undertaken as a district council-led project, Springburn carried on as a type of CDA dominated by the expressway construction (see below) while Govan was identified as an economic priority area by the Region and the SDA, though progress was held up by the need to accomodate the garden festival. When the problems of the peripheral estates came to the fore, they were not seen as presenting the required economic opportunities to justify SDA involvement (chapter 6). So, rather than the first of a new series of integrated urban regeneration operations, GEAR represents the end of the comprehensive approach to urban renewal which marked the 1970s. In the 1980s, urban policies were to be increasingly fragmented (Keating and Boyle, 1986).

## Transport and Highways

Transport planning is central to the process of urban development for several reasons. The disposition of major transport infrastructure is a major influence on the location of other facilities and developments; the costs of capital investment in transport are very considerable; and the provision of differing transport opportunities and revenue subsidies can have a major distributional impact. We have seen that the early post-war plans for the city were largely built around transport and highway considerations, reflecting the influence in Glasgow, as in other cities, of the engineering profession in questions of urban design. While the assumptions of the Bruce (1945) Plan on housing were offically overturned in the early 1950s (albeit creeping back in practice), the guiding philosophy behind the highways and transport proposals survived.

Little happened in the 1950s, but in 1965 proposals were unveiled for a new highway system, on the lines of the Bruce plan. This followed the methodology of the time in taking traffic flows, projecting them into the future and recommending what roads would be needed to accommodate the projected traffic. In the meantime, the Buchanan Report, *Traffic in Towns*, had appeared in 1963, rejecting this simplistic approach and advocating instead combinations of traffic management and, in constricted areas, major urban redevelopment. Following this, in 1964, the Greater Glasgow Transportation Study group had been appointed, bringing together the Corporation, the Scottish Development Department, the local authorities of the Clyde Valley Regional Planning Advisory Committee, British Rail and the Scottish Bus Group. Although the Convenor of Highways was to claim later that the Highway Plan had been 'fully vindicated by the Greater Glasgow Transportation Study' which appeared in 1967, this was largely because the GGTS had ignored the Buchanan philosophy and simply built upon the earlier methodology (Starkie, 1982). Its population and traffic projections, in particular, proved wildly exaggerated. The population of the city was expected to decline by 21%, to 827,300 by 1990; as we have seen, the decline was much steeper than this, to 765,000 by 1981. The population of the remainder of the conurbation was expected to increase by 52% and that of Scotland as a whole by 20%, to 6,332,000. In the event, both have fallen, with Scotland's population just over five million by 1981. Private vehicle ownership in Glasgow was predicted to increase by 296% to 283,000 and that in the rest of the study area by 345%, to a total of 746,000 in all—a projection arrived at by first predicting national growth and then assuming that Glasgow's traditional low rate of car ownership would catch up with national levels and thereafter grow at the same rate. In fact, by 1981, there were just 95,000 cars in Glasgow and, with the rate of car ownership continuing to be well below the national average, there was no sign of the earlier prediction ever being realised.

The road plans reflected concepts developed in the post-war years (Starkie, 1982), of three concentric ring roads with a series of radials. The inner motorway box would enclose the central business district, within which traffic restraint measures would be taken; two new crossings of the Clyde would be incorporated in this. The next ring would run through the inner suburbs, the nineteenth century city, while the outer ring would encircle the conurbation. Radials would run from the inner box to the outer ring to link the principal suburbs and centres of population to the city centre (Figure 4.1). The main east-west trunk route across central Scotland was to form part of the system, taking the M8 motorway across the city centre and round the inner box. As much of the length of the roads was to run through the Comprehensive Development Areas, it was assumed that highway building would proceed along with the redevelopment programme, up to the end of the century.

Public transport provision in the 1960s was divided between the Corporation, which ran the city buses and a small 'toytown' circular underground railway popularly known as the 'subway', and various operators later reorganised in the Scottish Bus group, which ran services to and from the city and British Railways. Glasgow, unlike most British cities outside London, had inherited a substantial urban and suburban railway system including underground sections. With the drastic Beeching cuts in the British Railways system, decisions had been taken in the early 1960s to close large parts of the city's rail system while modernising and electrifying what was left. Only the most heavily used sections were thus modernised, leaving a rather piecemeal system, or rather two systems, one serving south of the river, centred on Central Station and the other, serving points north of the river, centred on Queen Street Station. Care was taken, however, to 'safeguard' the routes of closed lines from adverse development proposals and preserve the tunnels in the hope of reopening them in the future when funds might be available for modernisation. This was a challenge taken up by GGTS which proposed the retention of all existing lines plus the reopening of closed lines to link the north and south systems. Although some rail enthusiasts were disappointed that there were not to be more reopenings, the proposals promised to give Glasgow a system of modern, integrated rail transport unparalleled in the UK with the cost minimised through the use of existing infrastructure— further development was not ruled out, with the continued safeguarding of the abandoned routes. Prospects for the system appeared to improve markedly with the 1968 Transport Act, which established the Greater Glasgow Passenger Transport Authority as a consortium of local authorities, to take over the city buses, together with the responsibility for subsidies and planning of rail services. The PTA was an example of the conurbation-wide planning which formed such an important argument for local government reform and in 1975 the new regional council became the Passenger Transport Authority, continuing to operate through a Passenger Transport Executive which, while constituting a department of the council, has a large measure of operational autonomy. Indeed, the precise relationship between the PTE and the council is a source of some mystery to councillors themselves.

Local government reform also saw the introduction of a new policy planning system for transport, the Transport Policies and Programme (TPP) system. The TPP is a rolling four-year programme for transport, updated each year and submitted to the Scottish Office. On the basis of TPP proposals,

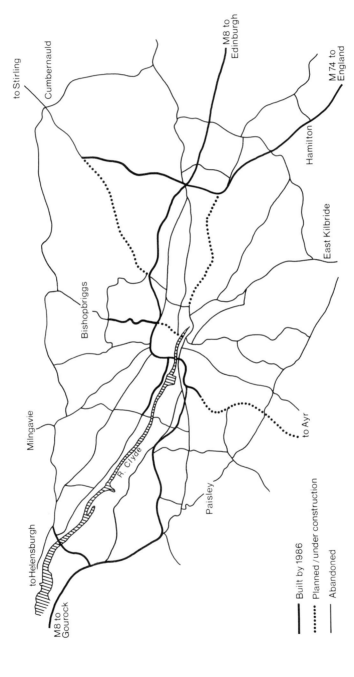

FIGURE 4.1  Highway Proposals of Greater Glasgow Transportation Study and their Implementation.

the Scottish Office then makes capital allocations to regional councils for transport and highways. Within this capital total, the region is in principle free to determine its own priorities among items like highway construction, investment in railway improvement or buses. One objective of the system was to eliminate bias in favour of particular types of activity, notably highway construction, which until then had enjoyed a higher rate of central government subsidy. The TPP is thus a very indirect instrument of control. Central government cannot veto proposals in the TPP or, indeed, oblige a region to adhere to its own TPP priorities; but it can restrict overall capital spending allowances to regions pursuing policies of which it disapproves. Further complications arise from the fact that, while the regional council is at the centre of the planning process, a variety of other actors is involved. Although it is the regional council which provides operating subsidies to rail services, British Rail, a nationalised corporation continues to operate the services themselves and, if it wants to close a service, must obtain permission from the Secretary of State for Transport—a London minister, as railways do not come under the Scottish Office—with considerable confusion of responsibility. While the regional council invests in rail provision under the TPP, British Rail itself also invests in the services, which may also be eligible for central government and European funding so that a venture such as a line electrification may involve putting together a complicated financial package. Bus services are operated directly by the PTE but inter-urban buses are operated by the Scottish Bus Group (SBG) which, until the early 1980s, was bound by a pre-war monopoly arrangement and could not carry passengers whose journeys were entirely within the boundaries of the former city. So a SBG vehicle setting down passengers on its way into the city centre would have to refuse permission to board to travellers at the stop, who would have to wait for a city bus. This restriction was later abolished and some integration has been introduced, with the Transcard, a season ticket allowing change between the four modes (PTE bus, SBG bus, rail and subway), though legislation in the mid 1980s put this under threat (see below).

Highway construction is similarly complex. The regional council is responsible for local roads and for major roads within the boundaries of the former city of Glasgow and former burghs—an inheritance from pre-reorganisation days. It does not require central government permission for road building but, clearly, major developments such as the M8 motorway, which pass in and out of the boundaries of former burghs, will need joint planning. The region, as a developer, also needs planning permission from the district council for roads, though a refusal can be appealed to the Secretary of State.

By the early 1970s, then, Glasgow had ambitious plans for road and railway development to the end of the century. The climate, however, was increasingly hostile to both. Spending restrictions became tighter, particularly on capital programmes and a 1971 GGTS report had proposed a limited programme for the 1975-80 period. In addition to work committed up to 1975, including the M8 across the city, incorporating the north and west flanks of the inner ring road—the Clydeside Expressway and the Great Western Road Expressway—this proposed building the Ayr Motorway, the Stirling Motorway, the Maryhill-Lomond Motorway and the Springburn Expressway—a total extra commitment of £57 million. Recognising the impracticability of the long-term proposals, the 1972 review of the Development Plan trimmed them down a little by cutting out lengths of the intermediate ring road but retained the inner and outer rings and the radials. GGTS' rail proposals for action in the 1975-80 period were the reopening of the Central Low Level Line and the St John's Link, connecting up the north and south side systems on both east and west, with complete electrification of the Hamilton Circle, for a total of £10.24 million. Even this limited programme was to be stalled in its implementation.

By this time, opinion was turning against large-scale urban motorway schemes, with environmental groups increasingly active at a national and local scale and more public awareness of the disruption caused by highway development. In 1974, a joint report by a group of amenity and public transport lobby groups complained that the highway schemes were based solely on savings in vehicle time and that 'no comprehensive assessment was made of the social and environmental costs of motorways cutting through communities, generating still more traffic and aggravating accidents, noise and atmospheric pollution' (SAPT et al., 1974). On the left, too, there was a greater appreciation of the redistributive impact of highway building, which benefits those with the means to travel by car while the inconvenience and disruption are often borne by those in the poorer areas. Among planners, there was more awareness of the problem of blight, with large parts of cities sterilised for years awaiting road building which, with revised estimates for car ownership, might never materialise. In Glasgow, these questions took on an added edge. The city has the lowest level of car ownership in Britain, yet it had one of the most ambitious urban motorway plans. The most cursory inspection of the plans showed, too, that most of the radial routes were intended for car commuting by the middle-class residents of the suburbs which had struggled for so long to stay outside the city's jurisdiction; only a minority of the routes could claim any economic or industrial significance. The routes of the ,highways through the city, on the other hand, went through poor neighbourhoods, often designated as comprehensive development areas. Yet, support for urban motorways within the Labour Group on Glasgow corporation and then Strathclyde region remained more solid than in other parts of the country.

Partly, this was a matter of civic pride. Glasgow was Britain's second city and must have the biggest and best of motorway systems. Motorways were synonymous with progress and modernity and English cities like Birmingham and Newcastle had their own schemes. Glasgow's persistence so long after other cities had turned against motorways is also attributable to the strength of the road engineers within the council and the preferences of the highways and transport convenors of the corporation and regional council, who tended to be captured by the professional advice of their permanent officials. One former Glasgow councillor, indeed, wrote of the programme as a 'techno-cratic blight' (Cable, 1974). Within the council, the highways department and committee tended to go their own way and be widely regarded as more 'technical' than 'political', an attitude confirmed by our survey of regional and district councillors in the late 1980s, in which few could be brought to give an opinion on transportation matters. By the early 1970s, certainly an anti-motorway faction had developed within the Labour group, calling for more investment in public transport, but its influence was very limited.

If there was little controversy in the council, one might have expected more on the ground. In cities throughout western Europe and North America, highway development has proved one of the most contentious issues in neighbourhood politics and a powerful force in mobilising communities which otherwise might be politically inert. Where highway users are middle classes but the environmental cost must be paid by poorer people through whose neighbourhoods the roads will run, one would expect a dimension of class conflict to run through the controversy. Opposition to the Glasgow schemes, though, was muted by the routing of the main highways through com-prehensive development areas, the populations of which were keen above all to get themselves rehoused. While most of the residents wanted to be rehoused within their own neighbourhoods rather than consigned to the peripheral estates, the imperative to get a decent house and the movement of population out in the course of the rehousing programmes did inhibit the development of community-based protest groups, except in a few areas such as the Gorbals where comprehensive development had taken place early and the community had already begun to mobilise around issues of housing (see chapter 5). In one or two cases, highway developments were proposed for middle-class areas of high environmental quality and aroused storms of protest both from residents and from conservationists, especially when, in the early 1970s, Glasgow's Victorian architectural heritage began to gain attention both loc-ally and nationally. This was the case, notably, with the proposals for the western approaches of the city (Keating, 1978) which provoked the New Glasgow Society, a conservationist lobby group to comment:

> The 'traffic versus amenity' issue raised by the Great Western Road proposals is bound to be revived when the detailed plans are published for the Ayr motorway, which skirts the Pollok estate, and the Lomond Motorway, which touches the Westerton/Canniesburn area of Bearsden. The days when Glasgow could build its motorways through decrepit redevelopment areas are past and this is bound to lead to more public reaction and criticism. (NGS, 1973)

In that case, the conservationist lobby lined up with the middle-class residents of Great Western Road to demand that the traffic should be put through the working-class comprehensive development area of Maryhill. A well-organised campaign was mounted, drawing on the skills and contacts of the middle-class professional residents and the proposals to widen Great Western Road were defeated (Keating, 1978).

By the mid 1970s, however, the conservationist lobby had begun to turn against urban highways in principle on the grounds that, wherever they were built, they would cause environmental damage and that resources would be better applied to public transport. This was one of the pressures on the new regional council, from 1975. At the same time, revised population estimates and the energy crisis of the 1970s were raising serious questions over the feasibility of the whole scheme. Glasgow district council, without transport responsibilities of its own, became extremely concerned about the blighting effects of highways on its own redevelopment programmes, the more so as it moved away from the comprehensive development area approach towards rehabilitation and piecemeal improvement (chapters 1 and 5). The prospect of sterilising large derelict areas of the inner city up to the end of the century and beyond, waiting for the highway schemes to be built, was quite alarming. Even central government, which had previously encourged motorways, became concerned and criticised Strathclyde's first TPP for its excessive bias to highways. With restrictions on capital spending, it was in any case obvious that resources would not be available for the programme and in 1975 a major review selected seventeen high priority schemes which had a reasonable chance of completion within ten years. Soon after, the 'safeguarding' of the other routes, that is the ban on all building which could interfere with the highway plans, was lifted, allowing redevelopment to proceed—in Maryhill, this produced the 'Maryhill corridor' initiative, a major programme of redevelopment and improvement coordinated by the district council.

The battles did not end there, however, for the seventeen surviving schemes included the east and south flanks of the inner ring road and several other major roads, which were incorporated into the 1979 structure plan. At the Examination in Public (the statutory public inquiry before a reporter appointed by the Secretary of State) of this, objections by a range of amenity and conservationist groups pointed to the damaging impact of these, particularly in the city centre. The objections were largely sustained by the Reporter in his submission to the Secretary of State. By this time, the Conservatives had returned to power in central government and the extraordinary spectacle ensued of a Labour council seeking to build more highways while the Conservative Secretary of State tried to stop them—the reverse of contemporary events in Edinburgh where the more familiar pattern of left-wing opposition and right-wing support for roads prevailed. In his comments on the structure plan, the Secretary of State deleted one major highway proposal, modified another and required a review of the need for an environmental impact of the east and south flanks of the ring road. Opposition to highway building was now developing within the regional Labour Party. Both the district Labour Party and the district council were already opposed and the latter had shown its teeth by turning down planning consent for several schemes, forcing the region to appeal to the Secretary of State to overturn the decision. In the Gorbals, a group calling itself GRIM (Glasgow Resistance to Incoming Motorways) had been launched, arguing that a working-class community was being threatened for the benefit of middle-class commuters. The argument is hardly suprising—what is surprising is that it had not been effectively put in Glasgow much earlier. By this time, the highway programme was well behind schedule. Of the 1975 programme of committed works, all that had been completed was the through route of the M8 (incorporating the north and west flanks of the ring road), the Clydeside Expressway and the

Springburn Expressway. The inclusion of the latter in the priority list was something of a mystery as the road does not really go anywhere but was justified at the time in terms of the industrial needs of Springburn. A typical example of the highway plans of the 1960s, it was to go through a CDA, with redevelopment organised around it and serve the commuter belt beyond the city. In 1975, on the eve of reorganisation, a Planning Policy Report of the Corporation was still insisting that it 'is an integral part of Springburn Comprehensive Development Area proposals and serves two main commuter suburbs, Bishopbriggs and Lenzie (so) this is an essential project' (Glasgow, 1975)— and its construction has held back the redevelopment of the area until the 1980s. Where it joins the M8 motorway, there rose in the late 1980s an extraordinary monument to Glasgow's road building ambitions, the Townhead Interchange, a highway junction of awesome proportions growing year by year to serve as the nerve centre of a motorway system that will never be built. On a lesser scale, the flanks of the motorway are littered with relics of the earlier plans, roads stopping in mid-air and pedestrian bridges untrodden.

The railway development proposals, in the meantime, had been steadily downgraded. At the request of the Scottish Development Department, the GGTS study team had postponed consideration of the full railway proposals until the alternative of express buses on the radial routes had been explored— but this in turn could not be done until the highway proposals were resolved. Its 1971 report on proposals for 1975-80 had disappointed many by failing to recommend the full implementation of the earlier proposals, going merely for the reopening of the Central Low Level line together with the St John's Link and some minor proposals (GGTS, 1971), to a total of £10.4 million. This was firmed up by the 1974 *Clyderail* report, a cost-benefit analysis with design details. As the report complained, 'physical implementation of the public transport recommendations (of the 1968 GGTS), apart from those progressed independently by British Railways, had made little progress in contrast to the committed highways plan to 1975 which has proceeded apace. This has resulted in an imbalance of investment in roads and public transport, a situation which will worsen so long as the public transport sector continues to be neglected' (Clyderail, 1974). Despite a favourable cost-benefit analysis, the plan proved too ambitious for the Scottish Office, whose approval was needed and was cut down to the reopening of the Central Low Level line. At the same time, approval was given for the modernisation of the Glasgow Underground (the subway), which was still using the original nineteenth century trains. Again, the rationale for this was unclear since, apart from the stretch between the city centre and west end, the Underground largely reflects last century's pattern of urban development rather than contemporary settlement patterns. While the routes recommended in the 1968 GGTS together with the Kirklee line continued to be safeguarded, it became increasingly unlikely that they would be reopened and the 1981 review of the structure plan duly abandoned the safeguarded routes, including the preserved tunnels. So was lost the opportunity for an integrated urban railway system whose cost would have been a fraction of the motorway programme. Instead, there is a system which serves considerable areas on both sides of the river but which links up only at Partick, in the west. Indeed, Partick, where there is a connection with the Underground, forms a rather curiously-sited hub for the system. Figure 4.2 shows the 1968 proposals and the extent to which they have been implemented but does not include the Kirklee and Parkhead lines which, while safeguarded for a number of years, never featured in firm proposals.

Glasgow corporation and Strathclyde region's antipathy to railway development is perhaps as puzzling as their attachment to urban highway building, given Labour's assumed preference for public transport. One factor was certainly the worry about the commitment to revenue support, which is particularly heavy for railways, a form of transport which is often further assumed to be used predominantly by the middle classes. The 1975 Glasgow Corporation *Planning Policy Report* on transportation emphasised that support for railways could not be justified as a means of redistributing income but only as a means of easing congestion in the city centre in the peak hours. There is indeed much evidence to back this up, particularly in the case of the lines to Bearsden and Milngavie and the south-side electrics. On the other hand, roads, too, are predominantly used by the middle classes and the proposals for reopened lines were to serve working-class communities in the north and east of the city. The reopened Central Low Level line has attracted a large working-class clientele and among the abandoned proposals were the reopening of lines to serve the region's priority areas of Maryhill and GEAR. There is evidence, too, from the reopened Central Low Level Line as from elsewhere that investment, by reducing manning requirments and increasing usage, tends to reduce rather than increase the need for revenue support. The abandonment of the St John's Link between the north and south side systems, involving the construction of a mere 200 yards of line (inset, Figure 4.2), is particularly mysterious, the product of extremely short-term financial thinking. The obvious contrast is with the Newcastle conurbation in north-east England where in the early 1970s a commitment was made to an integrated system of light rail and bus transit, using an existing infrastructure rather poorer than Glasgow's (requiring new tunnels and bridges), which has proved immensely popular.

Revenue support for transport services has continued to present problems in the climate of financial stringency of the 1980s, with the regional council complaining that, because it was one of the few local authorities with an urban rail network, it was providing a third of the total local authority support to British Rail in the United Kingdom. In 1983, despite a vigorous campaign, the line to Kilmacolm, scheduled for electrification in the 1968 GGTS report, was closed following withdrawal of revenue support by the region, which had been meeting some 75% of its operating costs. By the 1984-9 TPP, it was warning that, with 61% of the council's public transport support going to rail, which carried 11% of passengers and 29% of passenger miles, cuts would need to be made. With passengers contributing just 44% of total costs, the railways appeared a hopelessly uneconomic proposition, comparing badly with buses which accounted for 69% of passenger miles, covering 90%

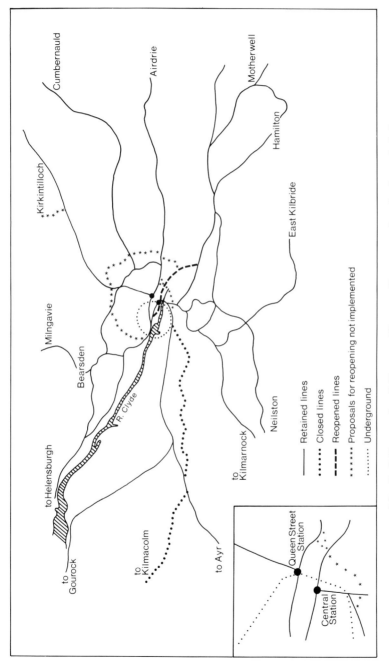

FIGURE 4.2 Rail Proposals of Greater Glasgow Transportation Study and their Implementation.

of their costs. The problem is that, despite these figures, the rail services account for the bulk of peak-hour journeys into the city centre, so serving a vital economic and environmental role. Nor are the cost comparisons always entirely fair, with railways having to carry the capital costs of the permanent way as well as operating expenses. The effect of this is particularly pronounced on the modernised Underground which, carrying high capital loan charges, covered only 27% of its costs in fares.

Strathclyde's low subsidies to bus services have also come in for some criticism, in that they have resulted in some of the highest bus fares in the country. Again, the local policy has contrasted with that of other Labour councils such as South Yorkshire and Lothian, where low fares policies were introduced in the 1970s for both social and environmental reasons. Certainly, Glasgow faces a particular problem with the peripheral estates which are expensive to serve by bus and, while three of them do have railway lines, these skirt the edge of the schemes. High fares to the city centre and other areas of work, shopping and leisure have added to the problems of residents on the periphery and to the unpopularity of moving to the schemes. The contrast with low rents is interesting. Low rents were an article of faith in the old Glasgow Labour tradition and had to be maintained even at the expense of housing standards (chapter 5). Low fares, on the other hand, never became a political rallying cry so that Glaswegians consigned to the peripheral estates faced penal costs in trying to come into the city centre. This is another legacy of the 1950s and 1960s single-minded concentration on house-building, to the neglect of wider questions of urban planning, in contrast to other European cities such as Stockholm, where urban expansion was integrated with transport planning to concentrate development along the transportation lines (Heidenheimer et al., 1983).

Another planning failure was the lack of integration of rail and bus services themselves. The very comparison, bus costs with those of railways, is, in fact, very misleading for it suggests that the two modes are in competition. With an integrated transport system on the lines of the Tyne and Wear Metro, they would, instead, be complementary, and so support each other. Buses, serving small or larger areas (such as the main housing estates) could feed into rail services for the longer journeys, including those into the city centre, making the best use of each mode. Glasgow never seriously considered this option when the opportunity was available but insisted on scrutinising each element of the system separately, with systems that were neither integrated nor competitive. Transportation policy was never adequately integrated with other elements of development policy and opportunities for the development of rapid transit systems were lost at the time when the resources were available. Nor can central government escape its share of the blame. By short-term restrictions on capital expenditure, it has discouraged investment in rail transport which, by increasing usage, could have cut back on the revenue support needed. These are the mistakes of the past but in the late 1980s a greater challenge faced public transport in the city. Having failed to secure an integrated transport system, the city was presented with the necessity of adapting to the opposite principle, of unregulated competition between modes, by a move which threatened much of the investment made over the previous decade.

The 1985 Transport Act was the brainchild of Transport Minister Nicholas Ridley, a fervent free-market right-winger. Although his writ did not run in Scotland, the Scottish Office appear to have gone along with a Cabinet decision to implement his scheme, making no effort to have Scotland excluded, though it is highly improbable that, left to its own devices, they would have come up with anything of the sort. The principle of the legislation is to allow unrestricted competition in urban transport, with the PTE and Scottish bus group competing against each other and private operators. No permission is needed to run a service—it is merely registered. Where the regional council wish, for social reasons, to provide a service which is not commercially viable, they must put it out to tender. The PTE's own bus fleet is hived off as a separate company (though still owned by the regional council) which must compete both on the commercial routes and in the tenders for subsidised services. The whole scheme has come under heavy criticism on the grounds that in its simplistic application of market principles it ignores the need for planning and integration in urban transport. With buses, rail and underground forced to compete for business, there is no incentive to integrate their services to make the most effective use of resources. Rather, all will tend to concentrate on the most profitable routes, with wasteful duplication while leaving large areas ill-served. Indeed, as there is no obligation on anyone, including the PTE's own fleet, to tender for the subsidised routes, the regional council no longer has any means of ensuring that transport will be provided. The subsidised rail services are put in peril with sporadic competition which may not provide an equivalent comprehensive service but may be enough to destroy their viability, while there is no control at all on the congestion caused by competing buses in the city centre. The Glasgow Underground, which could never be seen as an independent transport mode, is separated from the buses and will have to compete on its own.

In its defence of the legislation, the Scottish Office tended to play down its significance, claiming that services were likely to remain much as before, with useful additions. Since deregulation day in October 1986 the indications are that, in Glasgow at least, the flood of private transport entrepreneurs of which the London ministers had dreamt has not been occurring. PTE and SBG (both then publicly owned) were locked in competition, with a serious question mark over the rail system. Strathclyde, of course, has never had an integrated transport system. Had it had one, the damage might have been greater. Prospects for the future at the time of writing are not entirely bleak. A review of the rail system was suggesting that threatened closures might be averted as a result of cost-cutting exercises and that there might even be some limited opening of new stations. The opportunity for a fully integrated urban transport system, however, must be considered lost for ever.

# 5  Housing

## Introduction

Housing has always been central to politics in Glasgow as for decades central and local politicians concurred on the need for ever more houses. In the post-war years, there had been conflict as to where and how the building should take place, but by the 1960s space was being developed almost wherever it was available, with building on the periphery seen less as a substitute than as a complement to overspill. For local politicians, housing was significant in another respect. It was, through control over rent levels and the balance struck between rents and rates, one of the few ways in which local government could effectively redistribute disposable income. Glasgow, like the west of Scotland generally, had a long tradition of low rents and poor investment in housing and, with the spread of municipally-owned housing, the tradition was reinforced by electoral pressure to keep rents down. The annual rents decision in a city where over 60% of households are council tenants is clearly of major significance and Labour has always sought to keep this as low as possible. In 1960, for example, Glasgow covered only 31.6% of its revenue costs in housing from rents, compared with 68.2% in Birmingham, 47.1% in Liverpool and 54.8% in Manchester. Conservative central governments, on the other hand, have tried to get the rents up since the 1950s and even Labour governments have from time to time regarded Glasgow rents as too low. It was the Labour Government in the 1960s which acted to push up rents so that they overtook the Rate Fund Contribution as the major element in the housing revenue account (Figure 5.1) and the Heath Government (1970-74) introduced the Housing Financial Provisions (Scotland) Act obliging councils to raise rents and eliminate subsidies. Several councils defied the Act and its English equivalent and the Labour group in Glasgow was split on whether it should comply or risk illegality by defiance. In the event, the law was repealed by the incoming Labour Government (1974-9) and the right to set rents restored to councils.

Renewal policy for most of the post-war period was council-led and based on new-building in the periphery together with comprehensive redevelopment in the old inner-city areas, the whole undertaken by the corporation (later, the district) with help from the Scottish Special Housing Association, a central government agency providing houses on similar terms to the council. As Table 5.1 shows, the peak years of new building were the late 1960s, with

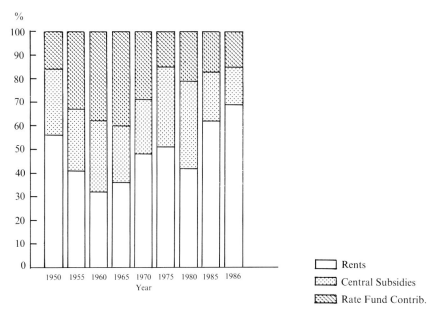

FIGURE 5.1   Housing Revenue Account % Income, Glasgow, 1960-86. *Source*: Glasgow District Council.

around 5,000 houses a year being completed, around 98% of them in the public sector.

As a result, the tenure balance in the city shifted dramatically. Renting from private landlords, the dominant tenure form in the old inner city tenements, virtually disappeared. In contrast to other parts of the United Kingdom, however, there was relatively little increase in owner-occupation (Table 5.2).

Glasgow's figure of over 60% of housing publicly owned compares with 53% for Scotland as a whole and under 30% for the United Kingdom and is surpassed only in some of the other Clydeside towns where the figure exceeds 80%. The result has been to increase still further the salience of housing issues, particularly in the politics of the district council. Municipal socialism on Clydeside became almost synonymous with the building of cheap rented houses on an ever larger scale. As Checkland (1975, p.92), exaggerating a little, puts it 'whereas before 1914 the Corporation was seen as a joint-stock company run by the middle classes, since 1933 it has been increasingly a social service run by the Labour Party, centred upon public-sector housing at low rents.' The work of the local councillor was dominated by housing questions and his success largely judged by his ability to get his constituents demands for rehousing met. At one time, access to housing was seen as an aspect of individual patronage and, though the introduction of a points

TABLE 5.1    HOUSING COMPLETIONS IN GLASGOW, 1960-85

| Year | Council | SSHA | Housing Association | Private Sector |
|------|---------|------|---------------------|----------------|
| 1960 | 3,255 | 72 | n.a. | 92 |
| 1961 | 2,885 | 164 | n.a. | 108 |
| 1962 | 1,949 | 56 | n.a. | 234 |
| 1963 | 3,164 | 328 | n.a. | 215 |
| 1964 | 4,308 | 482 | n.a. | 197 |
| 1965 | 4,159 | 601 | n.a. | 164 |
| 1966 | 3,638 | 1,372 | n.a. | 57 |
| 1967 | 4,423 | 1,156 | n.a. | 99 |
| 1968 | 4,059 | 440 | n.a. | 160 |
| 1969 | 3,950 | 627 | n.a. | 210 |
| 1970 | 2,587 | 258 | n.a. | 206 |
| 1971 | 2,672 | 72 | n.a. | 164 |
| 1972 | 2,492 | 0 | n.a. | 446 |
| 1973 | 1,741 | 0 | n.a. | 100 |
| 1974 | 1,770 | 0 | n.a. | 119 |
| 1975 | 1,856 | 0 | 303 | 107 |
| 1976 | 1,923 | 0 | 384 | 426 |
| 1977 | 1,733 | 20 | 1 | 530 |
| 1978 | 1,430 | 193 | 96 | 347 |
| 1979 | 615 | 85 | 11 | 817 |
| 1980 | 385 | 79 | 20 | 897 |
| 1981 | 588 | 972 | 470 | 1,079 |
| 1982 | 161 | 254 | 69 | 1,201 |
| 1983 | 63 | 147 | 102 | 1,299 |
| 1984 | 4 | 92 | 171 | 1,369 |
| 1985 | 140 | 237 | 192 | 1,665 |

Source: Glasgow District Council Housing Department.

system to qualify for the best housing removed the discretion of the elected member, the councillor was still expected to present his constituents' cases in the best manner and to find ways around the system. The biggest scandal in local politics in the 1970s, indeed, involved not large contracts or individual gain as in contemporary English scandals, but the procuring of council tenancies for friends and relatives of councillors. For the Labour Party, too, the provision of housing came to take on the character of collective patronage, the control and distribution of such an important resource being an part of the councillors' power base. Vested interests in preserving the high level of municipal provision were also created among people whose jobs depended on this, notably in council housing management and the direct labour department of the council, which was responsible for building and maintenance of council properties. The Conservative Party, for its part, has regarded the

TABLE 5.2    HOUSING TENURE IN GLASGOW %

|                              | 1961 | 1971 | 1980 | 1984 |
|------------------------------|------|------|------|------|
| Owner-occupied               | 17.1 | 23.4 | 26.6 | 28.3 |
| Council/SSHA                 | 38.0 | 53.9 | 63.5 | 62.7 |
| Private rented/<br>Housing Assn. | 41.2 | 22.5 | 9.9  | 9.0  |

Source: Gibb (1982); Glasgow District Council, *Annual Housing Review, 1984.*

growth of council housing with distaste and, in recent years, outright hostility, seeing it as the basis for Labour's electoral dominance in west central Scotland and as the antithesis of Conservative visions of a property-owning democracy.

A reappraisal of housing policy began in the early 1970s as a result both of a changing ideological climate and more strictly pragmatic considerations, but such was the weight of tradition and the identification of ideological soundness in the Labour Party with support for municipal renting that it was a decade before the new approaches were generally accepted. Thinking on the British left in the 1960s and 1970s had been increasingly influenced by decentralist themes and the need for participation by the recipients of state services. Critics within the Labour Party, both on the social democratic right and the libertarian 'new left' had begun to concede the justice of the charges of paternalism levelled against municipal authorities and admit that the tenants of schemes such as those on Glasgow's periphery had legitimate complaints about the standard of maintenance and the general environment of their properties. Locally, the key factor in sparking off the new thinking was the realisation following the 1971 census that the absolute housing shortage in Glasgow was about to end and that population decline had gone so far as to create problems of its own. Progress on the comprehensive development area (CDA) programme had been slow and, with the removal of families and partial demolitions, large parts of the city were seriously blighted, with empty and derelict property creating the impression of the aftermath of an air-raid. Of the 29 CDAs originally planned, only 14 had received government approval up to 1974 when the programme was halted and of the 48,800 municipal houses built between 1960 and 1972, only 14,800 had been in the CDAs. Comprehensive redevelopment was proving not only very expensive but disruptive and unpopular, breaking up old community patterns, moving people permanently or temporarily out to the hated per- iphery and producing when completed a bleak concrete environment. Con- cern was also expressed in a series of reports about the dominance of council housing in the city and the lack of opportunities for owner-occupation as a factor in the exodus of the upwardly-mobile though this was not generally considered a respectable sentiment within the Labour Party or in the Labour group on the council. Other housing policies of the 1960s, too, came under attack, with opinion turning against the tower-blocks which, with central government encouragement, Glasgow had seen as a solution to its land problem. At the Red Road flats, vandalism and malfunctioning of the lifts left the tenants, many with young children, as virtual prisoners for long periods of time with every tenant who was questioned wanting to leave (Worsdall, 1979). The extent of deprivation and environmental decay on the peripheral estates, of which signs had been apparent as early as the 1966 sample census (Sim, 1984), was beginning to gain wider recognition at least among officials at this time and the general destructiveness of highway development and proposals to find more land for council housing by pulling down good Victorian villas in areas like Pollokshields became an issue at a time of rising concern with the quality of the environment. In 1964, the Royal Institute of British Architects, meeting in Glasgow, had discovered its architectural heritage and Lord Esher in a 1971 report pronounced it the finest surviving Victorian city. A great storm in 1968 had caused much damage to the traditional buildings of Glasgow and pointed to the need for better maintenance and repair of what survived.

## Rehabilitation and the Rise of the Housing Association

The general thrust of the criticisms pointed to a more piecemeal type of redevelopment, with good buildings preserved and rehabilitated and, later, to a more diversified form of tenure. Observers in the 1950s (Brennan, 1959) pointing out that there was much structurally sound property in areas like the Gorbals, had advocated rehabilitation as an alternative to demolition and rebuilding and in 1970 a Scottish Office- Glasgow corporation working party specified the contribution which this could make to Glasgow's housing needs. This would not happen spontaneously even where generous grants were available. The Scottish tenement system meant that ownership of buildings is fragmented among owner-occupiers, private landlords and small shops and businesses; only one owner in a building needs to prove refractory for the whole development to be held up. Many old people among the owner-occupiers have no idea of the real value of their property and in Glasgow there is a historic reluctance to spend on items of mutual benefit—such as the common property in tenements—where the return is not exclusively identifiable to the owner of an individual dwelling. In any case, many of the owner-occupiers in decaying property—and some of the landlords, too—lacked the capital or income to pay their share of improvements, even with grants. Most non-council property is in the nominal care of factors, property agents who may collect rents on behalf of landlords and act as the agents of the owner-occupiers in arranging common repairs, but most factoring companies are firmly rooted in the nineteenth century and are essentially incompetent to discharge their contemporary tasks (residents of other cities, indeed, marvel at the Dickensian methods and general inefficiency of the Glasgow factors). So, to undertake the complex task of renewing properties across whole neighbourhoods, there was a need for public intervention.

The early efforts at this, however, reflecting the assumptions of municipal labourism, were not a success. It was assumed that if the city corporation was to rehabilitate the property then it must first acquire it, reducing the occupants, including the owner-occupiers, to the status of council tenants. This proved highly unpopular and acquisition caused serious delays in the work, with further delays as the council's direct labour organisation grappled with the problems of rehabilitation. The chairman of the housing committee in the 1977-80 Conservative administration commented on the first efforts, at the Old Swan, that 'it is safe to say that there is not a mistake which is capable of being made which we did not make' (Dyer, 1982). Officials in the council realised that rehabilitation—which was intended to overcome the disruption, planning blight and community disturbance associated with comprehensive redevelopment—was in practice causing as much trouble since residents had to be decanted and transferred and delays beset the programme (Rosengard, 1984). From the early 1970s, the solution for this was found in the form of the community-based housing associations, encouraged by the council and financed by the central government's Housing Corporation. Despite some suspicion by Labour traditionalists, these are free of the taint of landlordism and, as an alternative both to owner-occupation and council housing, have come to represent a 'third sector' of some importance in the city.

The inspiration for the housing association movement in Glasgow came from a number of sources (Rosengard, 1974). One element was the increasing resistance by residents in areas scheduled for comprehensive development or council-led rehabilitation to the dislocation involved. Another was the initiative of Raymond Young and a group of architects from Strathclyde University. Initially, the architectural profession had been rather dismissive of rehabilitation, their training being focused on design and building with little consideration of social questions but some sections of the profession now rejected this limited approach. In 1970, Young, as a postgraduate student, went to live in Govan and, gaining the support of the New Govan Society—a group of the remaining middle-class residents committed to improving the area—formed the Tenement Improvement Project, which later developed into ASSIST, an architectural practice initially based at the University and specialising in advising community groups on rehabilitation and improvement. In several parts of the city, protest was thus turned into positive proposals for alternatives. At the same time, as central government seized on the problem, the legislative climate was improving. The Housing Corporation, set up in 1964 to coordinate the work of housing associations in response to a drying up of the private rental market, had done little in Scotland before 1974. In 1969 and 1974, however, legislation increased its powers and scope and gave it funds to provide capital and revenue grants to local housing associations engaged in the rehabilitation and improvement of property. In 1974, as a result of the personal interest in the city by the chairman, Lord Goodman, the Housing Corporation established an office in Glasgow under Raymond Young. The final element was a change of attitude on the part of the then city corporation, whose officials had become increasingly concerned about the continued growth of council housing and the inefficiencies of the municipal approach to rehabilitation. By the early 1970s, they had a sympathiser in the person of Geoff Shaw, leader of the Labour group, a rather unconventional politician who had shot to prominence through his work in communty politics, following the shake-out of the Labour establishment in the defeats of the late 1960s. There was still intense suspicion in parts of the Labour Party about the break with the municipal tradition implied in the encouragement of the housing association movement. Some councillors regarded associations as rivals to the council in housing provision while others looked upon them as second class or a product of nineteenth-century philanthropic paternalism. The widespread feeling that housing provision and management was the business of the council alone died hard for, as Rosengard (1984, p.147) comments, 'there is no doubt that the municipal centralist tradition opposes that of voluntary and local initiative.'

The availability of Housing Corporation finance, however, was a powerful argument at a time of increasing restrictions on council spending and a pattern of partnership between the corporation (later Glasgow district council) and community-based housing associations was soon established. The basic arrangement is that community groups in neighbourhoods in need of improvement form a community-based housing association while the council for its part declares a Housing Action Area for Improvement to give itself the needed powers. The association then registers with the Housing Corporation and applies for the grant to undertake the programme of rehabilitation. This usually involves the association acquiring the properties to be improved though this is not necessarily the case and it can act as agent for the improvement of properties remaining in owner-occupation or even private rental. For the latter properties, finance for improvement comes via the council from its grants section. In fact, given the limited capital and incomes of the owner-occupiers in these areas, some 85% of the houses are purchased by the associations (Maclennan, 1984). The result of the new policy, then, has been to reduce owner-occupation from 45% to 8% in the neighbourhoods concerned, though many of the owner-occupiers themselves had previously rented the same properties until the landlords had sold out (Maclennan, 1983). Rents are set by rent assessment officers, who are also responsible for setting controlled rents in privately rented property, and initially were well below market rents though legislation under the post-1979 Conservative Government has led to increases. Tenants are entitled to housing benefit in case of need on the same basis as those renting from the council or private landlords.

Evaluations of the programme have shown that it is expensive, involving a high level of public subsidy (Maclennan, 1984) though to a group of residents who in the past have not enjoyed the tax breaks available to owner-occupiers with mortgages or to council tenants. Commentators, (Rosengard, 1984; Maclennan, 1984) are agreed as well that the benefits have gone to the lower income groups with none of the gentrification and displacement which have characterised improvement in other British cities. The programme has generally gained bipartisan support, appealing to the left as an alternative to owner-occupation and as rooted in cooperative and collectivist traditions, and to the right as an example of self-help and an alternative to munici-palisation—but equally, it has come under attack. We have noted the sus-picion of the Labour traditionalists. In the 1980s, the individualistic thrust of Conservative policy and the emphasis on individual owner-occupation was putting the associations, committed largely to rental, under pressure. As we have seen, they are an instrument of public policy, the recipients of public moneys. Inevitably, then, they are affected by changes in policy at the national level and after 1979 central goverment started to insist that they offer their properties for sale to sitting tenants on the same discounted terms as council houses (see below). By 1986, few associations had responded to the invitation and legislation was introduced to bring Scotland into line with England, with a statutory right to buy at specified discount for all tenants of publicly-assisted housing associations.

There is no doubt that the housing associations have tapped a potential for community self-help and cooperation dormant in Glasgow and by 1985 there were 40 at work in the city with some 10,000 improved dwellings to their credit. They are run by committees of local residents, often retired or unemployed people, with a sprinkling of professional and managerial people involved through local business interests or ideological commitment. Pro-fessional staff number typically between eight and fifteen and policy lead-ership is effectively shared between these, the committee and the outside agencies of council, Housing Corporation and central government. There are those in the housing association movement who see the current arrangements as a disguise for central control through the Housing Corporation rather than tenant control. Generally, though, this has caused few conflicts. Nor have their been serious clashes between the housing association movement or the Housing Corporation and the district council, as the associations have acted as the partners of the council in the area improvement strategy rather than as a totally independent housing sector. Indeed, this feature of part-nership, with the associations tied into the council's area improvement strat-egy, as well as the community base of the associations, marks Glasgow off from most other British cities.

While the contribution of community-based housing associations is mainly in the field of rehabilitation, several national associations are engaged in new building for specialised needs such as the disabled or the elderly. In recent years, central government, in line with its owner-occupation strategy, has been pushing the local associations to build for sale, but with little result as yet. As Table 5.2 shows, the number of new houses built by associations has never been high. On the other hand, the proportion of total housing expenditure accounted for by the associations has risen considerably with the move to rehabilitation and the cuts in council spending. In 1984-5 housing associations were responsible for around a quarter of all public sector capital expenditure. Glasgow has undoubtedly done well from its policy of encour-aging the voluntary sector, for by 1980 Strathclyde region was getting 75% and Glasgow alone 65% of the Housing Corporation's Scottish budget; Glasgow's allocation accounted for 15% of the whole UK budget. This was less a result of a strategic decision by the Housing Corporation than of Glasgow's preparedness with programmes of rehabilitation and the machinery for carrying them out (Maclennan, 1984) at a time when the problem for the Corporation was to spend its available budget. Later, increasing demand and public expenditure restraint put the budget under pressure and funds had to be rationed quite severely, so that by 1984-5 Glasgow was down to 47.3% of the Scottish total.

The impact of the housing association movement cannot be measured simply by the number of houses rehabilitated. Politically, it is of vital significance as the first breach in the municipal ownership tradition and a reversal of the trend towards a council monopoly of rented housing. There have been critics who have charged the associations with 'elitism' and with cutting off access to the improved stock, which circulates amongst the existing families. This implies that, if the houses were in owner-occupation or council tenure there would be more mobility, with greater opportunities, for example, for council tenants in the peripheral schemes to move into the city. In most cases, however, owner-occupation has simply not been viable given the need to improve the stock and the low incomes of many of the residents, while taking houses for improvement into council ownership does raise the general question of the desirability of a municipal monopoly. The housing association model also provided pointers to the future. As a community-based scheme under the control of the tenants (albeit within the limits of national and council policy), it provided a model for further developments in the cooperative field, as we shall see. On the other hand, the pressure on spending levels in recent years and the increasing central government control, as exemplified by the extension of the right-to-buy policy to the associations, has brought the movement more into the centre of political conflict.

## The Squeeze on Council Housing

Council house building, maintenance and rents have remained one of the most contentious items in Glasgow's politics and a source of frequent conflict with central government. Spending on capital account is limited by the capital sum known as the HRA (housing revenue account) capital allocation, together with receipts from council house sales, the money being found (apart from the sales receipts where these are in cash) from borrowing. The HRA allocation, like other capital allocations, is made by the Scottish Office on the basis of Glasgow's submitted housing plan. Revenue spending on housing, including maintenance and servicing capital debt, is met from rents, a central government grant known as housing support grant and the rate fund contribution, that is, the sum made available from rate income to subsidise rents.

Under the Thatcher Conservative Government, a central government offensive to break the pattern of municipal tenure was launched in earnest. Pressure was again applied on rents, with the introduction of a system whereby rate fund contribution limits were specified for each council in Scotland

and, if a council breached these, the excess was deducted from its HRA capital allocation. In other words, a council spending more than the Scottish Office wanted on the revenue side would have its capital spending cut, so bringing total housing spending within the centrally-determined total. The rate fund contribution limits were brought down sharply and housing support grant cut in an effort to force up rents. In 1985, the system was tightened up again when the rate fund contribution limits were given the force of law, so removing most of the council's discretion over the level of rents.

The second and complementary strand of Conservative policy was the sale of council houses to the sitting tenants. Council house sales had been encouraged under the Heath Government in an effort to diversify tenure but under Labour the consent of the Secretary of State was required. Under the Thatcher Government, a radical innovation was introduced in the form of the Tenants' Rights etc. (Scotland) Act. Its motivation was ideological, concerned with the promotion of owner-occupation but also unashamedly partisan, an attempt to break what was seen as the basis of Labour's political strength in the cities. By giving tenants the right to buy their houses at discounts from the market rate varying according to length of tenure, it attacked directly the whole tradition of municipal Labourism in places like Glasgow; and, whatever the academic merits of consumption theories of voting behaviour (chapter 3), British politicians firmly believe in the causal connection between municipal tenure and Labour voting. With the stick of high rents and the carrot of discounts for purchase, it was hoped to alter the whole balance between the private and public housing sectors.

The third strand of policy was effectively to stop the building of council houses on the grounds that Glasgow (and Scotland as a whole) now had an overall surplus of houses and that what was needed was a more diversified form of tenure and improvement of the quality of the stock. This could only come about, it was claimed, through private development. Of course, the strategic political motivation was at work here as central government was unwilling to see councils like Glasgow merely replacing sold stock with new council houses. So the housing revenue account capital allocation was cut by almost half between 1979 and 1984-5 (see chapter 2 for detailed figures), while SSHA spending, which is directly under central government control was cut from £24.6 million to £8.0 million (at 1985 prices), partly reflecting the completion of its programme in the GEAR area (Table 5.3).

Glasgow's initial reaction was to try and resist the new policies, to hold rents down at all costs and keep control of the housing stock. There were those who argued that rents should be increased as much as necessary as those unable to pay are eligible for housing benefit (formerly rent rebates) paid out of the national social security budget. In this way, the resource gain for the city would be maximised. This calculation was unduly rationalistic and proved politically unacceptable within the Labour Party (those advocating it were castigated as 'right wing'). The result was a series of penalties on the HRA capital allocation, which was cut by £10.71 million in 1981-2, £17.1 million in 1982-3 and £5.5 million in 1984-5. As Table 5.2 shows, council house building as a result tailed away to practically nothing, with the limited

TABLE 5.3    HOUSING INVESTMENT IN GLASGOW, £ MILLION (1984-5 PRICES)

|  | 80-81 | 81-82 | 82-83 | 83-84 | 84-85 | 85-86 |
|---|---|---|---|---|---|---|
| Glasgow District |  |  |  |  |  |  |
| (HRA capital) | 85.7 | 73.2 | 63.3 | 75.9 | 46.7 | 54.0 |
| SSHA | 24.6 | 16.2 | 15.9 | 14.1 | 11.1 | 8.0 |
| Housing Corporation | 40.7 | 47.1 | 53.0 | 55.8 | 47.2 | 43.5 |
| Glasgow District |  |  |  |  |  |  |
| (Non-HRA capital) | 18.9 | 20.7 | 35.9 | 77.3 | 80.5 | 37.5 |

Source: Glasgow District Council Housing Department.

capital allocation being needed for essential repairs and rehabilitation. This did not prevent a series of rent rises in the early 1980s as Housing Support Grant was cut back (Figure 5.1). On the other hand, Glasgow is one of the few Scottish districts still to receive Housing Support Grant at all and this, together with district council policies, held rents increases below the Scottish average in most years. The increases have, however, brought in housing benefit money—the percentage of claimants among Glasgow council tenants more than doubled, between September 1982 and September 1983, to stand at 70%. Since central government effectively took the powers to set the rents itself by imposing a statutory ceiling on the rate fund contribution, Labour councillors have been spared a great deal of agonising. On the other hand, the removal of the power to determine the level of subsidy has deprived the council of one of the few mechanisms which local government possessed to redistribute disposable income. In line with government policy, rents have met an ever-larger share of council housing costs. Critics point out that subsidies, in the form of tax relief, to owner-occupiers have not been constricted, as neither the Conservative Party nor its opponents at national level have felt able to face the political backlash from middle-class voters which a cut in these subsidies would provoke. The policy has also improved the attractiveness to council tenants of buying their houses.

Controls on capital spending not only brought the new-building programme to a halt; they also created serious problems in repair and rehabilitation of the city's stock. Pleas from local authorities, building employers and trade unions organised in the Strathclyde Housing Campaign, though, were rebuffed by ministers in the Scottish Office who insisted that capital allocations were adequate. By the mid 1980s, this question of the need to rehabilitate council stock had become one of the major housing issues in Scotland. It was accepted on all sides that Glasgow now had a surplus of housing, estimated by the district council as 16,464 in 1984, but there was still a shortage of good housing. Demand was still increasing as a result of falling household sizes, with a sharp increase in single-person households, and the waiting list was up from around 30,000 in 1979 to around 40,000. In 1986, it was estimated by the Grieve committee, set up by the council to examine the problem, that some £1,900 million needed to be invested in Glasgow's council housing, nearly all of it for repair and rehabilitation of the existing stock.

Council house sales have provoked great controversy within the Labour Party, with a section of the left and of the traditional municipal Labour forces regarding the policy as no different in principle from other forms of privatisation of public assets. Others have sympathised with the aspirations to owner-occupation among the working class and have become aware of the political attractiveness of the policy. In between, argument has ranged over the issue of discounts, the problems for councils' management of their stocks and the fact that it is the best houses which are likely to be sold, with councils prevented by capital spending restrictions from replacing them. Although some Scottish Labour councils tried to slow down the implementation of the Tenants' Rights Act, there is really no way in which the law can be resisted even by a council prepared to go into illegality, as the tenant can gain possession without its cooperation. So in some districts with attractive council houses, significant numbers have been sold. For example, 14.4% of new town houses in Scotland were sold between 1979 and 1983. In England in the same period, 10% of the local authority stock was sold to its tenants. In Glasgow, by contrast, just 1.5% of the stock was sold over the period and this predominantly in the attractive inter-war estates of Knightswood and Mosspark. In some parts of Knightswood, sales reached 25% of stock by the end of 1984, compared with 0.3% and 0.4% in the peripheral estates of Easterhouse and Castlemilk. The fear that the best stock would be sold is further borne out by the fact that 7.5% of semi-detached council houses and 4.8% of the larger, 5 room flats had been sold but very little tenement or multi-storey housing. In an effort to boost sales of tenement flats, discounts were further increased and while these may increase sales of four-in-a-block properties in the more desirable areas, much of the stock remains unattractive and is occupied by low income families without a wage-earner. Council house sales are transforming the tenure balance in some English cities and towns. In Glasgow, local authority renting is likely to remain the predominant tenure form for many years to come but within a steadily deteriorating stock. So council housing will remain high on the local political agenda.

## Alternative Strategies

The pressure placed on the conventional council housing programme was one of the main political assets of those officers and councillors in the 1970s and 1980s arguing for a 'third way' in Glasgow—forms of housing tenure breaking away from the conventional council form while recognising that converting most of Glasgow's tenants into owner-occupiers is unrealistic. We have seen that the housing association experience in the 1970s had breached the tradition of the municipal monopoly and ended the extension of council ownership in the rehabilitation areas. New policies for the existing municipal stock took longer to arrive. Retirements and local government reform brought in a new generation of officers more sympathetic to new ideas and prepared to say that the large-scale developments of the past, particularly in the peripheral estates, had been a failure but in the early days of the new district council they had little influence, though the region's structure plan consistently argued for housing improvement and the widening of tenure choice. Council housing was the credo of municipal Labour and to criticise it was to appear positively anti-working class. It was the defeat of 1977 which began the sea-change in Labour Party thinking. The party was soundly defeated on the peripheral estates which, for three years, were represented almost entirely by Scottish Nationalists. The old leadership was wiped out and younger figures who had survived the slaughter, such as Jean McFadden (group leader) and John Kernaghan (housing spokesman), came to the fore. Kernaghan's (1982) view on Glasgow's traditional approach was unflattering;

> Glasgow councillors are often described as the 'city fathers' and historically there never was a more apt description; paternalism became a way of life. There was a reluctance to listen to what people were saying. Apparently, a new councillor went through a Pentecostal experience during which wisdom was imparted from on high. 'Solutions' were often applied without problems being properly identified.

The initiative for the new ideas, however, came from the officials in the period of the 'hung council' of 1977-80. Their policy-making capacity was considerably strengthened with the creation of a unified housing department in 1979, responsible for public and private sectors and with a research capacity, and the introduction of the corporate management system by the new chief executive in 1979-80. In 1978, officials from several departments and the SDD produced the report, *Implications of Population Change to 1983*. Like many such exercises, this was to see its population forecasts belied by events but its proposals were to play their part in changing official and political thinking in the years to come. The report painted an alarming picture of population decline, particularly in the peripheral estates, with vacancy rates of up to 40%. The latest estate, Darnley, on the periphery of the Pollok scheme, had become an area for priority treatment as soon as it was completed and there was a serious problem about lack of tenure choice and the quality of housing.

This was the period of the minority Conservative administration in the district and the council's response proposed a radical change in past ways. Large-scale demolition of tenements in the peripheral estates was suggested, with replacement by houses with gardens for sale or rent. Houses would be sold to improve the tenure mix and a wide range of responsibilities would be devolved to tenant cooperatives, including the 'power to decide what balance to strike between rent levels and the corresponding amenities.' Elsewhere, the council should create a hierarchy of housing stock by the improvement of some of the stock to higher than normal standards, with correspondingly higher rents. At the lowest rent levels, only basic standards would be provided.

It was a deliberate break with the old municipal Labour tradition, with tenants themselves allowed to opt for higher rents if this gave them a better standard of property. The aim was to 'reproduce in each of the peripheral estates the character and *esprit* of a medium-sized town by endeavouring to make the estates desirable enough to attract and hold people of all classes in socio-economic terms. The more ambitious and thrusting members of the existing communities to be given the chance to satisfy their ambitions within the townships to be created.' Although some of these ideas were directly in conflict with the egalitarianism of the municipal Labour tradition, the promotion of owner-occupation and social mobility had been part of the bipartisan consensus in British national politics since the war. The suggestion that the peripheral estates were such a failure as to merit the treatment given to the inner city in the 1950s and 1960s, however, still touched raw nerves in the Labour Party. Moreover, the estates themselves were now represented largely by Scottish Nationalists. So the Labour Group opposed moves to add the peripheral estates to the existing priority areas of GEAR and Maryhill (Campbell, 1984). In any case, the decline in population proved an over-estimate and it was soon clear that money would not be available for large-scale capital works. In 1979-80, there were changes of power at both national and local levels as Labour lost power at the centre but regained control in Glasgow. Public expenditure cuts were high on the agenda of the new Government and it was plain that there could be no return to the old capital spending levels. What emerged as a result was the so-called 'Alternative Strategy' of 1980, largely prepared by the permanent officials under the 1977-80 council but sold to the new Labour Group, aimed at maximising the use of existing resources and encouraging the flow of private resources into housing, while avoiding the wholesale privatisation favoured by the Con-servatives. This has sparked off a series of initiatives heralding a radical change in housing policy.

An early initiative had in fact appeared in the mid 1970s in Sumerston, in the form of a tenant management cooperative. Management cooperatives were seen by officials as a means of promoting community cohesion and identification as well as reducing alienation from local government and improving the efficiency of maintenance. The arrangement is that tenants take on the responsibility of managing the houses, arranging repairs and allocating tenancies, receiving from the council a standard maintenance allowance per house. Because the houses remain in the ownership of the council which receives the rents, this cannot be seen as tantamount to pri-vatisation and, while some councillors worried about the loss of control implied, the experiment was generally supported. Since then, the principle has been extended and by 1986 there were some fifteen schemes in existence or under consideration, including one in the Kennishead multi-storey flats, a particularly challenging venture given the lack of community feeling normally assumed to be a feature of such tower blocks.

A more controversial initiative started in 1981 has been the 'homesteading' scheme in which the council sells at their (low) valuation price council prop-erties which would otherwise be due for demolition. Made no more than wind and watertight, these are handed over to people prepared to renovate them themselves. A council mortgage is available for the purchase and loans and grants can be given as to other owner-occupiers for renovation. For some of the Labour left and the municipal traditionalists, this was merely privatisation by another name, a back-door method of selling council houses. Supporters of the scheme, apart from making the obvious point that the houses in question, being due for demolition, could not have remained in the council stock, argue that it is firmly within the tradition of working-class self-help tapping extra resources and energies for the improvement of the housing stock. Evidence from the first scheme, at Glenelg Quadrant in Easterhouse, indicates that, unlike some of the equivalent schemes in England, it has not served to 'gentrify' working-class areas; the homesteaders are over-whelmingly working-class people from the area, in employment but on relatively low incomes and formerly renting from the council (Purkiss *et al.*, 1983). This is unsurprising as, in contrast to many of the inner city and riverside locations in British (and American) cities, it is impossible to envisage a rush of the 'yuppie' generation to Glasgow's peripheral estates. The second homesteading scheme, at Shettleston, involved nineteenth-century tenements where the council had acquired the property with a view to refurbishing it but did not have the money to do the work in the foreseeable future. This caused more opposition, as it was not simply a case of saving buildings from demolition but the scheme proceeded, attracting mainly young single working-class people living in privately rented accommodation. Thereafter, opposition within the district Labour Party and among the Labour group on the council resurfaced and, despite the wishes of the leadership, the homesteading programme came to a halt.

A radical initiative in the mid 1980s was the scheme for 'par-value' coop-eratives. The idea originated with officers and the motivation was again a mixture of idealism and financial pragmatism—the successful experience of tenant management cooperatives, and the need to tap new sources of finance for renovation and repairs. As we have seen, the finance for building and refurbishing council property—the HRA capital allocation—was cut in the 1980s. At the same time, the spending limits of grants for private house renovation—the non-HRA capital allocation—were increased, in line with the Conservative government's emphasis on the private sector. The effect was a major shift of resources from the peripheral estates to the owner-occupied areas of the city while the council's pleas to be allowed to transfer capital spending between the HRA and non-HRA allocations were refused.

If the allocations cannot be transferred, though, the properties can be shifted from the public to the private sector. Of course, this is central govern-ment policy, but in the case of the run-down property in the peripheral schemes the tenants have neither the inclination nor the means to buy. So a scheme was drawn up for the council to transfer the ownership of the prop-erties to tenant cooperatives at the valuation price. Purchase would be financed by bank and building society loans and the cooperatives would be able to claim interest subsidy from the Treasury under the MIRAS scheme for owner-occupiers. Tenants would then rent the houses from the cooperative at higher than council rents, but claiming housing benefit where eligible (as most of them would be). Grants for improvement of the properties would then be made from the non-HRA allocation.

The response of tenants, though occasionally tinged with suspicion, showed considerable enthusiasm, with groups of tenants in all four peripheral estates agreeing to proceed. Steering committees were elected and, in line with the participative philosophy of the scheme, allowed to appoint their own solicitors and consulting architects to prepare detailed proposals for property transfer and refurbishment. Potentially, this was a solution to Glasgow's council housing problems capable of bridging the ideological divide which had bedevilled policy in the past. For the right-wing government, it offered the prospect of demunicipalisation of part of the housing stock, a large breach in the council monopoly on the peripheral estates and the promotion of self-help ideas. For the left, it could be presented as an alternative to individual house sales and firmly within the cooperative traditions of the Labour movement. This was not lost on the politically astute officers who devised the scheme and the briefing papers are larded with quotations from impeccable socialist thinkers, old and new, extolling cooperation, decrying state paternalism and calling for popular participation and control over the welfare state. Not everyone was convinced and there were those in the district Labour Party and the council Labour group who insisted that this was mere privatisation, the disposal of public assets and quite unacceptable. More opposition came from the local government officers' union NALGO, fearful for the future of the unified, unionised housing service and the jobs of its members. Unlike the manual unions, NALGO is not affiliated to the Labour Party but many of its activists are delegates to constituency Labour parties and the district Labour Party and able to make their weight felt. A resolution from the committee of the Glasgow branch declared it to be 'outright privatisation which must be opposed in line with National Policy.' It took a motion proposed by the housing officials concerned, at a special meeting, to overturn this. The new resolution recognised the proposals as 'a variety of cooperative and common ownership in line with the traditional aspirations of the Labour Movement'—this after assurances had been received on job prospects, with council officials having the first refusal of posts with the new cooperatives.

The response of the Conservative ministers at the Scottish Office was to support the idea in principle but at the same time to raise a series of practical difficulties. The first problem arose in relation to the surrender of the co-operative tenants' individual right to buy through their becoming private tenants (who have no such right). Second, government consent is required to sell the houses at less than the best market rate, though the viability of the schemes hinged on a discount equivalent to that which the tenants could obtain automatically if purchasing as individuals under the right-to-buy legislation. Third, consent was needed for council guarantees on private loans for the purchase and these could count against the council's non-HRA capital allocation. Finally, the scheme depended on central government assistance for mortgage subsidy through MIRAS (automatically available for private purchasers), plus housing benefit and improvement grants. The crucial objection—and one senses the hand of the Treasury in London here—was that tenants could not qualify both for MIRAS as mortgagees and for housing benefit as tenants. Without the dual subsidies, however, rents in the schemes would be too high. So the Scottish Office gave its approval in principle but declined to endorse the mechanism. Instead, it suggested that the Housing Corporation be brought in to finance the schemes with a combination of grants and loans, as either par-value cooperatives or community based housing associations—this would have to be accommodated within the Housing Corporation's existing Scottish budget.

After consultation with tenants, it was agreed to proceed on this basis for the first three pilot schemes. For the next group, however, with no promise of further Housing Corporation funding, a different approach was adopted, with the council offering the cooperatives an annuity for purchase of the houses and using a different legislative provision to provide 90% improvement grants—the balance of the improvement cost to be met by non-guaranteed loans from banks and building societies. In this way, the need for Scottish Office consent would be eliminated but the cost to the council would be greater. There would be no immediate capital receipt for the sale of the houses and the council would be able to claim a smaller proportion of the improvement grant back from central government. In neither scheme would the purchase of the houses by the cooperative be eligible for MIRAS subsidy though the tenants will qualify for housing benefit.

The implications of the break in the municipal housing monopoly are immense, given the close association which we have noted between Glasgow municipal labourism and council housing. It is interesting, too, to note the twofold inspiration for the change in direction. On the one hand, there was a gradual change of thinking among officials and certain councillors, reflecting changes in the Labour Party more widely; on the other hand, these might not have prevailed without the financial constraints which forced the council to look for new sources of funds for housing. For its part, the central government was able to use financial pressures to push a form of demunicipalisation. With a unitary city government able to raise and spend resources at will, many of the new initiatives might not have seen the light of day. This is an illustration of a theme mentioned earlier (chapter 2), the benefits of pluralism in city government in opening up new avenues for urban policy. Yet our story, in all its complexity, also illustrates the limitations on urban governments. Even where there is general support for an initiative, financial and legislative restrictions may make it extremely difficult to assemble the necessary package of measures. Central rules and regulations are often ill-designed for the needs of specific cities and this is a case in point. A policy for housing tenure designed for Glasgow, where low incomes and poor stock make owner-occupation often unattractive yet where council tenure has its shortcomings, found no ready-made legislative formula into which it could fit.

## Special Initiatives

As part of its strategy of maximising the use of its limited resources, the district council designated in 1981 four Special Initiative areas in 'difficult-to-let' parts of the peripheral estates. Later, another two were added in Springburn and at the Red Road multi-storey blocks. Here, it is recognised that there is a need for extra resources for improvement of the housing stock as well as a need to harness private moneys and improve the tenure mix. Broadly, the aim of the iniatives has been (Sim, 1984);

—to halt and reverse the decline suffered by the areas;
—to bring the dwellings to an acceptable standard of repair and amenity;
—to afford adequate security to all residents;
—to stimulate community regeneration and development;
—to upgrade and maintain the environment and encourage a concern for that environment among residents.

Action has varied from one area to another. At Garthamlock and Lochend in Easterhouse, there has been large scale demolition to provide open space and simply to remove unlettable houses. In Easterhouse and Pollok, there have been public-private partnership deals whereby partially demolished and derelict estates have been transferred to private developers for rehabilitation and rent (see below). It seems that the developments at Easterhouse and Pollok had neither the visibility and emotional significance of the Gorbals case nor the wide-ranging implications of the community ownership strategy. It is also the case that it is difficult to sustain a conflict on too many fronts at once so that these schemes, while frowned upon by the left and the traditionalists, as attacks on municipal ownership, did not become the focus of major battles. At Kingsridge/Cleddans in Drumchapel, attention has focused on management improvements, including improvements to the repairs service. In Castlemilk and the Red Road flats, properties which had proved impossible to let to families have been converted as residences for students. At Red Road, provision has also been made for differing types of tenant at different levels, with elderly people on the lower floors, single people and childless couples at the next level, then students and, on the top two floors, executive/professional accommodation.

At a more general level, major efforts have been made to improve the workings of the housing management system for the city, with decentralisation to area offices, the introduction of the council's area management system (chapter 3) and involvement of tenants in management questions. This has meant that matters such as the clearance of part of the Barlanark scheme involving demolition of 1950s council property has been carried out with greater skill and sensitivity than the city clearances of the 1950s and 1960s (Sim et al., 1984). All this reflects the efforts to break the old image of municipal parternalism and insensitive housing management which had so alienated many of the council's tenants in the past.

## The Return of the Private Sector

In the rush to rebuild the city in the 1950s and 1960s, the private sector had largely been neglected. The council saw its task as rehousing slum-dwellers as quickly as possible and itself as the agent to do it. Owner-occupation was considered as beyond the means or aspirations of most Glaswegians and, for large parts of the Labour Party, as politically undesirable. So the expansion of the owner-occupation market was taken up by the suburbs outwith the city boundary, such as Bearsden, Milngavie and Newton Mearns; and the outcome of the local government reform battle was to ensure that these areas remained outside the city.

In the 1970s, some concern began to develop about the imbalance of the tenure stock as a factor in the emigration of the upwardly mobile from the city and, in a more general way, at the undesirable effects of the council housing quasi-monopoly. The impetus for a change of direction, though, again came largely from the force of circumstances. With the decline in new building and the end of the absolute housing shortage in the 1970s, sites previously zoned for council housing could be released and land was made available initially at Sumerston, Crookston and Cambuslang. These were fairly 'easy' sites, located neither in the inner city nor in the peripheral estates, some already prepared and serviced and the response from builders was encouraging. On the other hand, though originally intended as low-cost developments, these came out as fairly standard suburban estates.

The next stage, under the impetus of the structure plan with its emphasis on the inner city and of the alternative housing strategy, was to move into the inner city and the periphery. This was altogether more difficult as it rapidly became apparent that the market could not on its own work to produce the desired results here; private development would simply be too expensive for the people likely to want to live in these locations. So an element of subsidy would be required, at a high enough level to allow development to proceed while at the same time 'levering' the maximum amount of private investment, controlling developers' profits and targetting development to the areas and income groups of highest priority. As it happened, the council was in a position to give subsidies to private developers for both new-building and rehabilitation even when it lacked the money to undertake the work itself. This was due to the housing finance arrangements distinguishing the HRA and non-HRA elements of its housing capital account and the more favourable treatment given the former by central government in the early 1980s. A complex public-private arrangement, though, would be needed to manage such schemes and, apart from the technical problems involved, this was a political minefield. In Edinburgh, the council was coming under heavy criticism for its generous policy of grants to private developers who subsequently made large profits while in some English cities the Labour Party had set its face against similar arrangements. In Glasgow, the first joint schemes were in the periphery, at South Rogerfield in Easterhouse and at Priesthill in Pollok. Developers were offered a mixture of run-down properties and land and invited to submit proposals for rehabilitation and new-building, the council offering the land on favourable terms and giving grants under its non-HRA capital allocation for the renovation. Given the element of grant and subsidy, the council was able to stipulate the permissible profit for the developer and, by adjusting subsidy levels, determine the selling price of the houses. Cost inflation was built into the arrangements but it was understood that the prices of the new and renovated properties would not be influenced by market factors. There was some suspicion of these schemes, from locals fearful of a middle-class invasion and from Labour Party activists opposed to privatisation but the Easterhouse and Pollok schemes went ahead. Although the financial targets proved optimistic, with profit levels having to come down and subsidy levels go up, the target market was reached. The houses sold very quickly and at South Rogerfield, some 40% of buyers came from the local area. So a substantial part of the benefit was going to locals rather than incomers, who, it had been feared, would take advantage of the scheme. 60% of the buyers were former council tenants. At Priesthill, 50% of buyers were locals and 60% were former council tenants. At South Rogerfield, it was even remarked that some of the buyers came from the local homesteading scheme, indicating the beginnings of a local housing market, complete with filtration. To indicate the value of its investment in the programme, the council was able to point to a leverage ratio of 1:4 between grant and private investment at South Rogerfield, with later developments aiming for a ratio of 1:8, and considerable job creation.

Proposals to extend the idea to the Gorbals, however, hit insurmountable local and political objections. We have referred (chapter one) to the award-winning Gorbals-Hutchesonstown development, the first of Glasgow's Comprehensive Development Areas. Built in stages between 1958 and 1973, this consisted of a series of multi-storey towers and eight-storey flats. Opening the first of the flats, in 1962, Secretary of State Michael Noble had talked of the 'miracle of redevelopment in the Gorbals' and called them 'one of the most imaginative pieces of municipal enterprise in the history of Scotland.' Proposals in the plans for flats with 'hanging gardens', designed by Sir Basil Spence, had been approved in 1959 but only on condition that they did not set a precedent, the Scottish Office being worried about the cost of providing more than the basic amenities. By 1968, central government was moving against multi-storeys and Secretary of State Willie Ross, approving the details of the Spence plans, criticised the tower blocks, particularly for young families. These nevertheless went ahead and in 1969 work started on the low-rise flats at Hutchestonstown E, using the Tracoba system of industrialised building, whereby prefabricated panels are assembled on site and in 1972 the development was officially opened by the Queen.

The whole scheme proved a social and architectural disaster. The prefabricated flats, based on techniques pioneered by a French company in the arid climate of Algeria, were plagued with damp. This could be kept at bay only by constant use of the all-electric heating, an impossibility for the tenants at a time of rapidly rise energy prices, especially following the oil crisis of 1973. The Spence tower blocks, too, were plagued with damp as well as defective lifts and a host of other structural problems—structural repairs on these were eventually started in 1983. Estimates for repairs to the lower-rise 'Hutchie E' flats were in the region of £500,000 (later shown to be a gross under-estimate) and by 1977, just seven years after completion, suggestions were first made that they might have to be demolished. Meanwhile, the tenants had mobilised, forming an Anti-Dampness Campaign, launching a rent strike and appealing to have their rates reduced. Politically embarrassed, the council feared to take the tenants to court and offered a rent cut of one-third, an offer refused by the campaigners. Succeeding in their appeal on rates, the tenants kept up the pressure and by 1980 had forced the council to improve its offer and not only cut rents but pay compensation totalling some £500,000.

By this time, nearly all the tenants had been moved out but the stakes had been raised, with demands not for the repair of the blocks but their demolition and replacement with council housing for present and former tenants who did not want to be decanted to the peripheral estates. This faced the new Labour council with a problem. It did not have the money within its HRA capital allocation to redevelop the site and, with demolition alone estimated at £2 million and some £4 million of debt still outstanding on the properties, councillors could have faced legal penalties for wasting public moneys. Hence the proposal to bring in a private developer, on the lines of the schemes going ahead in the periphery.

Councillors soon had it brought home to them that the Gorbals is not the periphery. The Anti-Dampness Campaign had mobilised the community and gained great sympathy within the Labour Party. In 1982, after the Labour Group on the council had voted 21-19 to accept sale to a private developer, locals formed a Stop the Sale Campaign, supported by the District Party which condemned the move amid veiled threats about the prospects of the offending 21 councillors when it came to reselection as candidates for the next local elections. The objection was partly based on localist feeling, a belief that a working-class community would be dispossessed by alien owner-occupiers—though the evidence from the peripheral schemes is that the buyers of the refurbished and new properties would have been working class and the Gorbals flats are as unlikely a place for gentrification as Easterhouse. The Gorbals, with its signficance in Glasgow working-class history, also served as a focus for the underlying unease among the left and the municipal traditionalists about the extension of private development. Above all, the campaign over the years, taken into the media and around local Labour parties in the city, had presented 'Hutchie E' as a great council failure which it was the council's duty and obligation to the people of the area to resolve. So progress stalled until the district elections of 1984 after which the new Labour Group, its left-wing strengthened and bound by the manifesto commitment against land sales (see below), quickly cancelled the proposals. Instead, the flats would be demolished until such time as capital could be found for new housing.

The expense of demolition and the prospect of vacant land now began to pose problems of their own, both to the council and to local residents and by

1985 proposals began to emerge from the development company City Link, for a mixed development of shops and houses. The developer would meet the cost of demolition and, out of his profit on commercial and private housing, supply the council with some houses for rent. This was seized upon by councillors and even city party activists as a means of getting off the hook, though it is unclear why it should have been more acceptable ideologically than the earlier scheme. If anything, indeed, the idea of allowing a company to make a substantial profit on commercial development as a way of getting a small amount of council housing built could be seen as more in conflict with socialist principles than low-cost owner-occupaton. Nor would the shops be there to serve the local low-income community. To be viable, they would have to be high-class outlets, drawing people in by car from the southern suburbs of Glasgow and Eastwood. Some people in the Labour Party, includ-ing the local MP and regional councillor, stuck to the line that it should be council housing or nothing. The regional councillor, himself an owner-occu-pier in the suburbs, put the intransigent line in classic terms; 'We are trying to dismantle capitalism. Any plan which involves the private sector just helps to build it up.'

For the regional council's planning committee there was a more serious problem. The whole scheme was contrary to the structure plan and would threaten major commercial developments under way just across the river in the city centre. The Gorbals had not been intended for large scale commerce and the region was not prepared to see it happen merely as a by-product of the district's embarrassment over the 'Hutchie E' site. In technical terms the problem is one of 'planning gain', whether the granting of permission can lever sufficient resources out of private developers for public purposes to justify it. In the region's view there was not and the proposal was called in and turned down. By that stage the issue had become academic for, after the proposal had been approved by the district council Labour group and was on its way to the planning committee, the chief executive intervened to warn the council that, by failing to go to tender for the development, it might be in breach of the law. So the process was halted and tenders invited. With the publicity over the scheme and the prospect of a commercial development so near the city centre but convenient for south-side commuters, developers rushed in and six tenders were submitted, while several other proposals were publicly aired. In the event, the decision went for Frank Lafferty, a local builder, who in partnership with Barrett (the original intended purchasers!), proposed a complex of shops, leisure facilities and housing. In return for the site and planning permission, he would include houses and building services worth £6.4 million to the council, a considerable advance on the financial return from the City Link proposals. Again the proposal was called in by the regional council, who had shortly before discovered that the chairman of their planning committee was on Lafferty's payroll, a disclosure which led to his removal from the post and expulsion from the Labour Group!

'Hutchie E' is a tangled saga of ideological *idées fixes*, expediency and community activism, illustrative of the difficulties of formulating housing policy in Glasgow. Council leader Jean McFadden and housing chairman

John Kernaghan were both seriously damaged politically by the affair, on policy grounds and because of the suspicion that they had sought to push deals through without consulting the Party. By 1984, Kernaghan had left the council and in 1986 McFadden lost the leadership.

Building for owner-occupation in the inner-city raised different problems again, to do both with ideology and with the initial reluctance on the part of private developers to get involved here. To show the way, the council undertook its own scheme of building for sale in the Saltmarket although this development took longer than anticipated. After 1980, a major effort was made to get private housing on to redevelopment sites and smaller gap sites and, once again, subsidy was needed to overcome market disadvantages and reach the lower income groups. The Priority Purchase scheme was the result. Here, land was made available free for low-cost development, with priority for purchase (at a fixed price) going to council tenants, people on the council house waiting list and first-time buyers. What was revealed now was a strong desire on the part of purchasers, particularly those from council tenancies, for semi-detached houses rather than the traditional Glasgow tenements. The schemes, by aiming at the bottom end of the market, also showed a considerable potential for expanding owner-occupaton, even in the city centre. Take-up by developers improved and, by 1983, with the collapse of local authority house-building, some 80% of completions in the city were in the private sector (table 5.1). What was particularly encouraging from the point of view of urban renewal is that over half of these completions were on 'brownfield' (redeveloped) sites. Some misgivings have been expressed as to the quality of development at the bottom end of the market. Former council tenants and tenement dwellers may be initially delighted at the prospect of a semi-detached house with 'garden' ('English' style) but space standards can be very confined and privacy in practice a great deal less than in the traditional stone tenement. With all facilities installed and 100% mortgages, the purchaser can find himself borrowing over thirty years for the depreciating assets like carpets and cooker as well as the bricks and mortar and appreciation on resale may not be the same as for traditional owner-occupiers. It is sometimes suggested, indeed, that the new property will have a life expectancy, not of centuries like the stone tenements, but of decades so that the future of the city will be of continual change and redevelopment.

Yet again, this policy has run into political objections, amid fears in the Labour Party that the balance of policy was swinging too heavily towards owner-occupation and that, when some future Labour central government allowed spending on council house-building to resume, there would be no sites left. By 1984, the opposition was strong enough for the district Labour Party to insert a clause in the manifesto for the local elections banning the disposal of council-owned land to private developers. The initiative for this had come from the Gorbals campaigners but it struck a chord on the left and as a manifesto commitment rather than merely a recommendation from the party to the group, was binding and at one point looked set to stymie the whole policy of private development. In practice, reinterpretation of the clause by the council leadership started as soon as it was written and the effects were limited. The first major breach was connected with the garden festival (chapter 7) when land in the hands of a private developer was needed for the festival works; the district party agreed that a swap could be done with land in the council's hands. Thereafter, disposals to developers were made under 'licence', whereby the council retained ownership of the land during development and then gave it on the usual free or discounted terms to the house purchaser—with the disadvantage that the council now had to bear the cost and administrative burden of conveying the individual houses. Further complications arose in the case of houses being disposed of for rehabilitation as, if the council retained ownership, it could not finance the work by grant under the non-HRA account, though, on the other hand, it could claim exemption from value added tax. The balance of advantage in each case, then, was complex and not easily accommodated in an apparently simple policy such as that of the district party.

An area of particular importance in the regeneration of the city centre is the old Merchant City. This is an eighteenth- and nineteenth-century quarter, formerly the residence of Glasgow's tobacco lords who lived above their work. Later, the residents moved out but the area continued to be important as a commercial centre, with warehouses, markets and wholesale distributors. By the 1960s, it was run-down, blighted by highway proposals and scheduled for comprehensive redevelopment. In the 1970s, with the new emphasis on the inner city, the outstanding character of the buildings came to be more generally appreciated and the potential for a revitalised Merchant City realised. Since then, the policy has been to encourage refurbishment of the old warehouses for flats and to create a mixture of residential, leisure and commercial development as an experiment in inner city living. Again the market, left to its own devices, could not secure the desired results, so subsidy was introduced, with grants for the renovation and conversion of property and, in this case, a substantial input from the Scottish Development Agency. Although housing is hardly part of the SDA's remit, it saw in the Merchant City opportunities for the application of its LEGUP grants, a central government scheme for urban economic projects administered in Scotland by the Agency. So, with a combination of district council improvement grants and SDA help, residential flats were created, wine bars and fashion shops opened and the Merchant City set to rival the West End as the fashionable part of town. This sort of development, of course, has parallels in many cities in North America and some in Britain and clearly responds to a new demand for city centre living. Critics point to the limited range of living space, geared towards the 'yuppy' generation and catering for the upper-income brackets, to suggest that the redistributive impact of the programme was regressive. This is a sensitive accusation for a Labour coucil and called for a response. Certainly, prices in the Merchant City are beyond the range of young working-class people and there is no family accommodation, but there have not been the astronomical prices seen in the London docklands for converted warehouses. By the mid-1980s, with the momentum for redevelopment established, there was an increasing feeling that the Merchant City should be able to stand on its own, attracting only private capital for its further development.

The LEGUP grants from the SDA are in any case repayable as projects mature and the prospects for the capital appreciation of property led the district council to the view that private capital could be persuaded to finance further work. So the idea of a City of Glasgow Development Trust, bringing together the council, developers and financial institutions in a formal way to plan progress, was born. This would raise a bond to finance the development programme for the city centre, leaving the district council free to spend its limited non-HRA moneys on the more deserving categories elsewhere in the city for whom grant aid was conceived in the first place.

## Conclusions

Housing policy in Glasgow has come a long way in the 1980s. Under the influence of officials, key councillors and the pragmatic need to mobilise resources from wherever they can be found, a decisive break has been made in the old municipal-centralist tradition. The ideological suspicion of owner-occupation has all but disappeared and imaginative ways of dealing with the council stock have been introduced. Private capital has been brought into the city centre and harnessed to a public strategy, regenerating the older areas. A dent has even been made in the council housing monopoly in the peripheral estates. For the remaining council stock, which is likely to house the majority of Glaswegians for the foreseeable future, new management systems have been introduced to break down the bureaucratic barriers which had alienated so many tenants in the past.

The city's housing problems, however, are far from being solved. Cutbacks in capital spending imposed by central government are damaging both public and private sectors. The council house building programme has virtually ended, preventing the replacement of substandard stock, while the repairs and renovation backlog is increasing. In the private sector, too, much remains to be done. Our discussion has largely been confined to area-based initiatives. Spread over the city, however, is a large number of tenement properties in need of improvement and renovation, including rewiring and, in many cases, renewal of roofs. While the primary responsibility here lies with the owner-occupiers, the tenemental nature of the property makes it inherently a collective exercise. A variety of grants is available, including a 50% grant for major repairs, adminstered by the council under its non-HRA allocation. The council also has the power to serve compulsory repairs notices, usually at the behest of an owner seeking to coerce his recalcitrant neighbours. False perceptions of property worth and the diffuse nature of a benefit like the roof (traditionally of little concern to those not living on the top floor) meant that, even with grants, progress on improvement was slow. In 1982, in a burst of pre-election Treasury generosity, the rate was increased to 90% throughout the United Kingdom. In England, owner-occupiers rushed to take advantage but in Glasgow the system was unable to cope with the demand. The council could not keep up with the pressure of inspection and administration of grant and, when the scheme came to a sudden end in 1984, with a reduction of the rate to 50% and strict limits on the amount available, many owner-occupiers found themselves with compulsory repairs notices (sought by themselves to expedite progress) but no prospect of grant. The incident illustrates the capricious nature of central interventions, which in this case was not unconnected with the date of a General Election in which support for private sector housing was a major plank in the Governent's platform.

There is no doubt that financial pressure has played its part in forcing Glasgow to reappraise its housing policies. The danger now is that financial pressure will prevent it carrying through its new ideas, creating yet another housing crisis by the end of the twentieth century. Amongst those pushing for more spending on housing, the most sensitive issue is how far rents should be increased to cope with the burden. Some local government officials have strong views on the matter which they take little trouble to hide and ask why rents in Scotland in 1987 should represent just 7.9% of average earnings while in England and Wales they were 9.5%. This is a theme which ministers have pursued for many years and Secretary of State Malcolm Rifkind has claimed that low rent policies had 'damaged the housing stock almost irretrievably'. Low rents, he insisted, meant that tenants could expect a 'second class service'.

By early 1987 the Government was taking the offensive. Invited by the housing convenor of the Convention of Scottish Local Authorities to dissociate himself from remarks made by English housing minster John Patten, calling for the break up of council estates, Scottish Office housing minister Michael Ancram did the opposite. While recognising that in Scotland, with half the stock in council tenure, councils would continue to have a large role to play, he insisted that this did not mean that they would have to own and manage such huge property holdings. Constrasting the large amounts spent on housing with the poor conditions resulting, he placed the blame squarely on the local authorities themselves. They had used council housing to create 'over-large council empires'; their very size made it difficult for them to run their operations efficiently, with 12,000 houses lying empty. The problems were particularly acute in the multi-storey blocks and peripheral estates where 'mistaken social planning and poor subsequent management have contrived to create a frequently depersonalising and alienating environment.'

One can quibble about the historical accuracy of some of this. The blame for tower blocks and peripheral estates in the 1950s and 1960s lies as much with central as with local government; their development resulted less from planning than its abandonment; and the number of empty houses owes a great deal to restrictions on spending for repair and modernisation. What is undoubtedly true, though, is that the large peripheral estates have not been a social, environmental or economic success story. The Conservatives' solution is to diversify tenure, away from 'the concept of the 1930s and 1940s'. Large estates should be transformed into smaller communities. There should be experiments with different forms of social renting and new approaches to management. Private sector investment should be attracted in and people should be given greater involvement in the management and ownership of their homes. The implication that there should be a combination of privatisation, cooperative housing and other forms of tenure, was expanded on by Secretary of State Malcolm Rifkind in 1987. The problem of peripheral estates and multi-storey blocks, he claimed was 'not primarily lack of resources' but poor planning and management and councils, the principal culprits, should divest themselves of a large part of their stock.

As we have seen, Glasgow had for some time being reappraising its past policies. In November 1986, it published the hard hitting and radical report of an inquiry which it had commissioned under the chairmanship of Professor Sir Robert Grieve. The report produced some sombre figures about the state of housing in Glasgow. Although there was an overall surplus of some 17,800 houses, there was an acute shortage of good housing. The council waiting list stood at 40,000 and the specific needs of young people and old people for smaller houses and of large families for larger ones were not being met.

The four peripheral estates raised problems of their own. There was little demand for houses within them but a great deal of pressure to move out. Design and layout were poor and maintained open and private space limited. A large scale exodus had been avoided only by the shortage of good housing elsewhere. Without fundamental changes, there could be 'an irreversible decline into ghettos of the poor and unemployed.'

For the city as a whole, some 15% of houses were below the tolerable standard and no less than 43% needed repairs costing more than £3,000. The problem was compounded by overall levels of deprivation and low income. Unless drastic action was taken, warned the committee, then within ten years Glasgow would be faced with the need for a new slum clearance programme comparable to that of the post-war years. The total investment required to meet the need was some £2.9 billion, some two-thirds of which was neeeded for the council's own stock.

Investment was not the only problem highlighted by Grieve. The lack of tenure choice in the city reduced mobility and opportunities for young people. Opportunities for tenants wanting to move out of the peripheral estates was particularly limited, while the council house sales policy further reduced opportunities in the more popular estates. Rent differentials between various areas did not reflect their relative popularity but were based on a type of rough egalitarianism which penalised those living in the less attractive areas. But the main problem was the council monopoly which reduced choice between rent levels, areas and housing standards. The committee's solution was demunicipalisation, expanding the approach which the council had been developing in the 1980s but which would have been regarded as heretical in Glasgow Labour Party circles a few years ago. Some 25% of the council stock should eventually be disposed of to cooperatives, housing associations and the private sector, to produce a better social and tenure mix, particularly in the peripheral estates.

For the remaining council stock, there should be improvements in management, on the neighbourhood principle, with local repairs teams covering some 500-1,500 houses, known and accessible to the tenants. Participation in management should be improved, with a 5p per week levy on tenants to finance tenants' associations. Encouragement should be given to housing cooperatives. In the peripheral estates, special measures should be taken through a joint programme involving the community, district council, regional council, Scottish Development Agency, Scottish Special Housing Association, housing associations and the private sector. A special funding package of £255 million over five years should be financed jointly by the district council and central agencies.

The critique of past practice on which this is based now has wide political support. We can see a reflection of some of the comments of Michael Ancram on the failures of peripheral estates and the shortcomings of council management, as well as the undesirability of municipal monopoly in such large areas of the city. Within the district and regional councils such a message has become increasingly acceptable as an older generation of councillors gives way to newer thinking and the Labour Party itself revises its old paternalistic and centralist views. While it would be too much to claim an ideological identity between Labour and Conservative views of the problem, there is enough common ground in their proposed solutions to give an agenda for action for some years—an illustration perhaps of the theory of Charles Lindblom and the incrementalist school that consensus on immediate policy can be achieved in the absence of consensus on its fundamental objectives.

The problem, as usual, came down to money. Grieve makes it clear that without substantial extra resources its proposals will not work and that Glasgow is heading for another of the massive housing crises which have regularly marked its history over the last hundred years. Investment capital can be raised in a variety of ways, through public and private channels but it eventually has to be paid off. There are are only three sources of money for this—central government taxpayers; ratepayers; and tenants. The government's strategy is to transfer the burden onto tenants through higher rents and privatisation, though where individuals buy their council houses they come back into subsidy through mortgage interest relief. Grieve recommended spreading the burden across all three sources. Low rents were recognised as a problem, preventing proper standards of maintenance and enviromental work and, in another blow at Labour muncipal orthodoxy, the committe recommended a £2-£2.50 per week rent increase to support the improved repairs service and another £1 if the peripheral estates package was to be financed from rent income.

The capital programme raised financing problems of an altogether different magnitude. If all capital and service improvement costs were to be met from rent income, a rise of £5-£6 per week would be necessary. While many tenants would recoup some of this from the housing benefit which three-quarters of Glasgow tenants at present receive, others would face unacceptable increases and be pushed further into the poverty trap. Central government limits on rate fund contributions could be relaxed to allow rate funding of the peripheral estates package but Grieve insisted that the main help would have to come from central government. Capital spending limits should be increased and the added debt burden paid off through extra Housing Support Grant.

An alternative which the committee floated is for the Government to 'write off' the council's borrowing from the public works loan board, though it is recognised that it might be difficult to justify such generosity for Glasgow alone. In addition, extra capital spending was called for from the Housing Corporation and in grants to private sector housing, this to come from central government.

These were radical proposals and, at the time of writing, their future is uncertain, but the very fact that they were put forward by such an eminent group of people indicates both the seriousness of Glasgow's perennial problem and the new thinking that has been taking place. Without a massive injection of finance, though, the problem will remain intractable and Glasgow will retain into the twenty-first century its reputation as the city with the worst housing problems in Europe.

# 6 Attacking Poverty—The Social Strategy

## The Problem of Poverty

An earlier chapter (chapter 1) traced the 'rediscovery of poverty' and the growing concern in the 1970s about urban deprivation. Combatting multiple deprivation was one of the two key objectives of Strathclyde's 1976 regional report and following the lead of the old corporation in its last days, Glasgow district has devoted increasing attention to the subject. The region's response to the problem was formalised in its anti-deprivation strategy, later renamed the social strategy, coming, as befits a corporate objective, under a sub-committee of the policy and resources committee.

Curiously, the Labour Party in the region, as opposed to some Labour councillors, has given little attention to the issues of urban poverty and the need for positive discrimination in local services. It is partly that the party feels uncomfortable with the selectivity implied in such measures which jars with the universalism of traditional Labour views of the welfare state, while some on the left complain that local ameliorative policies merely take the edge off the class struggle. On the Labour right, a common feeling is that the council is there to run services, with redistribution the responsibility of national government. For the most part, though, there is merely indifference. The issue is not at the forefront of party debate and work on the social strategy has fallen to a small group of councillors working closely with committed and often politically sympathetic officials of the chief executive's and social work departments, later finding its way into election manifestoes as an uncontentious and rather technical item. Indeed, when it came to drawing up the 1982 manifesto, there were no resolutions of the regional party available on the subject and the relevant section was based on drafts prepared in the regional council by the permanent officials, rather than on party sources. There are, in any case, serious problems in using local government for the purposes of redistribution, here as elsewhere. Surveying experience in Europe and North America, indeed, Heidenhemer et al. (1983, p. 276) conclude that: 'Broadly speaking, local governments are not very good vehicles for promoting a redistribution of resources from the more affluent to the less affluent segments of the population.' This is because of their restricted tax base, because individuals and firms have the choice of moving to another jurisdiction to escape high local taxes and because of the territorial limitations of local government, which may not encompass both wealthy and poor citizens and neighbourhoods. It is also the case in Britain that cash benefits are paid out exclusively by national government, while local services are in kind and less amenable to interpersonal discrimination. In Strathclyde, some of these constraints may be less severe than elsewhere, given the large size of the region, which both facilitates redistribution within it and reduces the prospects of individuals and firms relocating beyond it, if they are to carry on business or work within it. Indeed, the capacity to redistribute is frequently claimed by regional councils and officials as one of the advantages of the regional system. Nevertheless, this capacity is in practice severely limited by the restricted tax base and the small margin for financial manoeuvre once the statutory services have been provided. This emerges clearly from the description later given by Strathclyde of its first anti-deprivation strategy of 1976:

   (i)  To bring pressure on central government and its agencies—the DHSS, the Health Boards, the Gas and Electricity Boards—to deal with the problems of poverty.
   (ii) To pressure the Government—and through our own efforts—to tackle the severe unemployment problems of the poorer parts of Strathclyde.
   (iii) To encourage district council housing departments and the Scottish Special Housing Association and the new towns to stop concentrating disadvantaged families in selected areas. We also asked them to achieve a more balanced community mix.
   (iv) On our part we would try to make sure that the services provided in the poorer areas were as good as—if not better than—those in the better off places. These services would be run well, more direct and relevant to people's needs.
   (v)  Finally, we would back up communities which wanted to plan and run their own projects to help their own areas (Strathclyde, 1982).

Much of this has to do with pressurising other agencies in the realisation that the solution to the problem of poverty lies largely with central government's redistributive services, particularly cash benefits. The redistributive potential of the district housing function is also recognised as an essential element but beyond the region's control. Much effort has indeed been put into pressurising other agencies. Campaigns have been run to increase awareness and encourage application for national social security benefits in the region, to the intense annoyance of the post-1979 Conservative Government. In 1982, for example, it was estimated that, in addition to the 250,469 supplementary benefit claimants, there were an additional 107,201 eligible non-claimants, so that the benefits campaign was a very effective way of bringing more resources into the region and into the hands of those in most need. In Glasgow, the need to pressurise the district council has been overtaken by the district's own new housing policies—they would be unlikely in any case to take kindly to pressure—but work has proceeded on health matters with the health boards, identifying problems and seeking joint solutions.

As far as the region's own policies and administration are concerned, the main efforts have been in seeking to challenge professional and departmental preconceptions about the nature of social problems and services and in a series of area-based and client-based initiatives. Area-based initiatives seek solutions to the problems of poor localities. Client-based initiatives are those which confront the problems of particular disadvantaged groups, such as the unemployed or under-fives, throughout the region.

## The Area Approach

The area based approach has emerged as a major instrument of policy. It rests on three key assumptions about the nature of poverty and deprivation. The first is that the problem consists of *multiple deprivation*, with an individual or household suffering from one type of deprivation being more than likely also to suffer from the others. Closely related to this is the theory of a *cycle of deprivation*, according to which deprivations are mutually sustaining. So a child brought up in a poor household in a deprived neighbourhood is likely to be an educational under-achiever and thus to end up unemployed or in a low-paid occupation and suffer from poor housing, health and environmental conditions. A vicious circle of under-achievement thus sets in, consigning whole areas where these conditions prevail to poverty. The goal of policy should thus be to intervene in the cycle at key points to improve the life chances of individuals born into such environments. This was the reason for the strong emphasis on primary education in some of the early anti-deprivation policies in Britain, an emphasis which is still visible in Strathclyde's approach. The third assumption about the nature of the problem stems from the other two. This is that deprivation is concentrated in specific neighbourhoods.

In recent years, the cycle of deprivation theory has gone somewhat out of fashion, both on the right, where it is regarded as an excuse for indolence and on the left, where the focus on the deficiencies of the individual is seen as a form of 'blaming the victim' of poverty rather than the structural factors which sustain it. Academic studies, too, have cast doubt on the transmission of poverty through 'problem families' (Holman, 1978) and pointed to the importance of environmental conditions in sustaining multiple deprivation. The emphasis on the area approach has been maintained, though this, too, has come in for some criticism. Most studies have shown that there are intense concentrations of deprivation in specific parts of cities; but this does not mean either that most deprived people are to be found in those locations nor that the majority of people in those locations are deprived. For example, in a city of 100,000, divided into ten wards of 10,000 each, there may be 10,000 deprived people (on whatever measure is used). If 4,000 of them are concentrated in one ward, this will give a deprivation index (the proportion of deprived) of 40% for that ward, compared with an index of 6.6% for the rest of the city—an apparently clear case of area deprivation. Yet, in the deprived ward, there are more non-deprived than deprived people, while outside the deprived ward are more deprived people than within it. So a strategy of targetting resources on *areas* might not be effective in reaching the target population.

In Glasgow and other parts of Strathclyde, it is nevertheless argued that an area strategy is justified on the grounds that deprivation is indeed strongly concentrated as a result of the pattern of urban development, especially since the war. This, as we have seen, resulted in a marked social segregation, particularly around the periphery of the city, between the low-income council estates and the better-off owner-occupied suburbs. It is further argued that, in the past, the allocation of local government resources has resulted in a form of *negative* discrimination in that demand-led services such as post-compulsory education are supplied in larger quantities in the middle-class areas and that in services like libraries and road repairs, spending patterns reflect the intensity of use. It is also the case that residents in the better-off areas are better organised, more articulate and better-connected and so able to play the system to more effect. A final argument for area discrimination is more practical. Local government services are, by and large, supplied into areas and, unlike national cash benefits, are not amenable to inter-personal discrimination *within* areas.

So both Glasgow and Strathclyde have adopted area-based approaches to combatting deprivation. The district's approach is related to its revised housing and urban renewal strategies (chapter 5) and was developed in the late 1970s, concentrating on GEAR, the Maryhill Corridor and the four peripheral estates (Figure 6.1). The region's policies have been more elaborate and developed earlier. Partly this is because of the region's statutory responsibilities but it also seems that regional politicians were less inhibited than some of their district colleagues about the peripheral estates, especially in the 1974-77 period when many of the district leaders were prominent figures from the old corporation, reluctant to admit to past failures.

For the purposes of the area strategy 114 small areas were identified, using the 1971 census data, as having unacceptable physical and social conditions. With information from the region's own departments, notably education, police and social work, the list was then narrowed down to 45, which were designated as areas of priority treatment (APTs). Of these 24 were within Glasgow, covering 300,000 people, 35% of the city's population and located largely in the periphery and inner city (Figure 6.2). In 1981, the number of APTs was increased to 75, with further modifications of the list as the 1981 census data became available. These areas were to have priority in applications for support from the urban aid budget, a central government programme providing grants for projects in needy urban areas. What was potentially of greater importance is that there was to be discrimination in favour of these areas in the allocation of capital and revenue from 'mainstream' budgets. This involved getting departments and committees of the

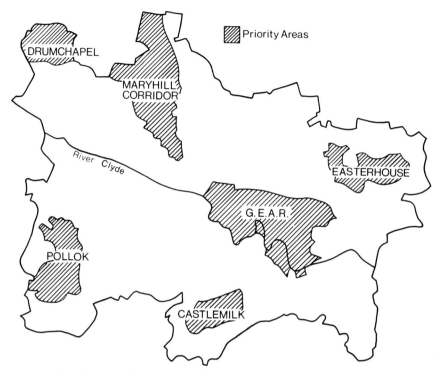

FIGURE 6.1    Glasgow District Council Priority Areas. *Source*: Glasgow District
Council.

council to change their allocation criteria and absorb the philosophy of the
new strategy. It was also seen as essential to break down barriers between
local authority departments and professions, to establish a unified approach,
focused on the needs of client groups and areas rather than the traditional
service needs. Such an approach could not, of course, be confined to the
region alone but would have to take in district services. The early experience
here was not encouraging. Glasgow district's director of planning had produced his own report on multiple deprivation in 1975, noting that the problem
areas were easily identifiable as the inner city residential areas and the major
peripheral and post-war housing schemes, with overcrowding being particularly acute in the periphery and low incomes in the inner city. As we have
seen, the district was not yet ready politically to concede the scale of the
problems of the periphery, but work continued at an official level. In 1977,
the director of planning responded to the invitation to comment on the
region's proposals in critical terms;

> It is stated . . . that the identification of the 45 APTs within Strathclyde followed
> after consultations with 'the Districts most heavily affected'. I am not aware that

FIGURE 6.2    Strathclyde Region's Areas of Priority Treatment. *Source*: Strathclyde
Regional Council.

> any such discussions took place and at no time have I or other officers from
> this Department had access to the information obtained from Social Work,
> Education and Police, nor have I obtained any details as to how this information
> was used in order to arrive as the conclusions contained in the paper (Rae, 1977).

He went on to note that the region had failed to link its priority areas in the
multiple deprivation report with those of the structure plan or the transport
policies and programmes.

   By 1978, though, there was a more cooperative approach and as an experiment on the lines of the 'action research' projects undertaken in the past
through the national Community Development Project and Comprehensive
Community Programme, seven of the APTs were designated as special initiative areas. Three of these were in Glasgow, two in the inner city and one in
the periphery. Here joint programmes were mounted by the region and
relevant district council with the objectives of helping problem identification
and policy formulation through grappling with the issues on the ground; coordinating the delivery of services at the area level, breaking down professional boundaries; and developing community awareness and self-help.

Area co-ordinators were appointed, seconded from district or region, to assume the lead role in each initiative. They were assisted by part-time area teams of field officers from the main regional and district departments and health boards, and local councillors. At regional headquarters, there were link-men for each service to ensure the application of positive discrimination and an officer of the chief executive's department was to act as a corporate link to the area co-ordinators, giving access to the top of the regional hierarchy. The co-ordinators reported to the regional and district chief executives and the initiatives were monitored by the multiple deprivation sub-committee of the policy and resources committee and the urban deprivation officers group corresponding to it on the official side. So the initiatives were designed to secure both co-ordination of services on the ground and access to the centre to allow positive discrimination in resource allocation.

This was a challenge to traditional methods of running services, superimposing *horizontal* integration on the usual *vertical* hierarchy and challenging the universalist criteria of resource allocation. On the other hand, as a series of very small-scale initiatives, the experiment was marginal to the work of the authorities as a whole and did not challenge the existing power structure. This created problems for all the initiatives, firstly at the political level. While the corporate strategy of the authority might officially favour positive discrimination, this was not always reflected in the decisions of the service committees. Nor was it always supported by councillors wearing their constituency hats who could not accept the consequences of diversion of resources from their areas to neighbouring initiatives. The problem of the adequacy of area as an indicator of need also arose, with councillors having to explain to needy consituents that a less needy individual along the road has priority in the allocation of council housing because he lives in a deprived *area*. This problem was particularly acute in small districts where small absolute amounts going into one area can be seen as a proportionately large loss to neighbouring parts of the district. For the region, a similar amount would represent a smaller part of the budget and, locally, the councillor could represent the money as coming from outside the locality. In other words, redistribution raises fewer political problems within a larger jurisdiction.

Problems also arose from departmentalism and professionalism, the very features which the initiatives were meant to tackle. Individual departments often proved unwilling to relax their own functional or technical criteria for taking action, though these might not coincide with each other or with those of the initiative. In the case of some departments, indeed, their duties and functions are prescribed statutorily, inhibiting novel approaches to problem-solving. Career structures within departments were found to reinforce the tendency, with field officers putting greater emphasis on conforming to the wishes and norms of their functional departments where their career interests lay than in engaging in new initiatives which might undermine the basis on which the departments were founded. Because the departmental hierarchy remained the basis of authority, there was a constant need for officers at the field level to refer back to higher levels for permission to take decisions, making horizontal co-operation across departments more difficult. To some extent, this problem was overcome by the provision of direct access from the initiative areas to the centre but, as we shall see, this was not a channel which could be used too frequently. There was a further problem, in that many of the decisions of the scale relevant to the initiative were taken within the divisional organisations of departments and here functionalism was as strong as ever.

The problems of coordination were compounded by the inter-agency dimension. Involved in the initiatives were not only the regional and district councils but also health boards, *ad hoc* agencies like the Manpower Services Commission, central government (through urban aid) and community groups. Each had its own priorities and decision-making systems not always compatible with one another. Of course, these are the very problems which the coordinators were appointed to deal with. It was part of their task to see that the margins of choice in resource allocation were widened and exploited to the full to produce positive discrimination. Their own political resources, however, were slight—they had no line control over departmental officers, only nominal financial resources and were young and relatively junior officials who faced the prospect of returning to departments after the conclusion of the initiatives. They approached their task in a variety of ways.

Some saw their role as 'trouble shooters' or 'fixers', dealing with individual, small-scale problems and measuring their success by their record, often a very good one, in dealing with these individual cases. Others sought to build up a network of contacts with field and divisional officers in departments, believing that consensus flowing from frequent discussion provides the best basis for action. Others adopted a more combative role, attacking departments locally and at the centre. All, however, faced a basic dilemma in dealing with the regional administration. To make the initiative work, a coordinator needed to gain the support and cooperation of departmental field officers. If these were unwilling or unable, because of departmental policy, to take the appropriate decisions, the coordinator had the right to go over their heads to departmental headquarters or to his contact in the chief executive's department. Yet, if he did this too frequently, he would damage his relationships with the field officers. Hence the tendency to consensus working at local level and to concentration on small-scale immediate problems which are manageable.

The difficulties in working through the regional administration to achieve transfers of resources increased the importance of two other aspects of the coordinators' work. The first was the management of urban aid programmes. As urban aid represents new money for the local authority, it can be used to broaden the margins of choice to finance new projects without threatening existing programmes—though after three years, a decision has to be made on whether the new projects will be carried on mainline budgets. While the region has long been allocated an informal quota of the Scottish urban aid budget, it still has to present lists of projects to justify it. Some of the coordinators had remarkable success in tapping this source and between 1976 and 1980, 30.1% of all urban aid in Strathclyde went to the seven initiative areas. This represents real positive discrimination, though amounting to under 2% of total spending. Bending mainline programmes towards the initiative areas proved altogether more difficult, particularly in a period of overall retrenchment when the best that could be hoped for was often simply the maintenance of existing programmes.

The second aspect of the coordinators' work which assumed greater importance was the fostering of community consciousness, an aim which all the coordinators stressed as important and which occupied a considerable proportion of their time. This would not bring them into conflict with local authority departments or require large amounts of resources. It had the further advantage that, if strong community organisations were built and local self-confidence increased, local people would be able to look after their own interests when the initiative finished. There was clearly a delicate balance to be struck here between reliance on the coordinator as 'fixer' and development of the community's own capacity to deal with the bureaucracy and the various coordinators struck different balances.

The original seven initiatives were terminated over a period of years after their initial three-year terms. Assessment on them was mixed, with some having succeeded in mobilising community energies while others were little more than an extra layer of administration. Lessons were drawn for the future of the area policy and for the next range of initiatives, notably that political commitment was needed as well as good region-district relations, that the terms of reference of initiatives needed to be specified precisely and that there should be proper training for staff and line managers to inculcate a sense of responsibility for the success of the initiatives.

One innovation which was made in 1981 was the establishment of divisional deprivation groups (DDGs) for the six divisions of the region. We have seen that the divisional level, where many key resource decisions are taken in departments, had created problems for the small area initiatives, but there was great reluctance in the early years of the council to provide a political mechanism at this level for fear of encouraging separatist feeling in the old counties and city. By 1981 these fears had lessened and the DDGs consisted of a number of councillors, all from the majority Labour Group, with the divisional directors of each regional service together with urban aid officials in attendance (Martlew, 1986). They were chaired by senior councillors and their chairmen collectively comprised a reconstituted social strategy sub-committee of the policy and resources committee. The DDGs lacked an executive role but they vetted all urban aid applications for their areas and acted as a forum for initiatives crossing departmental boundaries. Not surprisingly, this has given rise to conflict between the area perspective of the DDGs and the professional or service perspectives of mainline departments and committees—indeed, they were intended precisely to produce a 'creative tension' of this sort. The atmosphere in the DDGs was freer than in normal committees, with more opportunities for intervention and suggestions from junior staff and this in itself caused some suspicion that hierarchies were being subverted (Martlew, 1986). Again, of course, radicals in the council would insist that this is precisely what they were there for. Indeed, while there was wide agreement on the usefulness of the DDGs in the course of the third council (1982-6), the proponents of the social strategy still considered them too weak, with no control over officials in their divisions and insufficient power in relation to mainstream departments and committees. So, in 1986, the system was strengthened with the establishment of divisional community development committees reporting to the new strategy sub-committee of policy and resources committee (see below).

Other area-based structures have developed in a more *ad hoc* manner. A dozen or so area liaison committees were established in Glasgow in response to local needs and demands, bringing together local councillors and officials, sometimes with an input from the district council. Local grants committees have been established to administer the variety of grants to local community organisations previously dealt with centrally by departments. As well as cutting down on the decision time, these provide a source of considerable satisfaction for the local members who chair them, who are able to provide tangible benefits for their constituencies. Strathclyde regional councillors are also represented on the district council's area management committees (chapter 3) and, in the case of Maryhill, the existing initiative coordinator was appointed as the district's area manager. The fact remains, though, that despite the efforts which have been made from time to time, district and region have maintained their own separate area structures, the main exception being in the Easterhouse and Drumchapel joint initiatives launched in 1986 (see below).

## Client-Based Initiatives

As well as the area-based strategy, the Region has approached deprivation from the point of view of specific client groups, an approach which also cuts across departmental and professional hierarchies. A device which has been used to get into these issues is the officer-member group in which elected councillors and permanent officials, including fairly junior officials and field officers as well as headquarters staff, study a problem and produce a report for action. Examples of problems studied are services for the unemployed; provision for under-fives; post-compulsory education; disablement; and community business. Fitting the workings and the findings of the officer-member groups into the traditional departmental hierarchy has not always been easy and, like area initiatives, they are suspected of subverting the established order. In particular, given the leading role of social workers in the development of the social strategy, there is a suspicion by other professions that they are seeking to expand their domain. This is a problem of some years' standing. As a relatively new profession and one which defines its concerns in client terms rather than in traditional service-providing terms, social work is constantly colliding with the entrenched domains of other professions, notably teaching, medicine and the police.

The pre-fives group, for example, was concerned with the division between play groups, day nurseries and other social work initiatives on the one hand,

and nursery education on the other, as well as the imbalance of provision, with generous provision in some of the better-off areas and little in many of the APTs. Its recommendation for the total integration of services, however, caused some opposition from the teaching profession, who insisted that what the pre-fives needed was education, not mere child-minding and were worried about possible closures of existing nursery schools. The issue was particularly difficult in that nursery education, despite its centrality to the social strategy, is not a statutory service recognised for rate support grant purposes and so is an obvious target for cuts. Eventually, agreement was reached on the establishment of an under-fives' committee to plan all services for under-fives, together with an under-fives unit to integrate all the services within the education department—the latter accepted only grudgingly by some, as a concession to the teaching profession.

The continuing difficulties in getting the social strategy accepted in the formulation of policies and priorities in departments and committees was behind the proposals for reorganisation in 1986. These established a more powerful strategy sub-committee of the policy and resources committee, whose membership included the leader of the council and the chairmen of all the important committees, together with the chairmen of the new divisional community development committees. It was also intended that the new struc-ture should integrate the social strategy with the council's other main cor-porate priority, the economic strategy. The approach was the now-familiar one of establishing countervailing structures to the traditional departments and committees but, it was hoped, with more 'clout' now. The strategy sub-committee included the most powerful members of the council while provision was made for its chairman to attend the important pre-agenda meetings of other committees, including education and social work. Linked to this are the divisional community development committees (see chapter 3), with the potential to secure integration of services and respect for the strategy on the ground. How this will work out in practice will become apparent only in the years to come.

Evaluating the success of the social strategy is extremely difficult, as the recession of the 1980s and the increase of Strathclyde's unemployment levels from around 5% in 1975 to some 20% in 1986 has overwhelmed any efforts the regional council might be able to make in combatting poverty. Another problem is the familiar one of measuring the outputs of social policy, as opposed to the inputs. On the input side, certainly, the region can point to some achievements. In 1975, there was part-time education in many of the deprived areas of Glasgow. A decade later, this was no longer so and, indeed, some 390 teachers above the standard national levels were being employed in areas of deprivation under the Scottish Office's 'Circular 991' scheme. It should be said, though, that the elimination of teacher shortages in areas of deprivation was due principally to the fact that the overall supply shortage of teachers in Scotland in 1975 had given way to a large surplus in the 1980s. Social work, too, can point to advances in staffing. Again, this reflects national trends but the region has developed more sensitive indicators of need to deploy the social and community workers into the right areas. Decisions on capital spending on items such as roads and transport also take cognisance of the existence of APTs as a criterion, though it is often difficult to tell how far the rationalistic decision-making procedures in the transport policies and uprogrammes document precede or follow the concrete choices.

The social strategy, as well as a set of substantive policies, has involved a process of learning. Both regional and district councils have sought to explore the nature of the problem while tackling it. Indeed, much of the work done on a small-area basis must be seen as learning and experimentation, trying to find solutions which could be applied on a wider basis. The learning process also involves the organisation of the councils themselves, which have sought to overcome features of their traditional structure which may have hampered both the identification of problems and innovative solutions to them. This picks up a theme examined in chapter 2 where corporate management was seen, at least in part, as an attempt to create organisational forms more responsive to changing social problems. As in other policy areas, however, the capacity for innovation and for effective policies is limited both by the financial constraints on local government and the tight statutory definition of their powers. With most local government spending consumed by the provision of statutory services and the raising of extra revenues effectively prohibited by central government restrictions, the margin of discretion left to the local authority has become ever smaller. In a period of national economic recession, local government's efforts to tackle poverty are constantly overwhelmed by the scale of the problem.

From the late 1970s, it had been recognised that the social strategy would have to deal not just with the problems of the declining inner city but also with those of the peripheral estates, where the mistaken decisions of the 1950s and 1960s were bringing their toll of problems. Here, trends in the regional economy and the incidental effects of public policy decisions were combining to produce a major urban crisis in the 1980s.


## The Problem of the Periphery


An earlier chapter has described how the periphery was developed as a series of single-tenure, one-class estates. Easterhouse is typical. Some 95% of the housing was corporation-owned, predominantly in three and four storey tenements and there was always a substantial proportion of large families. High density building in the periphery was controversial from the start but as fast as houses were built more were needed. Faced with the magnitude of the problem, the city fathers opted for a policy of 'Tae hell with the planning, just give us the houses', eating rapidly into the green belt and with social and shopping facilities coming much later, if at all. So the discredited Bruce plan of the post-war years was, in practice, largely implemented. Easterhouse grew rapidly in the 1950s and 1960s and, if former slum-dwellers were at first pround of their new houses with modern fittings, disenchantment quickly set in. Lack of school building combined with teacher shortages to produce part-time education for a generation of children, while the first phase of the shopping centre was not opened until 1972. Easterhouse was by now marked as a low-income area and the second phase was never built. Recreation facilities remain sparse, though a swimming pool was opened in 1969. Reaching the size of a medium-sized Scottish town, with 56,000 people by 1971, much of the estate was bleak and monotonous, streets of council blocks lacking either privacy or the sense of communal living of the traditional city communities.

We must guard against the common tendency to romanticise the old communities, marked as they often were by poverty, squalor and violence; but if they had developed a sense of social solidarity, as they had, then presumably Easterhouse should have been able to do the same. Easterhouse, however, had its own early reputation to contend with. Crime and juveline delinquency received enormous publicity, despite evidence collected by Professor R E Nichol of Strathclyde University showing in 1968 that crime was no worse there than elsewhere and, indeed, was falling, in contrast to the rising trend for Scotland as a whole. In the late 1960s, the singer Frankie Vaughan took an interest in the estate, launching the Easterhouse youth project and a much-publicised 'arms surrender' by local gangs but not everyone was sympathetic. Baillie James Anderson, convenor of the police committee in the Conservative city administration of the time, was one of many who branded the area, describing proposals to improve the environment as 'pie in the sky idealism' and opposing a scheme to provide fenced gardens on the grounds that the posts would be uprooted and used as weapons. When, in the same year, the project's youth centre was temporarily closed (because of vandalism according to the critics, for lack of finance according to its supporters) Anderson pronounced the project a failure, adding that 'this is precisely what I prophesied' (*Glasgow Herald*, 18.10.69). Vaughan's efforts to turn the gangs' energies into peaceful channels was criticised by Lionel Daiches, former Sheriff-Substitute in Glasgow who lamented that 'before one can get public concern one must be a delinquent' (*Glasgow Herald*, 2.7.68). In 1969 it was revealed that nearly a third of Easterhouse residents had filed applications for transfers out of the estate, most wanting to go back to the Gallowgate in the old east end, hardly an urban paradise itself. With the resulting turnover in population, a stable community became ever harder to achieve.

The peripheral estates were developed primarily as residential areas, in contrast to the new towns rising at the same time at some little distance away, and employment opportunities were always limited. An industrial estate was established at Queenslie near Easterhouse but of the 10,000 jobs there less than a third went to Easterhouse residents (CES, 1985). Long distances, poor services and high fares on public transport were obstacles to seeking employment further afield in a community in which, by 1981, only some 15% of households were car owners.

## Measuring the Problem

The impact of the recession in the 1980s has exacerbated the problems of Easterhouse and Drumchapel, as an analysis of the 1981 census for the Easterhouse and Drumchapel APTs shows (Strathclyde, 1984). Deprivation was now clearly most widespread around the periphery (Figure 6.3). In Easterhouse, as befits a post-war development, practically all houses had the basic amenities, but no less than 29.5% were classed as overcrowded, against a Glasgow average of 15.9%. There were 6.4% of households with four or more children against 2.2% for the city as a whole and 15.9% of households contained single-parent families (against 7.0% for the city). Only 1.7% of heads of households were in professional or managerial occupations, compared with 11.0% for Glasgow and 16.2% for the region as a whole; by contrast 39.7% were in low-paid occupations (25.6% for the city). Male unemployment in 1986 was 40.3% overall and 47.8% among the 20-24 age group (19.2% and 24.0% for the city). The extent of low incomes can be judged from the fact that some two-thirds of households are on housing benefit. 85.1% of households are without a car (70.6% for the city and 54.6% for the region). The population of Easterhouse has been declining along with

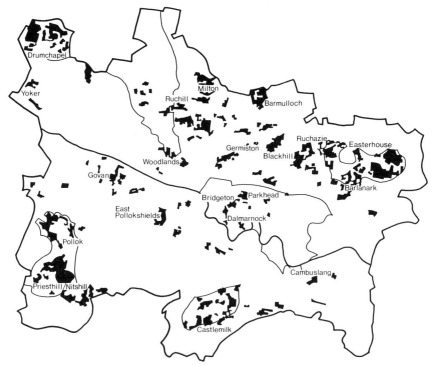

FIGURE 6.3　Social Deprivation in Glasgow. Worst concentrations. *Source*: Glasgow District Council.

that of the city. Taking the greater Easterhouse area as a whole, rather than the more narrowly defined APT, the population declined from 56,483 in 1971 to 45,708 in 1981 (CES, 1985) but, because of diminishing opportunities elsewhere, this was not as great as had been anticipated in the late 1970s, when it was hoped that population movement could, if not solve the problems of the peripheral estates, at least make them more manageable. The age structure of the population, reflecting that of the estate, showed an increase in the 17-24 age group and only a small drop in that of 12-16, indicating that the unemployment problem is likely to increase. Overall, Easterhouse retains a younger population than that of the city as a whole and, with low levels of educational achievement, limited prospects of moving into employment outwith the area. Poor health is exacerbated by housing conditions, notably overcrowding.

Overall, then, Easterhouse exhibits the classic symptoms of multiple deprivation, a finding confirmed by the 1985 report from the Centre for Environmental Studies (CES 1985), which noted that it contained ten of the worst 30 enumeration districts in the city (seven of the others were in the other peripheral estates). Glasgow, in turn, was one of the worst off cities in Britain in terms of deprivation.

## The Impact of Public Policy

By the late 1960s, it was already widely accepted that the policy of building at high density on the periphery had been mistaken, however understandable in the circumstances of the time. Attention had been drawn to the plight of the periphery in the second review of the Glasgow development plan in 1972. This found, as we have noted, that the crude housing shortage would soon be over but devoted extensive coverage to the extent of multiple deprivation, confirming that this extended well beyond the inner city areas zoned for renewal, to the corporation's own post-war estates. At one point, it seemed that the problems of the peripheral estates might almost solve themselves, with falling population allowing for widescale demolition. A 1978 report from the district council raised the prospect of a massive housing surplus by 1983 but this was never formally adopted by the council and its predictions were soon seen to be unrealistic. Nor was the district council politically ready to admit to the failures of the periphery and moves to add the estates to the existing priorities of Maryhill and GEAR were opposed by the Labour group, then in opposition (Campbell, 1984). The district was nevertheless gradually changing its view of the periphery. The last peripheral development, at Darnley in Pollok, qualified as an area of need before its completion, an event much delayed because of inefficiency in the council's direct labour organisation while the political shock of SNP successes in 1977 had a major impact on thinking in the Labour group.

Meanwhile, the 1976 regional report of Strathclyde region had affirmed the commitment to combatting multiple deprivation and the areas for priority treatment (APTs) had been designated. The practical effects of APT designation in terms of resources are notoriously hard to assess, given the lack of a control sample but the district council has undertaken a series of exercises to assess the impact of capital investment by public and private agencies on the priority areas, GEAR, the Maryhill corridor and the peripheral estates. The figures for capital spending from 1979-80 to 1983-4 indicate a bias against the estates, with investment per head by all agencies amounting to £586 in Easterhouse against £2,415 in GEAR and £1,776 in the Maryhill corridor. For district council spending alone, the figures are £219 per head in Easterhouse, £604 per head in GEAR and £684 in the Maryhill corridor—though these figures exclude the district's non-HRA capital programme which provides grants for private house improvement. Given the lack of private housing in Easterhouse, inclusion of this would produce a further bias against the estate. What also emerged was the crucial dependence of the peripheral estates on council spending. While the district council was responsible for nearly 40% of all investment over the period, in the peripheral estates it is the dominant investor. In Drumchapel, for example, 85% of all investment was undertaken by the district. In Easterhouse, this figure was just 37.5% but this was due to the fortuitous circumstance of the Monkland motorway passing through the area, increasing sharply the contribution of Strathclyde region during the road's construction. There is no private investment recorded and only a token amount by the SDA, a finding confirmed by the SDA's own figures, which show Provan (including Easterhouse) as amongst the four Scottish parliamentary constituencies with the least amount of SDA current investment as at November 1984 (*Hansard*, 6.12.84). More detailed figures which have been produced by the district council for selected years up to 1984-5 confirm the picture.

What emerges, then, is that Easterhouse is critically dependent on public expenditure and, given its preponderance of public sector housing, vulnerable to policies such as prevailed in the early 1980s, when central government sharply diverted housing capital expenditure from the public to the private sector. For the city as a whole, the centrally-permitted expenditure on council house investment (the HRA account) fell from £62.6m in 1979/80 to £51.0m in 1984/5 while that for private sector grants and loans (the non-HRA account) increased from £13.3m to £84.5m. The balance was later reversed with the heavy cuts in the non-HRA programme, though in real terms council housing investment in 1987 remains well below the levels of 1979.

Figures on revenue spending are even more elusive. Under the *social strategy* Easterhouse is eligible for preferential treatment in the allocation of resources. In education, falling school rolls and the elimination of the teacher shortage has meant that staffing levels could be established on a proper basis and then extra staff appointed under the Scottish Office *Circular 991* scheme. This has certainly brought more teachers to Easterhouse, where staffing ratios are more generous than elsewhere in the region. In social work, too, extra staff have been provided since reorganisation and welfare rights workers have been deployed to try and ensure that people get the state benefits to which they are entitled. The fact remains, however, that many revenue services are demand-led so that those areas with more children staying on at school will tend to get more education expenditure and make more demands on the library service.

Other instruments of policy, however, may work against the periphery, notably in the fields of planning and industrial policy. While some of the declining industrial areas were to be designated as *economic* priority areas with the focus on bringing back industry, the main thrust of the measures for the peripheral estates were in the field of social policy. The development of the structure plan shows this up clearly. The first version, in 1979, talked of the need for 'priority for related action in the fields of housing, derelict and degraded land and planning blight both to improve employment opportunities and maintain the progress of renewal' in nineteen areas, including Glasgow's four peripheral estates. The 1981 revision, produced after the council had developed its economic and social strategies, claimed that 'there is a strong correlation between the council's APTs, the prospective joint economic initiative areas and the urban renewal priorities identified in the approved Structure Plan'. This coincidence did not, however, apply to the peripheral schemes which, while they were all APTs and 'renewal areas' were not 'early action' renewal areas or joint economic initiative areas (see chapter 4). When, for the 1984 revision of the structure plan, Glasgow district proposed adding Easterhouse to the list of early action areas, the region turned down the idea with the delphic comment that in Easterhouse 'the vacant land is concentrated on the periphery, which presents problems associated more with agricultural practice than urban renewal'!

Further evidence of the adverse effect of planning policies came in the early 1980s when proposals for a large retail development on the Goodyear site in Drumchapel and warehousing and retail outlets at Auchinlea Park at Easterhouse where 'called in' by the regional council and turned down or cut back as contrary to the structure plan's emphasis on the city centre and town centres elsewhere in the region—this outweighed their potential for local job creation. These decisions have proved highly controversial. The justification for the restriction on retailing is that shoppers should not be drawn into the peripheral estates from other areas as this would put retailing in those areas at risk. It is thus a policy of restraining market competition in the name of wider public policy goals. In the case of the peripheral estates, though, its effect is to prevent them competing for one of the few types of mobile investment available, which could draw wealth into the areas from better-off areas, wealth which could then be distributed among the estate residents in the form of wages. Another consequence of the restriction on shopping provision for incoming shoppers, together with low incomes in Easterhouse, is a lack of competition which allows prices in Easterhouse shops to be maintained above those prevailing in the city centre. Easterhouse, situated on the motorway, appears particularly well located for precisely the type of retail development which is prohibited. So the grievance often expressed in Easterhouse is that, not only have the planning decisions of the past worked against their interests, but, dependent on public spending in an era of cuts, they are not even been allowed to compete in an area where they have market advantages, so the dependence on the state is perpetuated. The corollary of this is that, if the public authorities are so assiduous in restricting market forces, they should recognise a corresponding obligation to provide employment themselves. Instead, the residents complain that they are getting the benefits neither of capitalism nor of socialism.

Nor have central government and its agencies given priority to the periphery in developing economic policies. Though the SDA has an input into the community business ventures there have not been the major investment programmes in Easterhouse which are to be seen in the city centre and we have noted the small amount of Agency investment in the peripheral schemes. The parliamentary constituency of Glasgow Central, on the other hand, was identified in 1984 as the recipient of by far the largest amount of SDA investment. The business group *Glasgow Action* (chapter 7) is an example of an SDA sponsored idea which is all but exclusively concerned with prestige city centre projects. Other intiatives, particularly in Easterhouse, have focused on community development and, in the absence of major industrial activity, the promotion of 'community industry'.

## Community Development

As already mentioned, one of Easterhouse's early problems was the failure to develop a 'community spirit' and the lack of the infrastructure of community development such as shops, schools and leisure facilities. Time, however, has been a major force in aiding the development of a community. In 1969, an action group emerged to combat the bad publicity given the estate. In 1972, the *Voice* newspaper was established, influenced in its early days by the Church of Scotland and later by the Labour Party. The Easterhouse festival society, formed in 1977 by church and community groups, sponsored community activities including job creation schemes, environmental improvements, amateur dramatics and gala days, drawing funds from the Scottish Arts Council, urban aid, district and regional councils and the Manpower Services Commission. These initiatives owed much to Ron Ferguson, a Church of Scotland community minister, with his philosophy of uniting the community to improve their lot. Community mobilisation and solidarity, though, are fragile. In the Easthall area, a residents' association is well established, but in other areas frustration easily gives way to demoralisation. The lack of political competition since the demise of the Scottish National Party does not encourage participation and there is a tendency for groups to turn in frustration on themselves and each other. In 1986, the festival society, beset by criticisms that, with its budget of over £100,000, it was privileged, elitist and dominated by officials, erupted in crisis and its director resigned. At the same time, the *Voice* was taken over by a collective of young radicals, unemployed locals sharply distrustful of all authority. The portraits of Mao and Ho Chi Minh on the walls of their offices and their hard-left rhetoric reflected more a defiance of the powers-that-be than a coherent political strategy and they appeared to have no links with outside organisations. Easterhouse youth as a whole is more sullen and resigned than rebellious and violence is largely domestic, turned inwards rather than at outside symbols of wealth and authority.

This is a recurrent pattern in areas like Easterhouse where the lack of a stable community structure and the existence of sporadic interventions by the public authorities with larger or smaller sums of money attached produces short-lived campaigns around particular issues and institutions. Often, though, the interventions are just enough to raise expectations while the resources are inadequate to resolve the problems. There is a constant questioning of the representativeness and legitimacy of local community spokesmen and a stable pattern of community leadership fails to emerge.

## Economic Palliatives

Easterhouse, built essentially to relieve Glasgow's housing stress, has never developed an economic base consistent with its size. Deindustrialisation on Clydeside and the recession of the 1980s have compounded the problem, hitting Easterhouse and the adjacent manufacturing areas of eastern Glasgow particularly hard. Yet the main thrust of spatial economic policies in Scotland has been directed to the new towns and the traditional industrial areas (Keating and Boyle, 1986), while we have noted the 'objective discrimination' inherent in the structure plan. This is not to say that the problems of employment in Glasgow's periphery have been totally neglected but the main initiatives have been in the field of 'community business' geared to satisfying the limited local demand rather than integrating areas like Easterhouse more fully into the regional economy.

Towards the end of 1979 the Easterhouse festival society (EFS) established the Easterhouse employment initiative group, from which a community company Provanhall Holdings Ltd developed in December 1980. It has converted flats into shop units and a school annexe into workspaces for the district council but, as a private company, was unable to receive urban aid or funding from charitable trusts. The Easterhouse community trust was therefore established as the company's fund raising arm. The Manpower Services Commission, urban aid, the Gulbenkian Trust and the regional and district councils have given financial and other support.

Another initiative which owes its origins to the EFS has been the Greater Easterhouse partnership. Formally launched in February 1985 as a company limited by guarantee with enterprise trust status, the partnership is supported by the two local authorities, the SDA and a number of private businesses. A community group and a funding group exist with the former identifying potential projects and the latter deciding whether to provide funds. This dual structure is reflected in the management of the partnership; a community manager and a business manager, the latter seconded from one of the partnership's private sector backers, work together to process applications from the local community. In this way, it is hoped to harness the business knowhow of the private sector to the needs of small community-based businesses though the impact on overall employment levels is likely to be small.

Easterhouse has also been the site of one of the Manpower Services Commission's (MSC) technical and vocational education initiative (TVEI) experiments. This originated in concern within the Conservative central government about the decline of technical education and a belief that this was one of the factors in the decline of the British economy (Moon and Richardson, 1984). It can also be seen as a bid by the MSC and Department of Employment to gain control of part of the education service to combat the liberal education traditions of the Department of Education and Science. There appears to have been no Scottish involvement in the evolution of the policy but in due course Scotland was given its share of the experiments and, within Scotland, Strathclyde region got two. In its origins, TVEI seems to have been conceived as a challenge to the educational establishment, with the usual consultative mechanisms being by-passed (Moon and Richardson, 1984). In the implementation phase, however, the policy has had to come into the schools and be put into effect by teachers, with the support and cooperation of the local educational departments. In this process, it seems to have experienced a type of goal-displacement familiar to the public policy literature.

TVEI involves introducing into a group of neighbouring schools a vocational education stream geared to specific skills, for pupils from 14 to 17 (or 18 in England). MSC money is provided for materials and equipment and it is intended that, as the training programmes progress, pilot industries will be established on school premises. As these mature, they will spin off into the community, being replaced by new ones developed in the courses.

Like other initiatives of the Thatcher Government (enteprise zones are an obvious analogy) TVEI might have been expected to arouse ideological opposition on the part of Labour local authorities implying, as it does, that comprehensive education has been a failure and that children should be trained vocationally from such an early age. On the other hand, it offered the prospect of extra resources in a time of extreme stringency. The same applies at the level of the school—indeed so worried were teachers about the precariousness of the MSC money that they exempted TVEI from the boycott of new development which was part of the long 'industrial action' of 1985-6—an invitation, if one was needed, for the government to give the MSC control of more of the education budget. Later the main teachers' union the EIS, changed its mind more than once about the scheme. Strathclyde region's response to the TVEI invitation was to place it in an area of social and economic deprivation on the ground that it was here, with low levels of educational achievement, that traditional education had been found most wanting. It was also claimed that training in vocational skills could assist in the economic regeneration of the area.

The Easterhouse TVEI was launched in 1984, with an emphasis on high technology. 'Computer Studies and units in the application of new technology (would) form compulsory elements of all years of the course. Equally important other units (would) reflect the technological bias of the course as a whole' (Strathclyde, 1984). According to the MSC, the emphasis on high technology emerged from surveys of youngsters in the area. It is evident, too, that the preferences of the teachers involved played a large part in the choice. What does not appear to have been considered at this stage is the appropriateness of high technology ventures as a viable industrial and economic strategy for youngsters with (by definition) no higher education, operating in a poor local market. Indeed, there seems to have been little serious economic analysis of the TVEI, with the question of whether the 'industries' generated would merely serve the local market or compete in regional markets glossed over. The initial list of industries seemed to suggest both, with proposals for boat building, house repair, graphic design, fast foods, a residential centre, burglar alarms, a community information service, a travel agency, school supplies and a community computer service. The emphasis was to change in the implementation stage.

The link with the economic development needs of the area, however, is weak. When the time came for the establishment of pilot industries, the real problems of breaking into the competitive economy surfaced and the list of industries was reduced to mainly low-technology ventures serving purely the local market, toys, 'cute cakes', a wrought iron works and leather patch-work, with some electrical assembly work as the nearest to advanced tech-nology. Nor was the establishment of the pilot industries connected in any way to the instruments of spatial development policy. There was no programme of help with premises, investment, infrastructure or business advice to tie in with the vocational training programme, though these were being sought after the industries had started. What emerges from TVEI is therefore some extra money for Easterhouse schools as long as the experiment lasts and perhaps some very marginal impact on the less competitive sections of the local economy. Much of the TVEI money and effort has in practice gone into providing courses of a more conventional kind, albeit not geared to the usual certificates. As a result of the teachers' insistence, there are to be programmes of 'life skills' to train children to cope with the needs of contemporary society. This is indicative of the assimilation of TVEI to traditional education and may help the children to compete in the tight local employment market, though an expansion of the remedial education facilities would do a great deal more. TVEI indicates that when central government determines on a programme, it will find the money to pay for it; at the same time, though, it has been cutting back on programmes which could have a direct impact on unemployment levels while, in the absence of reflation at the national level, job prospects for the residents of Easterhouse remain poor.

As for the regional council, it has been claiming the Easterhouse TVEI as a great success, though public statements from officials are extremely ambiguous on whether 'success' means that education in Easterhouse has become more vocational and less liberal or that the MSC's initial objectives have been subverted and the TVEI money used for conventional education. The region's main concern appears to be to keep the MSC money and, for this, they have been prepared to collude in some extremely dubious claims made about the success of the project and its 'pilot industries'.

In the context both of community development and economic activity, it is important to remember the housing initiatives in Easterhouse discussed in chapter 5. The introduction of a private housing market is intended to alter the socio-economic character of the area by providing an opportunity for the modestly upwardly mobile to stay there, while at the same time bringing in private capital for housing rehabilitation and new building. There is, as we noted earlier, some evidence of success here.

## The Drumchapel and Easterhouse Initiatives

The argument so far is that the main thrust of physical and economic development policy has largely passed the periphery by, leaving estates like Easterhouse dependent on local social policy initiatives and the limited moneys which can be obtained through urban aid. Concern about them had been building up for some time, however, stimulated by the 'social strategy for the eighties', Glasgow district's area management and decentralisation structures and the work of the region's Glasgow divisional deprivation group. By the early 1980s, the peripheral schemes were on the policy agenda (Campbell, 1984), with general agreement that 'something should be done' by way of a simultaneous attack on their social and economic problems. Just what should be done and how the resources could be found was not so obvious.

In October 1983, proposals were put forward by the chief executive's department of the region identifying the problems, outlining the broad objectives of joint economic and social initiatives for Easterhouse and Drumchapel and discussing the strategy and programmes. It was stressed that the gestation period for the initiatives should not be as long as that which preceded GEAR. A steering committee was to be established consisting of elected and senior officers of the two authorities as well as other agencies, the Scottish Development Agency, Greater Glasgow Health Board, and possibly the Scottish Office and Manpower Services Commission. In the event the part played by the central agencies was negligible or, in the case of the Scottish Office, nonexistent. Each agency and each department was asked to prepare briefs and various ideas were to be considered in the lead up to the formal establishment of the initiatives. Community involvement was regarded, at least on paper, as an essential component in the inititiatives not only to lend credibility to the ideas but also to foster community spirit in the areas.

The following year and half or so, to the Summer of 1985, saw very slow progress towards the establishment of the initiative. Partly because some of the most senior members of both authorities were involved, who were obviously pressed for time, partly because of the need to seek advice, views and ideas from a range of departments and officials, and partly because of poor relationships between the district and regional council, it took more time in arriving at the point when a formal agreement could be reached. Training seminars were run, consideration of the administrative structure and constitution of the initiatives and the nature of community involvement were discussed. Until this stage there had been almost no communicaton with the local communities but during the summer of 1985, community conferences were held in each of the areas.

Interim planning groups (IPG) consisting of elected members and officials from the two authorities, other representatives from bodies such as the SDA and GGHB, and some of the members from the residents' forum met regularly from summer 1985, acting as the institutional lead-in to the formal establishment of the initiatives. One of the most contentious matters was the appointment of full-time directors for each initiative. The SDA, in one of their very rare examples of involvement in the areas and with the joint initiatives particularly, funded a consultant to draw up an advertisement for the post. Given the limitations on the powers and finance of the iniatives and the scale of the problem to be tackled, the jobs were criticised as needing [two 'supermen' and there was great difficulty in filling them.

The formal, legal establishment of the area management groups (AMG) for each of Geater Easterhouse and Drumchapel, replacing the IPGs, only occurred in April 1986. The AMGs, joint committees of the two authorities consist of equal numbers of regional councillors, district councillors, and community representatives. The limits within which the AMGs can operate, and indeed exist, as independent entities are tightly constrained by legislation, with little possibility of a major devolution of power and responsibilities. There is also considerable potential for clashes over 'who speaks for the area'. The (existence of 'community representatives' recognises the limited representativeness of the councillors, elected by very small proportions of the electorate but the representativeness of the community activists, chosen at local conferences which could so easily be manipulated, is by no means obvious.

The aims of the Easterhouse and Drumchapel Initiatives as set out in 1983 are:

1.  to generate the facilities and community organisation of the areas, which in the case of Easterhouse especially, was recognised to be comparable to a medium sized town.
2.  to meet the aspirations of the population both in the short term and also into the 1990s and beyond.
3.  to create jobs and (re)generate the local economy.
4.  to involve the local community.
5.  to develop the communities of Easterhouse and Drumchapel and their respective individual component communities.
6.  to make use of all possible sources of funding, encourage flexibility and innovation.

In effect, the aims come under two broad headings of social and economic development. However, while the projects have been described as social and economic initiatives and the local authorities recognise the clear links between the two aspects, what has emerged appears much more social than economic. In addition, it is hoped that they will also act as pressure groups for greater financial investment in the areas. The employment strategies envisage the maximum use being made of the various existing funds, including the Manpower Service Commission's job creation schemes, widely criticised as mere 'placebo' policies. There have been suggestions that public agencies in the area could adopt local recruitment policies, though this would have to be accommodated within existing staffing levels, given expenditure restraints, and might encounter difficulties with trade unions. While community businesses, too, can generate some employment, the scale of unemployment will require far more ambitious projects and there seems little likelihood that these will come the way of the Easterhouse and Drumchapel initiatives without the major funding which can probably only be supplied by central government. So far, though, the Scottish Office has shown little interest in, and even less taken an active part in the establishment of the initiatives.

The finances of the initiatives will inevitably determine their powers, the extent of their independence and, ultimately, their success. The bald fact is that there is no extra money available apart from a special pump-priming budget for 1985/86 which offered £50,000 to each of the areas. It is envisaged, of course, that greater priority for capital and revenue mainstream resources will feed into the areas as Easterhouse and Drumchapel AMGs articulate their proposals to the local authorities but these will have to compete with projects in other areas. In addition, the estates' expected share of urban aid moneys has been consolidated into a single block, amounting to some £200,000 for Drumchapel and £400,000 for Easterhouse in 1986-7. As the Scottish Office has refused officially to sanction this arrangement, however, applications will still have to come through the regional council for individual projects; so effectively there is merely another filter, the AMG. It is also hoped to lever support from the Greater Glasgow Health Board, the SDA, the MSC, the European Community and the private sector, though finance from these sources is dependent on opportunities being identified which can compete with those in other areas. In turn, this would require spending by central and local government, notably in providing infrastructure, premises and help with investment finance. It may also, if the region is serious about bringing in private capital, require some reappraisal of the structure plan.

Given the lack of financial resources and powers for the initiatives, it is difficult to hold high hopes for their future. They must be seen, at best, as a means of access to decision-makers in local government, an attempt once again to bend the criteria for resource allocation in favour of the deprived areas. There is an underlying theme, though, that somehow previous attempts at combatting deprivation by 'throwing money' at the problem have failed and that what is required are community-based initiatives to let the community solve its own problems. Certainly, centralised planning and housing policies have been at the root of many of the problems of the peripheral estates. Yet, for all the special initiatives in the areas, it is by no means true that money has been thrown at them. On the contrary, they have suffered from severe under-investment. Large injections of outside funding will be required to regenerate areas like Easterhouse and Drumchapel while, for all the virtues of community industry, it is simply not possible for a low-income economy to find prosperity by buying and selling to itself. An instructive comparison might be drawn with the Scottish new towns. These too were initially established largely to cope with Glasgow's housing problems, yet they were generously funded, endowed with the full range of commercial and leisure facilities and promoted as centres for industrial development. It is true that this was in the era of 'big spending' and that the competition for both spending and industry are now intense—but peripheral estates are of the scale of whole towns and solutions to their problems may have to be of that scale.

In the spring of 1988, the Scottish Office published its *New Life for Scotland*, which put considerable emphasis on the peripheral estates. Once again, there is no promise of extra funding but rather an emphasis on the private sector and financial restraint.

# 7   Jobs and Industry

## Economic Decline and the City

In the 1950s and 1960s, the problems of Glasgow, as of other British cities, were seen primarily in physical terms. In the 1970s, social policy issues came to the fore. The 1980s, in their turn, have seen the economic problem occupy centre stage. Partly this is the result of a redefinition of the syndrome of urban decline, with economic and industrial failure seen as the central factor, the root cause of most of the other problems. Mainly, though, it is due to the serious downturn in the urban economy in the 1980s, a phenomenon noted in many British cities and which, in the case of Glasgow, was the culmination of a long period of decline in the traditional industries. Yet, in relation to this central problem, local policy makers' powers are extremely limited. Such as they are, they have been used increasingly energetically but, inevitably, with only a marginal impact on the problem.

Unemployment rates in the west of Scotland have traditionally been higher than the UK average and at local government reorganisation stood at around 8% for the region, against 5.2% for Scotland as a whole and 4.1% for Britain. Bad as this appeared at the time, it would pale beside the 1987 figure of 18.2% unemployment in Strathclyde; nor could much consolation be taken in the fact that this was now a mere 1.5 times the national rate instead of double as in 1975. The main toll of jobs was taken in the recession of the early 1980s, with the peak of redundancies coming in 1981 to reduce total employment in the region from over one million in 1975 to some 800,000 a decade later (Figure 7.1). This poses a stark contrast with the optimistic forecasts of the 1974 *West Central Scotland Plan* of between 900,000 and 1,000,000 jobs in the 1980s. By 1987, Strathclyde accounted for 3.6% of British employment, against 4.3% in 1979 (Strathclyde, 1987).

In terms of broad sectors, the job loss was concentrated in manufacturing industry, which accounts for nearly the whole of the 200,000 net job loss, with changes in other sectors more or less balancing out. The process can be seen clearly in the case of the traditional industries. In the Glasgow conurbation (comprising 71% of the Region's population), 38,416 people were employed in shipbuilding in 1961; by 1981, the number had fallen to just 12,750 (Lever and Mather, 1986), with just two yards left within the city and large areas of empty ground by the river. Dramatic falls were also recorded in metal manufacture (down from 39,195 to 16,246 over the twenty years),

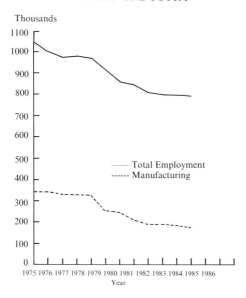

Thousands

Total Employment
Manufacturing

Year

FIGURE 7.1    Employment, Strathclyde Region, 1975-86. *Source*: Strathclyde Regional
Council.

and mechanical engineering (down from 86,467 to 33,086) (Lever and Mather, 1986). Glasgow district council (1985) drew attention to decline in three types of firm: (1) those operating in metal manufacture, with the virtual elimination of iron and steel industries in the closure of the nationalised Clyde Iron, Tollcross, Hallside and Clydebridge works and the privately owned Parkhead Forge between 1977 and 1983; (2) large establishments, foreign-owned, such as Singer at Clydebank, Goodyear at Drumchapel (closed), nationalised such as Leyland, Rolls Royce, British Rail engineering (cutback or closed) and large UK companies such as W D and H O Wills, Wm Collins and British Bakeries (cut back); (3) firms largely dependent on export markets such as Weir Group and Distillers. Between 1971 and 1983, while Glasgow had lost 45% of its manufacturing jobs, no manufacturing company of any scale had set up in the city. Strathclyde region as a whole, which in 1978 accounted for 4.6% of all British manufacturing employment was down by 1985 to 3.4% (Strathclyde, 1985).

Much was made by central government in the mid 1980s about the number of new jobs which were being created in Britain; this they insisted was more significant than the unemployment levels. Critics pointed out that the vast bulk of these jobs were part-time and low-paid; they were also predominantly taken by women which, however welcome in itself, did not solve the problem of how to replace the lost full-time jobs for men. In any case, not even this consolation prize was available in Strathclyde and Glasgow. Service employment in Glasgow grew more slowly than in any other British city in the 1970s and then fell off in the recession of the early 1980s, leaving no net increase.

Urban economic decline in Britain is a topic which has attracted attention for some years (Cameron, 1980) and several attempts have been made to explain it (e.g. Fothergill and Gudgeon, 1982; Lever and Mather, 1986). Unfortunately, economic analysts, for all their efforts, have been unable to reach any consensus, though there is general acceptance of the view that, whereas British spatial economic disparities were seen in the past as *inter*-regional, now they are as much *intra*-regional, with the older and larger urban areas losing out to the smaller towns around them. In the case of Glasgow, though, we have a declining conurbation *within* a declining region, recognised as such since the 1930s. This does help to simplify policy choices in some respects, eliminating the conflicts and contradictions between 'regional' and 'urban' approaches to spatial policy which have caused problems in some parts of England (RSA, 1983); but it means that Glasgow's problems are on a correspondingly daunting scale.

Recession and decline have had differential impacts within the Glasgow conurbation. As in other conurbations, there has been a drift of activity from inner to outer conurbation, with the former's share of employment declining from 66.8% in 1952 to 58.2% in 1981 but, while absolute numbers in employment had fallen steadily in the inner city, in the outer conurbation they had grown until the mid 1970s (Lever and Mather, 1986) with the expansion of service industries. Examination of *unemployment* levels reveals at first sight a rather different picture, though getting an accurate picture of long-term trends can be extremely difficult given the Department of Employment's repeated revisions of the method of calculation (which have all served to deflate the figures). There has been a steady increase of unemployment in both inner and outer conurbations but the growth has been faster *outside* the city than *within* it. While Glasgow's male unemployment rate was worse than that of the rest of the region in the 1970s, by 1986 it was marginally better, at 22.1% against 22.9% (Department of Employment figures). These findings can be made compatible with what we have noted for changes in employment when we remember that the city, and particularly its inner areas, have experienced rapid population decline, so that a relatively poor record in job creation can go along with a *relatively* less poor record in terms of unemployment. The term *relative* must, of course, be emphasised. Overall unemployment by the mid 1980s was at chronic levels, with Strathclyde in sixth worst place in British regions and counties and the regional council estimating that, if it were not for the measures taken by central government to 'massage' the figures, overall (male and female) unemployment in the region would register at 26.5% in 1987 against an official figure of 18.2%. The official Department of Employment trends are given in figure 7.2.

Within the city of Glasgow, too, there has been some change in relative performance. Drawing on census figures, McGregor and Mather (1986) show that, within the city, unemployment increased between 1971 and 1981 less fast in the inner areas than in the outer areas, a reflection of the crisis of the

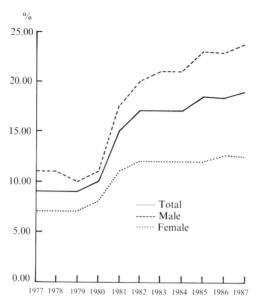

FIGURE 7.2 % Unemployment, Strathclyde Region at April, 1977-87. *Source*: Department of Employment.

peripheral estates discussed in chapter 6. Again, these findings are *relative* and unemployment in 1985 continued to be highest in the city centre and east end and the peripheral estates, with male unemployment of 57.7% in Fairfield and 55.1% and 55.0% in the Glasgow Green and Dalmarnock areas (both in GEAR). Easterhouse West and Castlemilk East both stood at 42.3% while Drumchapel West stood at 40.7%. So the economic crisis reflects the now familiar spatial pattern of the city, most severe in the old central areas along the river and in the new peripheral estates.

Glasgow's industrial decline has not been accompanied by a compensating growth in other types of activity. Foreign investment in high technology, once spoken of as Scotland's industrial hope for the future, has tended to go to the new towns or other locations outside the city. Nor has the city enjoyed much spin-off from the North Sea oil boom, apart from the location of the Britoil headquarters there. There have, however, been one or two more hopeful developments. Glasgow in 1985 had about 100,000 people working in offices, making it the principal business centre in Scotland and the seventh largest commercial office centre in the UK and the mid 1980s have seen a small boom in office development, concentrated in the central business district on the western side of the urban core. The most striking case here is that of Britoil. In 1976, as a regional policy measure and to ward off nationalist pressure, the then Labour Government announced that the headquarters of the British National Oil Corporation (BNOC), established to give the public sector a share in the oil boom, would be located in Glasgow. The choice of Glasgow was a little controversial since, if the activity were to be dispersed from London, a location adjacent to the oil fields (such as Aberdeen) might have been more logical. Glasgow, however, was in Scotland, providing a defence against the nationalists and it was in a development area, not to mention a solidly Labour city. The complete build-up and construction of purpose-built offices was to take a decade, during which time the Conservative Government had privatised the company as Britoil, abolishing the regulatory function which the BNOC had additionally carried out. Britoil, nonetheless, opted to stay in Glasgow, making it the first major enterprise to locate in the city for decades. Its impact was considerable, with a direct employment of 1,568 people and, according to a study by the Fraser of Allander Institute (1985), a multiplier effect on the local economy which accounts for almost as many permanent jobs again. Britoil employees are disproportionately well-qualified in relation to the regional average, with higher incomes, 42% of them being in managerial and professional occupations. The office block is far the largest such private development in the city and the equivalent of about three years total normal development, creating some 1,973 man-years of work in the region. Britoil's purchasing policies have also drawn other firms to Glasgow while the effect on business confidence of having a major headquarters and not a mere branch plant coming to establish itself in the city was considerable, an inspiration in the mid 1980s to *Glasgow Action*. Even this success, though, was highly qualified. The privatised Britoil never carried through the original BNOC plan to go into 'downstream' refining and retailing activities and, since it confined itself to exploration and recovery, was particularly vulnerable to the fall in the oil price in the mid 1980s. In 1986, it was obliged to lay off a third of its workforce and cancel plans for a second phase of the headquarters complex.

Generally, then, the economic outlook for Glasgow in the 1980s was not hopeful, hence the efforts by local agencies to frame new policies for economic and industrial renewal.

## Local Government Efforts

Local authorities by their everyday activities have a considerable impact on the local economy. Both Strathclyde region and Glasgow district are large employers, though central government pressure and fiscal constraints have forced them to cut back. In 1986, Strathclyde employed a total of 108,325 people and Glasgow district another 14,145. Of course, central government will argue that staffing cutbacks thus frees resources for spending on other goods and services, creating new employment, but as we have seen (chapter 3) withdrawal of central government subsidy has prevented corresponding cuts in rate levels. Capital expenditure reductions will have had some direct effects on local employment, especially in housing where, as we have seen, they have been particularly severe.

As far as more explicitly economic and industrial policies are concerned, both Strathclyde and Glasgow have been active within the severe statutory and financial constraints laid down by a central government which regards economic and industrial matters as its own, with local government confined to a facilitating role. In Strathclyde, combatting unemployment is one of the two key corporate objectives and the chief executive's department houses the economic policy group responsible for general economic matters including research, lobbying and joint projects, and the industrial development unit with operational responsibilities for implementing aspects of the strategy, including the promotion of inward investment. On the members' side, there is an economic and industrial development committee with a wide-ranging remit. In 1980, Glasgow district reorganised itself to give greater priority to economic and industrial development, with an employment sub-committee of the policy and resources committee, responsible for economic policies and initiatives. In line with the district's preference for interdepartmental corporate structures rather than a large chief executive's department (chapter 3), the task was allocated on the official side to an economic development bureau grouping five departments, which produces a rolling five-year plan.

Both councils undertake the routine work of providing land and factories. Under policy guidelines produced in 1983, the region identified its role as the provision of units in the 500 to 1,000 square foot range, an area not met by the private sector or the Scottish Development Agency. By April 1986, some 147 units totalling 163,000 square feet had been provided on 35 sites. In addition, the region has developed 'new enterprise workshops' for people in the initial stages of developing new products, small business centres to provide short-term accomodation for new firms and 'integrated workforce units' in which total support is offered to new ideas for six months, with a view then to going to commercial backers. The district council identified its best prospect as the provision of very small factory/workshop units, with a target of 4,000 square metres per annum. A joint development between the two councils, the SDA and the two local universities is the West of Scotland Science Park, aimed at the commercial development of scientific ventures. Business advice is also offered by both councils. The district has two business development officers and and the Region has four; again these have identified distinct areas of work. Direct aid to firms is more limited, though the district does have a modest loans and grants scheme for very small firms and the region has used the European Social Fund to supplement its own resources in financing an employment grants scheme of wage subsidies for a limited duration where jobs are created or preserved.

At one time in the late 1970s, the promotion of inward investment, particularly from North America, was a major focus of attention. The SDA was active, as were most local authorities and new town corporations and after 1979 the industry minister in the Scottish Office started leading delegations overseas. All this gave rise to considerable confusion. The London-based Invest in Britain Bureau resented the independent Scottish effort under the SDA and demanded the closure of its overseas offices. After a good deal of wrangling, a compromise was reached under which inward investment promotion would come under a new unit, Locate in Scotland (LIS), jointly run by the SDA and the Scottish Office. This brought the effort more firmly under civil service and ministerial control (the SDA, as an 'arm's length' body, could get away with things which a government department could not) but has not entirely ended the rivalry and distrust between the British and Scottish efforts. In 1982, the local authority efforts were disciplined, too, with legislation preventing a district advertising for industry outside its own area without the approval of the region, and regions from sending abroad without the approval of LIS. So a local authority anxious to attract inward investment now had to get its sites and opportunities accepted in LIS's portfolio and hope that they would be promoted abroad. Many authorities by this time accepted that their independent efforts had in any case proved largely fruitless given the limitations on their resources and skills and were content to leave the task to LIS. By the mid 1980s, though, Glasgow was expressing worries that few if any of the new jobs attracted to Scotland by LIS were coming to the city.

With the free-for-all in inward investment promotion ended, Strathclyde concentrated on promoting the products of local companies through trade missions, publications and exhibitions. Glasgow, for its part, turned to the promotion of the city as a whole through the ambitious *Glasgow's Miles Better* campaign. This was a very broad-based campaign promoted by Lord Provost Michael Kelly (1980-4) to improve the 'image' of Glasgow, seen in England and abroad as dirty, violent and poor. The smiling 'Mr. Happy' figure was to be seen displayed on public buildings, car stickers and, in London, on hoardings and even the sides of taxis. Indeed, perhaps the only place in Britain the campaign did not penetrate effectively was Edinburgh where the municipal authorities took a dim view of their poor relation's efforts to better itself and Mr. Happy was banished from the Ediinburgh buses. At the same time, Kelly himself redefined the Lord Provost's role as ambassador for the city, getting extensive media coverage for his every action and courting businessmen and other decision makers, impressing them with the neglected potential of Glasgow. The campaign's aims were diffuse so evaluation of its success is necessarily impressionistic, but, after some initial scepticism, it does appear to have got Glasgow noticed, especially as it coincided with real opportunities for promoting Glasgow's new attractions, such as the Burrell Gallery and the Exhibition Centre.

One neglected area which Glasgow began to exploit in this period was tourism. Given the city's traditional image, the idea of it as a tourist centre might have appeared somewhat ludicrous, yet in 1982 some 560,000 visitors staying in the city had spent an estimated £62 million, generating £18 million in local income and sustaining some 5,400 jobs. This was notably lower than Edinburgh's figure of £100 million and holiday-makers accounted for just 26%, against 54% in the capital but Glasgow did have great potential both as a base for visiting the Highlands (which are on its doorstep) and for its own attractions. In 1983, the Burrell Gallery was opened, an imaginatively designed museum to house a collection left to the city after the war. Though the project was delayed for years and costs continually escalated, the district council stuck with it to completion to see it become in its first year the biggest tourist attraction in Scotland (it has since vied with Edinburgh Castle for the honour). The city's long-established art gallery and museum at Kelvingrove, too, is one of the major attractions in Scotland though the costs of the Burrell have led to complaints that it and the People's Palace at Glasgow Green (specialising in working people's history) were being neglected.

## Levering Resources

Given the very limited powers and resources of local authorities in economic matters, much effort has been devoted to lobbying other agencies including central government to change their policies and to seek resources from whatever sources are available. Lobbying activities include campaigning to retain development area status in the two major reviews of regional policy since 1979, so retaining investment grants for firms in the area; joining the campaign to keep open the Ravenscraig steelworks at Motherwell; and seeking (with very limited success) to persuade central government to disperse civil service jobs northwards.

Joint ventures have been of several types, with the depth of recession and the lack of powers and resources of their own leading both authorities into rather indiscriminate collaboration with whatever public agency or scheme does possess resources and is willing to spend them in Strathclyde. We have noted the eagerness to embrace the Manpower Services Technical and Vocational Education Initiative (chapter 6). Other Manpower Services Commission projects have been taken up equally enthusiastically as central government has entrusted the Commission with more responsibilities for managing the effects of the unemployment crisis. The community programme is a job creation scheme providing short-term employment for people who have been out of work for some time and Glasgow district is one of the largest of its sponsors, placing people in its own departments (mainly in parks and recreation) and, to a lesser extent, with other employers. In three years up to 1986, 13,200 people went through the scheme. The youth training scheme, regarded with extreme suspicion by the trade unions and the Labour Party in its early years, sets out to provide training for school leavers. Critics have claimed that it is merely a means of massaging the unemployment figures, with trainees often receiving little real training and being used as cheap and subsidised labour by employers. Between 1983 and 1986, 26,200 Glasgow youngsters entered the YTS programme which was extended from one to two years. The effect has certainly been to depress the registered unemployed figure in the 16-19 age group, though this still stood at 33% in 1985. People under 25 accounted for just over 40% of all the unemployed in Strathclyde, suggesting that the effect of YTS in most cases is to delay rather than escape unemployment. In all, in the period 1983-6, the MSC spent just over £100 million in Glasgow, a substantial sum which was welcomed by the local authorities but, given the strict British system for controlling public expenditure totals (chapter 3), this expenditure has a £100 million opportunity cost. In other words, the money could have been spent on other items and its spending by the MSC represents an equivalent reduction in spending possibilities elsewhere, for example in extending education, renewing the city's infrastructure or industrial development. Such choices, however, are not available to policy makers in Glasgow, Strathclyde or Scotland, who must learn to use whatever programmes are handed up from London.

A similar instance of having to adapt policies to programmes to which central government has decided to attach funding arises with the enterprise zone experiment. Enterprise zones were first suggested by Professor Peter Hall who, in 1977, proposed the creation of non-planning zones free of taxes, social services and government intervention of all kinds, to revive the depressed inner cities. In a modified form, the idea was taken up by Sir Geoffrey Howe, then Conservative opposition spokesman on economic affairs, who proposed zones, to be managed by a new type of agency, in which there would be:

—an abandonment of planning controls, industrial development certificates and office development permits (these were restrictions on development in congested areas which operated as part of regional policy);
—A reversal of the Community Land Act (a Labour measure effectively nationalising development land), with public authorities required to auction off their land holdings;
—exemption from development land tax (a tax on speculative gains on land dealings) and, possibly, local rates;
—guarantees against tax changes and nationalisation;
—no government grants or subsidies;
—no pay or price controls and a suspension of some or all of the provisions of the Employment Protection Act.

The idea was to free native entrepreneurial talent from bureaucratic restriction and taxation but, while the free market basis of the scheme was still evident, Howe's version of enterprise zones recognised the impossibility of withdrawing services such as police, fire, roads, sewers and education, particularly if the objective was to encourage industrial development. In doing so, however, he raised doubts about the whole basis of the scheme. If industrialists were to continue to receive the benefits of public services but be exempt from the obligation to pay for them, then this would, far from a return to native capitalism, be yet another form of industrial subsidy. More fundamentally, to confine the benefits to industrialists in specified zones interfered with one of the principal features of a free market approach, the freedom to locate in the best sites without costs being distorted by government policies. The argument about planning restrictions seems to have derived exclusively from London experience, where conflicts over land use and industrial dispersal policies had occasionally led to refusals of planning permission for industrial development. In Scotland, planning restrictions had been operated in order to protect areas of high amenity and encourage industry to locate in precisely the sort of area Howe had in mind, while industrial

development certificates ( a system for controlling development in the con-
gested areas of Britain in the hope of steering it to the depressed regions) had
never been required north of the Border. So here was another example of a
policy designed in the south being sent north, irrespective of its relevance to
local conditions.

When the Conservatives returned to office in 1979, Howe's enthusiasm was
translated into a Treasury initiative, considerably modified in turn by interdepartmental bargaining (Taylor, 1981). The Department of Employment,
under pressure from the trade unions, refused the suspension of the Employment Protection Act. The proposal to withdraw regional policy aids and
other grants and subsidies was dropped after pressure from both sides of
industry. The proposal to force public authorities to auction off land was
dropped as unworkable and probably very costly, though the intention was
declared to select zones without substantial public land holdings. On the
other hand, to maximise the attractiveness of the zones, the proposal for rates
relief was incorporated though, to satisfy the local authorities, rates are
not abolished but paid by the central Treasury, a straight subsidy to zone
occupants.

The implications of the proposal to abolish planning restrictions also
caused some problems in the consultation with local government. Controls
on nuisance-causing activities were accepted as unavoidable but later in
the elaboration of the proposals they were extended to include access to
infrastructure such as water and sewerage and to activities which would
impact economically on neighbouring areas. For example, if unrestricted
retailing were allowed, hypermarkets could come to take advantage of the
subsidy, presenting unfair competition to retailers outside the zone. This was
to be a particular problem at Clydebank, where there were also worries that
the zone benefits could be captured by whisky bonding, which requires large
amounts of space at low cost (for storing the whisky to maturity) but provides
very little employment.

By the time the final proposals emerged, the idea had drifted a long way
from the original free market concept and was beginning to look like an
instrument of traditional spatial policy, a means of subsidising industry to
locate in one area rather than another. There was, however, a continuing
reluctance on the part of government to admit this and an insistence that
the zones were not part of either urban or regional policy. In England,
implementation was given nonetheless to the inner cities directorate of the
Department of the Environment. In Scotland, it was given first to the urban
renewal unit in the SDD and then transferred to the SEPD (later renamed
Industry Department for Scotland).

For local authorities, enterprise zones were a mixed blessing. Few were
convinced of the analysis underlying the policy and many feared that, by
cutting across their planning and development policies, reducing their powers
and encouraging relocation of industry, they could cause problems. Indeed,
the whole analysis underlying the idea implicitly criticised the way local
authorities had handled industrial development in the past and suggested that
their role should be reduced. On the other hand, the zones did comprise a

package of financial incentives to industry at no cost to the authority while it was likely that central government would do all it could to see that the experiment appeared a success, by getting the zones filled with industry one way or another. Enterprise zone designation was also something to be used in advertising for industry in a competitive market.

For the first round of zones, sites were chosen by the regional offices of the Department of the Environment (in England) and the Scottish, Welsh and Northern Ireland Offices. The choice of Clydebank for the Scottish zone emerged from a Scottish Office working party set up after the closure of the Singer factory, which had also recommended the establishment of an SDA-led task force, which at that time was being set up. The Clydebank zone is not quite coterminous with the task force area but its 570 acres are included within it and its promotion was to be undertaken by the task force. The former Singer site, purchased by the SDA and renamed the Clydebank Business Park, accounts for 86 acres of the zone and is a central feature of the task force's efforts. In fact, though technically a single zone, the EZ consists of seven distinct, though contiguous sites, with 472 acres in Clydebank district and 98 in Glasgow. Planning restrictions were generally lifted, except for developments over 4,250 square feet and for food retailing and clothing but part of the zone is reserved for light industrial use and one area subject to the complete planning regime. Whisky bonding was not to be permitted without specific permission (Jordan and Reilly, 1981).

Most of the land was in public ownership or, like the Singer site, was taken into public ownership, the main owners being the Scottish Development Agency, Clydebank district council and the South of Scotland Electricity Board. Extensive site preparation, environmental improvement and factory building has been undertaken by the Agency. Infrastructure is the responsibility of Strathclyde regional council whose initial attitude was to welcome the zone but complain about the need to pay for infrastructure development without extra capital allocations though the problem now appears to have been resolved. Attraction of industry and matching incomers with sites and premises is the responsibility of the task force. To this must be added the whole range of government incentives available outwith the provisions of the enterprise zone scheme. As the task force points out in its promotional literature, firms in Clydebank are also eligible for maximum assisted area incentives, including regional development grants, selective financial assistance, aid under the Office and Service Industries Scheme and European Coal and Steel Community loans, as well as SDA assistance by way of fully serviced sites and premises, some at concessionary rates, loan and equity funding, business advice and loans from Clydebank enterprise fund, adminstered by the SDA and the Bank of Scotland.

Certainly, the zone has 'succeeded' in terms of attracting industry. By April 1984, 229 companies had moved into premises in the zone, with a projection of 2,557 jobs. Of these, however, 58 companies, accounting for 602 of the jobs, were relocations, firms moving to take advantage of the zone concessions. Perhaps the best known of these was Radio Clyde who moved from the Anderston Cross Centre, a city centre development already suffering from severe difficulties in attracting tenants and rapidly falling into decay. 1,551 jobs were in new companies and the rest in newly established branch plants. Most of the jobs, 2,098, were provided in SDA premises and this included practically all the new jobs, with jobs in privately developed premises being mainly relocations. It is clear, then, that the dynamic for new firm creation was coming from the provision of SDA premises and the offer of incentives. Overall, by Spring 1984, £19.5 million of public money had been invested in the zone, against £16.25 million of private money. The importance of the public sector effort was recognised by Roger Tym and Partners (1984) in their review of the zones for the Government, when they commented 'not only has the rate of development and employment been greater (at Clydebank) than in many other zones, but so has the degree of public sector involvement'. By this time, the original enterprise zone theme, of liberating private initiative by removing public involvement, had all but disappeared, though it was still necessary to pay it some lip service. Faced with the imbalance of public and private spending, the *Enterprise Zone Bulletin* (Spring 1984) ingeniously described the £19.5 million public investment as 'fast being overhauled' by the £16.25 million private contribution.

The Clydebank enterprise zone provided something of a propaganda victory for the central government at a time when it was cutting back on both regional development grants and financial support for local government. A large impact had been made in a small area and the displacement effects largely ignored. These latter were considerable. Reviewing the experience of all British zones, Roger Tyms (1984) calculated that some 85 of firms would be operating in the same region in the absence of a zone and that only 4-12% of new firms might not have started up without a zone. Of the relocating firms, some 90% came from the same region and most of those which migrated inter-regionally went to the English zone at Corby. We could draw any number of lessons from this experience. It shows, in direct contradiction to the original enterprise zone idea, the importance of public intervention and positive planning in urban economic regeneration; it also shows the danger that local supply side measures in the absence of an increase in aggregate demand or increased penetration of export markets will merely result in displacement effects. The political message received by local authorities, however, was that central government would back enterprise zones, not hesitating to rig the rules by massive public subsidy to ensure that the experiment 'worked' and that, if they did not get the advantages of a zone, somebody else would, so drawing industry away from them. When invitations to bid for a second round of zones came in 1982, then, Glasgow district eagerly prepared their application. They did not stand a serious chance, given that the first zone was already partly in the city and the political balance of Scotland determined that the next zone should go to the East (and preferably spill over into a Conservative constituency). So the zone went to Dundee, with a little bit hived off and sent up the road to Arbroath (Keating and Boyle, 1986). Meanwhile, another zone had been set up in the Highlands as the Government's response to the closure of the Invergordon aluminium smelter.

Another source of external funding which has received considerable prominence is the European Community. The principal funds involved are the European regional development fund (ERDF), the European social fund (ESF), funds from the European coal and steel community (ECSC) and loans from the European investment bank (EIB). The ERDF was established in 1975 following British accession to the Community, to overcome the bias of the common market to the so-called golden triangle at the centre but, as a result of wrangling by national governments it emerged less as an instrument of community policy than as a device for transferring resources among member states. National quotas were imposed, with a fixed share for each member state, with the moneys released in response to applications related to projects in the development regions. The United Kingdom, like the other states, then imposed a 'non-additionality' rule, under which ERDF money subsitutes for but does not supplement national expenditures; a practice according with the Treasury rule of imposing a ceiling on all public spending (chapter 3). This means that, where an ERDF grant is made to a private firm, this replaces an equivalent part of the national aid which the firm would be receiving. In practice, firms do not receive any money from Brussels at all. Central government merely labels projects which have benefited from part of its regional expenditure in terms of 'ERDF grants' and keeps the money itself. In the case of infrastructure grants to local authorities, the money is passed on to the authority and, coming in the form of a grant, helps it save on the loan charges it would otherwise have incurred. ERDF funding does not, however, allow any local authority to undertake any additional capital spending since projects must still be accommodated within its capital allocations (see chapter 3). So the real significance of the ERDF is for the authority's revenue account (through the saving on loan charges), not for its capital programme.

In practice, a fixed proportion of the United Kingdom's ERDF quota has been allocated to Scotland and a balance maintained between industrial grants and infrastructure projects, within community rules (Keating and Waters, 1985). From 1979, a non-quota element was introduced, amounting initially to 5% of the Fund total, to be available for major programmes in any development region of the Community.

The European social fund was established early in the life of the community to provide funds to cope with the adverse effects of industrial change, with the emphasis on retraining workers displaced by the decline of older industries. There are no national quotas and, in the UK, there is some relaxation of the non-additionality rules. A substantial part of the British receipts go to the Manpower Services Commission and to agencies such as the Scottish Development Agency and the Highlands and Islands Development Board, where they are treated as non-additional, but where local authorities have been successful in gaining revenue support they have usually been allowed to keep the money.

Strathclyde has been one of the most active of British authorities in the Community, retaining a liaison officer in Brussels to keep up with developments and inform it of opportunities. ERDF funding has been exploited to the maximum for infrastructure projects and the non-quota section tapped for projects in its steel and shipbuilding areas. It has also exploited the ESF for its employment subsidy scheme, with the regional council supplementing ESF grants to create or retain jobs which would otherwise not have existed.

For some years, the European Commission has been trying to reform its 'structural funds', to make them more of an instrument of community policy and to forge closer links between the recipients and itself. In 1981, it came up with radical proposals for the ERDF, concentrating quota aid on specific regions chosen according to Community-wide criteria, expanding the non-quota section and introducing 'integrated operations' of various sorts. Again, this fell foul of national governments and all that emerged was a loosening of quotas; the UK was to get between 21.4% and 28.56%, with the gap filled by development programmes. Programmes recognised as of community significance could get a higher rate of grant, at 55% instead of 50%.

Following precedents in Naples and Belfast, suggestions were made in the 1980s that there should be an Integrated Development Operation (IDO) for Glasgow, bringing together all the structural funds behind a coherent programme. Like much of the Community's funding activities, the IDO concept has a distinctly evanescent quality. When one looks for the practical effects, they tend to disappear. In Belfast and Naples, hopes of relaxing the eligibility rules (allowing funds to be used more flexibly) and the non-additionality rule had been dashed. Given the attitudes of the British Treasury, there was little prospect of anything different happening in Glasgow. Nevertheless, following approaches from Strathclyde region, with the support of Glasgow district, the commission financed a consultants' report on the possibilities. This (Roger Tyms, 1984b), frankly admitted that there is 'no new EC budget specifically for an IDO: benefits lie in increasing the effectiveness of existing funds, in increased priority accorded to applications and higher rates of grant, and in the unquantifiable gains following from a closer relationship with the Community.' The practical content of the proposal was in fact little more than a rehearsal of existing uses of community funds in Glasgow—but with no reference until the final section to the non-additionality rule—and a projection of them into the future. A 'forward programme' for £500 million over five years is talked about (not surprisingly this grabbed the media headlines) but figures like this are simply plucked from the air. Given the additionality rule, all projects must be kept within the limits of local authority capital allocations and neither council has the remotest idea of what these are likely to be for five years ahead. Neither the Treasury nor the Scottish Office has given any indication that additionality rules could be relaxed or that the grants awarded for industry under the ERDF (at present retained in London) could be put in the IDO kitty.

What had emerged by 1986 was a very limited scheme by which the infrastructure elements of the ERDF alone were put on a programme basis, allowing some stretching of the eligibility criteria, the consolidation of small projects which might not otherwise have qualified on their own and some eligibility for the higher, 55% rate of grant. The existence of the additionality rule, the way in which community receipts are treated in the rate support grant and accounting practices, make any attempt to quantify the benefits which Strathclyde and Glasgow have received from EC funds largely meaningless. Certainly, the benefit is not in proportion to the publicity given to them or to widespread beliefs in a pot of gold waiting in Brussels for any Scots enterprising enough to go and retrieve it; but, at a time of severe fiscal pressure, authorities must squeeze the last penny out of any source available.

## Area-Based Strategies

On its establishment, the SDA had been given only the most general of briefs which it had itself to translate into concrete policies and programmes. One specific task which it was given by the Scottish Office was GEAR (chapter 4) and in 1979 this was followed by the leadership of a special task force set up in Garnock Valley after a Scottish Office-led working party had examined the problems arising from the closure of the Glengarnock steel works. Similarly, in 1980, an SDA-led task force and enterprise zone emerged from a Scottish Office working party following the closure of the Singer factory in Clydebank. These were emergency measures for areas hit by sudden and drastic closures. Their spatial focus was narrow, their objectives to get as many jobs as possible to replace those lost and their methods informal. There was some success, though the 2,557 jobs in Clydebank did not come near to replacing the 10,294 lost between 1975 and 1980.

These remained special cases, however and the Agency began to worry not only about its stretched resources but also about the implications for its own forward strategy of allowing itself to be used as a 'fire brigade' by the Scottish Office, reacting to closures rather than seeking out opportunities. Formalising a forward-looking area strategy would have other advantages, bringing together the Agency's own area development functions and enabling it to put its relationships with local authorities on a clearer basis. So in 1981 an area development directorate was set up and a decision taken to spend 60% of the Agency's 'targetable' resources in area projects. These would be joint economic initiatives negotiated with local authorities and subject to formal project agreements. While the initiative for the new area approach appears to have come from the Agency itself, it was quickly accepted by the Scottish Office. It enabled an economic dimension to be given to urban policy without giving additional economic powers to local government. At the same time, the Scottish Office itself could avoid detailed involvement, and so direct responsibility, in urban development, a task which absorbed large amounts of energy in the Department of the Environment in England (Keating, 1985b).

The approach was not, however, without its ambiguities. The 60% target of resources for area projects represented an aspiration rather than a target and was susceptible to endless redefinition. Some forms of spending, for example on environmental improvement, can be allocated quite easily to areas but investment proposals in area projects must satisfy the same criteria as elsewhere. This basic dilemma in spatial economic policy is further illustrated in the choice of locations for area projects. A policy of going to the areas with the worst problems or the highest unemployment is alien to the philosophy of the Agency, which is to seek out potential and to create in Scotland internationally competitive industry. Formalisation of the area approach and breaking with the 'fire brigade' model of Glengarnock and Clydebank was intended to enable the Agency precisely to seek out the most promising areas. Yet it remains under political pressure to provide a visible response to the needs of the worst-hit areas and to balance its geographical coverage. So the formula developed that it would go to those areas where there was the biggest gap between 'potential' and 'performance', allowing it to consider both opportunities and problems. In the first of the new-style projects, in Leith (Edinburgh), there were few difficulties of this nature. The site was chosen partly from political prudence, lest the SDA be seen as too exclusively a west coast agency, but also because it was capable of being pulled back from decline rapidly. The first area project in Strathclyde, for Motherwell, was less clear cut. Motherwell featured on Strathclyde Region's list of twelve economic priority areas and work had been going on for some time on possible responses to steel closures. Concern was mounting about the threat to the Ravenscraig steel works, reprieved after a long campaign in 1982 and there was clearly pressure on the Scottish Office to make a gesture to the area. The SDA, for its part, insisted that what brought it to Motherwell was the potential for improved performance in the local economy, pointing to its natural location, access to the rail and motorway networks and the availability of maximum regional development grants. Apart from the last advantage being far from 'natural', several other parts of Strathclyde could point to the same combination of features. So the decision to come to Motherwell must be considered both economic and political.

Meanwhile, Strathclyde region had developed, through its economic policy group, its own area strategy, launched with great publicity in 1981 (local elections were due within months). Sums of £300 million were bandied about, nearly all of which was to come from other agencies, including the SDA. While there had been discussions already about priorities and schemes, Strathclyde's motive in making the unilateral announcement was to seize the leadership in area development policy in the belief that the SDA was there to serve local government and not the other way around. In practice, agreement on the twelve areas highlighted by Strathclyde was not difficult, with Glasgow district also associating itself with the proposals. In addition to Motherwell and the task forces in Clydebank and Garnock Valley, area projects were launched for Coatbridge in Lanarkshire and Port Dundas in Glasgow. These involve a programme of environmental improvement, infrastructure renewal, factory building and business advice. Through the project teams of officers working in the area, businesses also have access to SDA investment finance and market and investment opportunities are sought out.

For the SDA the area project model offered considerable advantages over the approach adopted in GEAR. The Agency did have some freedom to choose locations and the scope of the projects was more purely economic and physical, without the social policy role which it regarded as a diversion from its true function. By the mid 1980s, though, the philosophy was changing again, firstly at a rhetorical level but then in practice. In its early days, the SDA had been regarded as a body to solve 'problems'. Repudiating this language in the early 1980s, it insisted that it was there to seek out 'opportunities'. By the mid 1980s, the operative phrases were 'business development' and 'market failure'. The SDA was there not to over-ride the market but to make it work better, not to replace business initiative but to make it work better, a considerable change in emphasis from Labour's ideas in the 1970s. This, of course, reflected the philosophy of its masters, the Conservative ministers in the Scottish Office and of the Treasury which put them through a major scrutiny in 1986, but ministers had not themselves in the past always been consistent with their own philosophy, responding to political pressures in sending the 'fire brigades' into Clydebank and Garnock Valley.

The more hard-headed approach did affect Glasgow, though, as the idea of a city-centre project on the lines of the Dundee or Motherwell initiatives was transformed instead into a series of business and commercial development plans. The proposed Govan-Kinning Park initiative, meanwhile, had become caught up in preparations for the garden festival. Glasgow's advantages came to be seen as lying in business and commercial development and this, rather than industrial renewal, was to be the focus of the SDA's efforts, going with the market rather than trying to control it. Interest in the potential of the city centre had been growing with the arrival of Britoil, the renewal of the Merchant City and, in the 1980s, the St Enoch development, the Scottish exhibition and conference centre and the garden festival.

The St Enoch development was a scheme for the city-centre site of the old St Enoch station (whose shell conservationists had tried unsuccessfully to retain). At one time, central government had planned to disperse large numbers of civil servants from the Ministry of Defence to new offices on the site but resistance from the London-based officials together with expenditure cuts progressively reduced the number, who were eventually accommodated on another site. Meanwhile, the SDA, in 1980, put together a development package for a large amount of retail floorspace together with an ice rink and applied for planning permission. The proposals, and a simultaneous plan for development in Buchanan Street, came up against the structure plan, with its commitment to limiting retail development and the region called both in, approving the St Enoch development (perhaps because of the SDA involvement) but turning down the Buchanan Street one, though later on, with changing attitudes on the role of the city centre, the principle of commercial development on both sites was accepted. With the SDA assembling a development consortium, work on the St Enoch site was started in 1986, though plans for Buchanan Street had not yet been finalised.

The Scottish exhibition and conference centre featured from an early stage in the SDA's plans for revitalising the Scottish economy. While on a smaller scale than the national (British) exhibition centre in Birmingham, it was to be a major development, a shop-window for Scottish business and a considerable boost for the area in which it was sited. In 1980, the SDA had a list of no less than 60 sites, each eagerly promoted by local interests and including Edinburgh (the capital) and Stirling (in central Scotland). With the list cut down to the serious contenders, a report was commissioned and eventually a site chosen on the abandoned Queen's Dock in Glasgow. As a major project, the exhibition centre needed approval from central government and the Scottish Office undoubtedly took a keen interest both in the siting and in the organisation. After the arrival of the Conservative government in 1979, it insisted on the involvement of private capital, ostensibly on a risk basis but in fact on very favourable terms, with the SDA and the two local authorities providing the rest of the funds. Much of the SDA and local authority investment, in site preparation and infrastructure provision, was written off before the centre was handed over to the operating company. This is a tripartite organisation, on whose board are represented the SDA, the private investors and the local councils. Profit is calculated on the basis of operating cost, with preferential arrangements for dividends to the private investors. They get the first share of dividend and only with profits above a certain threshold would the ratepayers gain any return on their capital. In practice, no dividend is expected to accrue to the SDA or local councils. So once again, it was public intervention which was bringing private capital into the city centre, though for political reasons central government was determined to give credit to the private sector. At the time of writing, the exhibition centre, opened in 1985, is too recent to judge of its success but the impact on the hotel and service industries does appear to be signifiant while, physically, the dockland area has been transformed. Further public subsidy, nevertheless, was necessary to bring a hotel to the site.

The garden festival has proved rather more controversial. The idea originated in Liverpool in the 1980s when Michael Heseltine, as Secretary of State for the Environment, had special responsibility for the city. The principle is that an area of derelict land is designated as the site of a national garden festival, with the public moneys which are available for land renewal put into it to reclaim the land and stage the festival. The city gets the improved land which, after the year-long festival, is available for development, a large number of visitors and publicity. After Liverpool, the idea was retained by the Department of the Environment as a permanent part of its urban programmes and a competition was arranged for a second festival, won by Stoke on Trent for 1985. When the third round was advertised, Glasgow complained about the competition being limited to England and Wales and it was extended to Scotland. The SDA, as the derelict land agency in Scotland, were involved at an early stage, backing Glasgow's application and helping to prepare the case. For the Agency, of course, this was more than a simple derelict land operation; it was an opportunity to put its land renewal funds behind the promotional and marketing strategy which it was developing for the city centre. Initially, Glasgow district had proposed siting the festival on Glasgow Green (where they had had similar plans in the early 1970s) but, examining the government's brief, which specified that what was to be created was not a park but a development asset to attract private investment, urged instead the merits of the abandoned Princes Dock, directly over the river from the Exhibition Centre. When Glasgow's bid was successful, responsibility was entrusted to the SDA, which must fund the whole development from its existing budget. The total cost is unclear but the SDA investment will be in the order of £37 million, of which they hoped, perhaps optimistically, to recoup some £26 million (Balsillie, 1986). In turn, the Agency handed over operational control to a wholly-owned subsidiary company, on whose board both the region and the district are represented.

The Glasgow festival differs from the earlier ones in England, which had the aim of improving and bringing into early development derelict inner city land which might otherwise have continued to lie idle. In Glasgow, the site chosen had already been allocated to a developer for private housing and, to get the land for the festival, the agency had to persuade Glasgow district to swap this for land elsewhere in the city. A by-product of the swap was the breach in the council's 1984 policy of not disposing of land for private house building (chapter 5). Nor was there to be much of a long-term environmental effect on the area. A few features were to be retained but, the more land is retained for permanent parkland and public leisure activities, the less opportunity the festival will have to make a financial return on the investment and the less opportunity there will be to use the festival to stimulate commercial development on the site.

The SDA see the garden festival as a shop window for Glasgow, a vital part of the promotional and 'image building' effort. This view is shared by both region and district, whose own promotional and publicity efforts it complements. They have an additional motive for enthusiasm in that the funding comes from the SDA which *might* otherwise have spent the money elsewhere. This point is a matter of some grievance elsewhere in Scotland where projects which in the past might have expected approval without argument have been held up because of the diversion of resources from an Agency budget which has itself been cut back. Within the city, there was some unease at the use of public resources for so apparently frivolous an event and at the fact that what will be left in the long term will not be a public asset but a facility for private developers. There was also some unease among the custodians of the region's social strategy that part of the opportunity cost of the festival was the Agency resources which they were hoping to get into the Drumchapel and Easterhouse initiatives (chapter 6).

Certainly, the festival reflects the general thrust of Agency policy towards commercial promotion in the city centre, a bias which was reinforced with the publication of a consultants' report in 1984 and the creation of *Glasgow Action*. This was to merge with the theme of reviving indigenous business leadership in the city to such a degree that we shall need to examine them together.

## Reviving Business Leadership

While analysts might disagree on the precise causes of economic decline in Glasgow, one phenomenon clearly observable is the decline of the local business community. The second and third generations of the industrial families of nineteenth century Glasgow have failed to maintain the business leadership of the past, with firms coming increasingly under external control and new firms and technologies failing to emerge. This is a complex issue, as much sociological as economic, and clearly Glasgow represents merely an exaggerated version of British industrial and economic decline. Scott and Hughes (1980) trace the decline in Scottish ownership of industry and the consequent fracturing of the Scottish industrial network of interlocking direc-torships and family holdings but admit that there is still much work to be done on the sociology of ownership, the histories of industrial families and their connections with the state. By the 1970s, the issue of Scottish control had come onto the political agenda and provided a motive force behind the lobbies to save Anderson Strathclyde, the Royal Bank, SUITS and Highland Distillers from external takeover. In the case of SUITS, the Monopolies and Mergers Commission had stated in 1979;

> The primary task of industry policy in Scotland today is to create the conditions which favour natural growth and strengthen indigenous enterprises . . . growth not simply in production but in key management activity including the conception, design and marketing of products from a Scottish base and, importantly, financial control of the company's operations. In other words, conditions have to be as favourable for head-quarters functions as for branch operations. (quoted, Fraser of Allander, 1985).

In their evidence to the Monopolies and Mergers Commission on the pro-posed Royal Bank of Scotland takeover, the Fraser of Allander Institute commented;

> The general pattern of post-war development in Scotland has resulted in the creation of branch plants and subsidiaries rather than the creation of new indigenously controlled firms. This growing element of external control makes it inevitable that the ablest young men in management have tended to gravitate towards the point of control and away from Scotland. . . The principal harmful effect of centralisation is the loss of some of that,very small number of people who have the capability of successfully realising new commercial opportunities. These are largely the same people who take responsibilities in public life. Conse-quently, their departure marks a simultaneous decline in the quality of public life. (quoted, Fraser of Allander, 1985).

Similar sentiments had been expressed on many occasions by the Scottish Council (Development and Industry) a semi-official economic development and lobbying organisation (SCDI, 1969;1973). In 1987, a research report commissioned by the Scottish Office showed that, while acquisitions by over-seas companies often benefited the companies concerned, the 'external effects' in terms of loss of research and development activity and local purchasing were, in balance, negative (Bain et al., 1987).

Most of the major developments in Scotland in the 1960s and 1970s were state-inspired, for example the vehicle plants at Linwood and Bathgate, the

Ravenscraig steelworks, the Invergordon smelter and the BNOC (Britoil) headquarters. The main exceptions were in micro-electronics and oil exploration and development, though here too state aid was important. Yet these major industrial developments had failed to spark off a cycle of indigenous development, a revival of Scottish entrepreneurship and, in the 1980s, Linwood, Bathgate and Invergordon were all closed and Ravenscraig only kept open through political pressure.

At the same time, business involvement in civic affairs had lapsed. Businessmen had ceased to sit on the local councils and the voice of business through the Chamber of Commerce was a weak and intermittent influence in municipal affairs. Even the Conservative Party, potentially a voice for business community, was fading out by the 1980s while the 1975 reform of local government had failed to rekindle interest in local affairs by industrial and commercial people.

These considerations were very much in the minds of the SDA and their consultants when a report on Glasgow city centre was commissioned in 1983. At this time, the Agency was putting increasing emphasis on private sector leadership in urban economic regeneration and on the need to exploit business opportunities, working with the market. So what emerged was not an integrated renewal project on the lines of those established in Dundee and elsewhere, but a number of separate initiatives, including the launching under SDA auspices of *Glasgow Action*, a group of leading businessmen together with the leaders of the regional and district councils. Clearly modelled on American examples (Boston and Baltimore are frequently cited), Glasgow Action aimed to restore business leadership, create and exploit business opportunities in the city and provide a channel of communication with, and influence over, local government. The organisation is informal, with no written constitution or programme of meetings though there is a full-time director paid and housed by the SDA and a part-time chairman, a leading local businessman. It operates through informal contacts and the interlocking directorships in Scottish and British firms of its members, seeking out opportunities for development in Glasgow and trying to get firms to move into the city. There is a particular emphasis on getting headquarters rather than branch plants in Glasgow, though it is recognised that developments like Britoil are few and far between. Generally, then, the organisation works to overcome imperfections and information blockages in the market and to inculcate a sense of civic responsibility which, in their view, is itself good for business.

Relations with the local authorities are necessarily a sensitive issue. Businessmen have a native suspicion of the Labour Party, particularly at the local level and some of them simply want to complain about the level of rates and the existence of so much council housing. On the council side, the suspicion is reciprocated and any suggestion that businessmen were being given a privileged position or influence over policy matters would go down badly in the city party and the constituencies. However, the more pragmatic mood prevailing in the mid 1980s, at least at elite level, helped relationships and the leaders of *Glasgow Action* and the regional and district councils appeared ready to accept each others' spheres of influence. *Glasgow Action* would confine itself largely to business development in the city and the council in turn would recognise the vital role of the private sector in economic regeneration. There were at one stage hints from on high that the Government might want to use *Glasgow Action* to channel money into Glasgow, by-passing the Labour local authorities—similar suggestions were floated in England—but the idea appears to have been dropped rapidly. Certainly, the last thing *Glasgow Action* wanted in its early days was to become a part of the state bureaucracy.

Nevertheless, the SDA, having established *Glasgow Action*, did proceed to hand over to it the lead role in developing policies and ideas for the city centre, including the implementation of the ideas in the city centre report. These included action to attract headquarters of firms to Glasgow, to develop a computer software industry, to develop exportable services and build up business in tourism and educational short courses. Fresh efforts were also to be made to improve the city's 'image'. Airlines were to be persuaded to improve their services to Glasgow, *Locate in Scotland* lobbied to bring more business Glasgow's way and electronics firms encouraged to fund university chairs in key technologies. Tourist attractions could include an aquarium, a science 'exploratorium' and a folk/emigration museum. All these would, of course, be universally regarded as desirable but the problem with their implementation is that they would involve the newly-formed *Glasgow Action*, ostensibly formed to get business leaders to take over the role of commercial development, lobbying to get public funds committed to its projects. The various tourist attractions, for example, would not be commercially viable and would require subsidies. The Greater Glasgow Tourist Board should, it was recommended, 'be given a budget of £500,000 per annum', but it was not specified who should pay. The SDA and the regional council should sponsor short courses at Strathclyde University, though, as they would be run by a separate unit, the University as a whole would not benefit. The impression of a plan written by businessmen for the benefit of businessmen is irresistible. If the report does not quite say that what is good for commerce is good for Glasgow it does describe business leaders as '"doers and achievers" with vested interests in the city's well-being', implying that civic and business goals must necessarily coincide.

While the report was essentially a business development plan, the consultants had not confined themselves to this but had gone into questions of urban design, albeit confined to the central business district. The resulting proposals, targeted at the 'image' problem were thus breathlessly described:

> The image to promote is of Glasgow as an available, accessible and open city. Just as the bars are open all day, this should be translated into different aspects of urban life. Glasgow should become a marketplace of urban contacts. . .It is rough, it rains a lot but it is not pretentious and it is the flipside of Edinburgh. Glasgow works, it tastes good, it is nourishing and it turns you on.
>
> The strategy proposed is that of implosion. By avoiding sprawl and concentrating the nerve centres of the city, the fire may start to burn. The aims

of this strategy can and should be achieved by a process of emphasis and a manipulation, rather than by drastic surgery.

But the centre has to catch the imagination. If not, then nothing matters. It is just a car without ignition. But for this to happen the centre needs a spark, a live wire, an axis that will epitomise the city. Buchanan Street is the only street that has this potential.

Beyond the mixed metaphors, the report presented a set of proposals for the long-awaited commercial development of Buchanan Street, to which *Glasgow Action* duly gave their backing in 1985. The centrepiece to the new development would be the church by Alexander 'Greek' Thomson, one of Glasgow's most distinguished nineteenth-century architects, transported from Caledonia Road in the Gorbals, where it now lay derelict and re-erected in Buchanan Street. A concert hall, long planned for the Glasgow-based Scottish Symphony Orchestra, would be included in the development. This essay in urban planning was not to the liking of everybody. Glasgow district's depute director of architecture believed that, in the words of William Morris 'good buildings should be left where they are', while the seasoned community campaigners of the Gorbals (chapter 5) were outraged at the idea of the one distinguished building left in the area being hijacked to the city centre. Commercial logic, town planning and community feeling now clashed, with one of the aspiring developers insisting that the Church must move;

> The site is blighted. It is basically a traffic island beside a container depot and a railway bridge and it could be affected by the proposed south flank ring road. I could see no commercial money being provided for it; it must be moved. (*Scotsman*, 24 Feb.1986).

If *Glasgow Action* had hoped to stay clear of political controversy, they were clearly going to be disappointed. It is too early as yet to make any judgement on the organisation but it does appear that the focus of the revived business interest is going to be the city centre and the commercial opportunities which it provides. We have noted the relatively bouyant property market there and, with the development of the exhibition centre, the garden festival and tourism, this is likely to continue. As yet, however, there is little sign of a revival of entrepreneurship in manufacturing industry or on the city's periphery.

Another private sector initiative in association with the public sector is Glasgow Opportunities (GO), an enterprise agency sponsored by the SDA and Scottish Business in the Community (SCOTBIC) in 1983. Funding comes from the SDA and private firms who, as well as contributing financially, second staff for varying periods of time and give free business advice as needed. GO's main function is advice to new and established small and medium sized companies, running some training courses in conjunction with the Manpower Services Commission and helping administer the SDA's Enterprise Funds for Youth (EFFY) scheme. The scale of the operation is small, with three full-time staff and five secondees, from three Scottish, one British and one American firm, and reflects the growth of the enterprise trust movement in Scotland in the last few years (Keating and Boyle, 1986).

A rather different type of operation is Strathclyde Community Business (SCB), set up by Strathclyde region with support from Glasgow district and the SDA. The focus of community business is on employment creation as a means of distributing income rather than on wealth creation and, indeed, Strathclyde's involvement grew out of its social strategy rather than its economic strategy. Community businesses are not expected to be internationally competitive, are all on a small scale and serve essentially local markets. SCB provides development finance, training and advice to community groups wishing to start business ventures and channels Urban Aid to them. Given the economic and social problems of the peripheral estates and their neglect by mainstream economic and planning initiatives, it is not surprising that community business has been promoted as an element in the Easterhouse and Drumchapel initiatives (chapter 6).

## Who Controls Economic Development?

In Glasgow, as in other cities, there is clearly a great deal of economic development effort going on. It less clear just what it all adds up to. It does appear that in the 1980s the dominant agency of public intervention is the SDA. It is true that the local authorities are 'geared up' for economic development. They have reorganised their structures, produced plans and sought to bend their programmes to the needs of development—but *politically*, economic development has not had a high profile and there is no particular ideological thrust to either authority's policies, which have been led by officials and the more pragmatic councillors. This becomes clear when we compare Glasgow and Strathclyde with some of the English Labour councils of the 1980s, particularly the Greater London Council and West Midlands County Council (both abolished in 1986) or Sheffield city council. In those areas, there have been attempts by left-wing councils to gain some control over the economic development function, to favour, for example, minority groups, women or workers' cooperatives or to promote 'socially useful' enterprises. Interventionist devices including the Greater London and West Midlands enterprise boards (which have survived abolition) have been set up, pension funds mobilised for local investment, and full use made of the limited discretionary power which local authorities have to spend the product of a 2p rate on non-statutory functions. Of course, it may be argued that the effect of such devices on the local economies is marginal but this is not the explanation of Glasgow's failure to follow this line. Rather, Glasgow's and Strathclyde's attitudes reflect ideological factors, an ingrained caution on the right of the Labour Party and a disinterest on the left, tinged with a suspicion of capitalism which is less marxist in inspiration than the product of years of industrial confrontation and decline. There is also the problem of resources. Both councils have heavy commitments to discharge with a limited fiscal base and maintaining service levels always has priority. Even the use of the limited discretionary rate power is subject nowadays to spending penalties if it should take a council over its guideline. Finally, there is the presence of the SDA, as the body which many councillors see as the proper agency to undertake the economic development role.

On the other hand, the two councils have become quite adept at levering resources from other agencies—including the SDA—and are widely regarded as amongst the most skillful authorities in this respect. Yet there is a policy cost. Control of development is taken out of the hands of local government into those of agencies, in this case the SDA and, to a limited extent, the Manpower Services Commission. The SDA, in its turn, has been redefining its role from that of an urban renewal agency to a facilitator of change, a promoter of business opportunities, particularly in the city centre. The problems of the periphery and other neglected areas, therefore, fall back into the lap of the local authorities, to be managed through social measures including non-competitive industry. There is little evidence of local councillors being aware of this problem. SDA money, like MSC money, is regarded as manna from heaven, to be welcomed uncritically. It is likely that, as the problems of the periphery worsen, questions will increasingly be asked.

In the context of the economic problems examined at the beginning of this chapter, however, all the interventionist efforts, including those of the SDA, must be regarded as marginal. The sums available to stimulate economic development are tiny in comparison with other public expenditure programmes and, as has been emphasised several times, overall public expenditure levels in the city have been under severe pressure. So, even with the most sophisticated policies, the local councils and the SDA would be hampered in the search for economic regeneration by lack of resources. The economic future of the city depends more on market forces operating at a national, European and world level and upon national government policies than on anything which might be done locally. Both international competition and national policy since the late 1970s have been extremely damaging to British manufacturing industry in general and the traditional industries in particular, with devastating effects in the Glasgow area. The main growth sectors in the British economy have largely passed the region by and unemployment has continued to mount. So all the efforts of local agencies appear to be swimming against the tide. It is to the implications of this that we shall turn in the conclusion.

# 8 Conclusion—Towards the Dual City?

We have reviewed in this book the progress of Glasgow's urban renewal strategy. In physical terms, it has undeniably had a measure of success. Glaswegians and visitors alike can see the evidence over large parts of the inner city. No longer do areas like Maryhill or the East End look like the aftermath of an air raid. Residents, including large numbers of owner-occupiers, have come back to the inner city. The buildings are cleaner, as is the air itself. The cultural life of Glasgow, too, has developed apace with a profusion of theatres and galleries—visitors are often surprised to discover that it is Glasgow and not Edinburgh which houses the Scottish National Orchestra, Scottish Ballet and the Scottish Theatre Group. Restaurants are better and more numerous while the notorious bars have improved beyond recognition from the gloomy, scruffy (often all-male) joints of ten or fifteen years ago. Of course, public policy can do little about the Scottish weather (although *Glasgow Action* does have proposals for glazing over the city centre) but, generally, Glasgow is, among British cities, one of the liveliest to live in.

It is largely free, too, of the racial tensions and communal violence afflicting many of its English counterparts. Racial harmony may, of course, be to do with the absence of racial divisions. It is true that the high levels of unemployment since the war have largely deterred immigration into the west of Scotland, even from the traditional source of Ireland, as the 1981 census figures show (see Table 8.1).

One must also, though, emphasise the degree of tolerance, if not integration prevailing in Glasgow (and elsewhere in Scotland) among different racial groups. Admittedly, Glasgow has its own longstanding ethnic problem, the historic Orange-Green (Protestant-Catholic) divide. The Orange parades pro-

TABLE 8.1    % POPULATION BORN OUTSIDE THE UNITED KINGDOM

|  | Irish Republic | New Commonwealth & Pakistan | Elsewhere |
|---|---|---|---|
| Britain | 1.1 | 2.8 | 2.3 |
| Glasgow | 1.2 | 1.3 | 1.0 |

Source: General Register Office for Scotland, Census 1981, Key Statistics for Urban Areas, Scotland (Edinburgh: HMSO, 1984).

vide the occasion for some disorderly conduct and general bullying of anyone unlucky enough to get in the way. Nevertheless, while the troubles in Northern Ireland have led to some renewal of sectarianism in Scotland, this has generally been kept under control within local communities (who have no desire to see another Belfast) and has made virtually no impact in the electoral arena. Certainly, there have been some attempts to import the Northern Ireland question into Scottish politics, with independent unionist candidates threatening to stand in the 1987 general election in protest against the Anglo-Irish agreement and an effort to exploit the issue by an SNP parliamentary candidate in the east end of Glasgow. Generally, though, the Irish issue has been kept out of local politics by Labour politicians who, unlike some of their London colleagues, are aware of the explosive potential which it could have at home. In this, they are in tune with the other established parties, which have sought to play down the historic links between the west of Scotland and Ireland. Recent trials show that Glasgow has been used as a base for paramilitary extremists from both the Republican and Loyalist sides but, so far, in order to carry out their operations outside Scotland.

The education issue remains a potential source of sectarian strife. Falling school rolls and the spread of secular values have put at risk many of the separate Catholic schools maintained by the regional council. Some of these have survived only by taking in non-Catholic children, including Moslem children whose parents value the non-secular ethos of the Catholic schools. In an unplanned way, this has produced some remarkably encouraging examples of racial, sectarian and even class integration but several bishops have been at pains to point out the threat which this poses to the separate system of Catholic education. Financial pressure on the regional council, as we have seen, has forced it to look at this issue of school closures, but it has been extremely wary of provoking conflict with the Catholic church by proposing the merging of the two school systems, an obvious means of achieving economies. For the Labour Party, the segregated education system remains the basis for the religious settlement in Scotland and there is great reluctance to challenge this. Yet, as long as separate education systems remain, the sectarian divide in Scottish society will persist, with its potential for social conflict in the future.

Images take a long time to change but the *Glasgow's Miles Better* campaign and the promotion of the Burrell gallery have done much to change perceptions south of the border and beyond. Indeed, the success of Glasgow's civic promotion has caused some rumblings in its rather staid neighbour, Edinburgh, seeing its assumed dominance in Scotland's cultural life and tourist effort threatened. In 1987, Edinburgh paid Glasgow the ultimate compliment by launching its own civic publicity campaign under the direction of former Glasgow Lord Provost, Michael Kelly.

In strictly quantitative terms, there is much evidence to support the impression of urban renewal. Some 75,000 houses have been built since 1960 and a large number rehabilitated. Private investment has been mobilised to build houses in the city after many years of municipal monopoly. The Burrell Gallery and the Scottish exhibition centre have been completed and the waterfront area is being transformed. Yet, for all the efforts of the region, the district and the SDA, public policy appears to have to run ever faster to stay in the same place, given the slide in Britain's economic fortunes.

Glasgow is the victim of a long-term national economic decline which has accelerated in the 1980s with the neglect of industry and reliance on North Sea oil to maintain a lifestyle of cheap imports for those fortunate enough to be in work. In the 1970s, the Scottish nationalists made much of the fact that 'Scotland's oil' was being used to prop up a decrepit British state and economy. In fact, it was not just Scotland but all of Britain's traditional industrial areas which suffered from the bout of 'Dutch disease' (an over-valued exchange rate based on energy exports) of the early 1980s. The collapse of the economy of the west midlands of England has been even more dramatic. Against these trends, the efforts of urban renewal agencies can only be marginal. Nor will it do to claim that the run-down of traditional industries is part of a healthy 'shake-out' in which resources will be redeployed into the industries and services of the future. Manufacturing has been the mainstay of the local economy in the past and was the focus of nearly all the regional development efforts of the 1960s and 1970s. Yet economic regeneration in the 1980s has been highly selective, touching the commercial and tourist sectors but passing manufacturing by, while unemployment continues at a high level. This is the first sense in which we can talk of the 'dual city'—the contrast of strong and weak sectors, of prosperity for those in work and poverty for those without a place in the new economic order. This, of course, is a reflection of Britain as a whole—but at least Glasgow may be more fortunate than some of the cities of northern England, which have no growing sectors at all.

The other 'dualism' is spatial—with successful physical and commercial renewal in the centre while on the periphery, in the housing schemes developed in the 1950s and 1960s as the solution to Glasgow's perennial housing problem, a new urban crisis has emerged. A whole generation in Easterhouse, Pollok, Drumchapel and Castlemilk is growing up with little prospect of employment or economic and social advancement. Here we do indeed have a cycle of deprivation, with few children going on to higher education (the university is regarded as a remote and alien place), little social mobility and a vicious circle of ever lower expectations. At the time of the 1981 Hillhead bye-election, some English observers—brought up on the *No Mean City* image of Glasgow as riddled with poverty and violence—were surprised to learn that the constituency had the highest percentage of university graduates in the United Kingdom. The peripheral estates, by contrast, have some of the lowest. (Glasgow as a whole has around 4/5 of the UK average).

As we have seen, the peripheral estates are now on the political agenda but many of the policy proposals must be seen as mere palliatives, managing the social consequences of decline. Indeed, there is a growing tendency to regard them as a self-contained problem, not part of the general social and economic life of the region. For example, left wing social workers have commented to me that it is unrealistic to present university education as a normal aspiration for children in the schemes who should instead be trained to cope with the problems of living where they are—thus perpetuating the very 'labelling' process which the Social Strategy was supposed to overcome. Other initiatives have been based on assumptions about the communities' ability to pull themselves up by their own bootstraps. It is clear from these pages that the lack of investment by public and private sectors, together with the low levels of cash income and remoteness from the markets represented by the better-off communities make this an impossibility. Where the estates do have locational advantages—as sites for out-of-town hypermarkets—planning policies prevent their being exploited though retail development is being actively promoted in the city centre. The argument that it is necessary to protect the city centre traders from competition sits ill with the crusading capitalist spirit of *Glasgow Action* and confirms the view that the revival of the city centre is due largely to the efforts of public policy. The peripheral estates, on the other hand, have ended up enjoying neither the benefits of a comprehensively planned economic and spatial system nor those of a *laissez faire* regime.

The danger, then, is of the peripheral communities being forced to look inward on themselves, to have increasingly to manage their own penury and forgo the integration into the regional economic and social system which alone could hold out hope for their populations. Such an outcome would present few problems of political management. Party competition in recent years has been non-existent, nor are the estates critical in electoral terms at central or local level. As long as they continue to vote Labour they run the risk of being taken for granted. Yet, if local community groups run their own candidates and succeed in getting them elected, they will be excluded from the deliberations within the Labour Party which are so crucial in deciding the policies of the the regional and district councils. In any case, we have noted the fragility of community organisation in the peripheral estates and the way in which even small-scale initiatives can provoke dissention which is all the more accute as it involves such small amounts of money. Electoral reform, as advocated by the Liberal-SDP Alliance, the SNP and a few Labour and Conservative figures, could help improve the quality of representation by increasing political competition. As it is, though, the peripheral areas of Glasgow are to some extent politically disarmed. Nor is there necessarily a serious danger of social disorder as, geographically isolated, alienated youth would have nothing to attack but their neighbours. Yet there must be dangers in the long run in a degree of alienation affecting the social cohesion of the country as a whole.

We have focused on the role of the local authorities as—economic development perhaps apart—it is they who have the prime role in urban renewal. Yet, as was emphasised in chapter 2, the government of the city is much more than this, including central government and its special agencies. The dominating theme of local government reform in the 1970s was the need for integration and planning in urban policies, though the terms of the central-local partnership were never explicitly spelt out. The new councils, however, came into being in a climate of retrenchment very different from that in which they were conceived and, since 1979, have faced increased pressure to cut their expenditure. At the same time the old consensus on the goals of urban development policies has largely disappeared and councils are being pushed into following central government policies which, left to their own devices, they would not have adopted. Planning, too, is out of fashion, rejected by a central government committed to market solutions to social and economic problems. So the comprehensive, integrated approach to the problems of the city envisaged in the early 1970s has not materialised. Instead, there is a degree of institutional pluralism, with differing agencies pursuing their own policy preferences.

This is not necessarily unhealthy or damaging. Indeed, it can be argued that institutional pluralism provides some degree of compensation for the lack of political competition in the city. Where no agency has the powers and resources to tackle a problem on its own, it is forced to look to others to cooperate and the resulting exchanges may throw onto the policy agenda issues and ideas which otherwise would not emerge. For example, the intervention of the SDA over the garden festival site forced the district to breach its 1984 policy of not disposing of land to private developers. Left to its own devices, the Glasgow Labour Party apparatus would have taken much longer to shake off the legacy of the old municipal building monopoly. Similarly, the early versions of the region's structure plan opened up the issue of rebuilding in the inner city. Central government pressure, for all its damaging effects, has caused the authorities to seek new sources of funding and new ways of doing things. The Manpower Services Commission may force educationalists to re-examine their ways of working, though there must be great scepticism about the beneficent effects of their interventions.

The danger, though, is of a complete disintegration of the various strands of urban policy, with the elected local councils reduced to mere pressure groups in the process of urban change. There is no doubt that, for all the criticism of local government reform (often used as a scapegoat for all urban ills since 1975), the performance of the new authorities represents a great improvement on the old. Management techniques have been improved and, on the political side, rigid attitudes equating socialist virtue with municipal bureaucracy have begun to shift. On the other hand, both Glasgow and Strathclyde stand out as fairly traditional authorities compared with their Labour counterparts elsewhere in Britain. Their initiatives on housing (Glasgow), deprivation (Strathclyde) and civic promotion stand out as bold and imaginative but even these have failed to make a great impact nationally. Glasgow's civic leaders are not national figures even within the Labour Party, in contrast to some of the new generation in England, and Glasgow's innovations have not fed directly into party policy.

This is partly due to the Scottish factor. The system of administrative devolution with no political devolution to accompany it does cut Scottish urban politics off from England while producing within Scotland a curiously depoliticised society. All the parties except the Conservatives are now committed to the creation of an elected Scottish assembly to assume the functions of the Scottish Office. It is generally believed that an assembly would not tolerate a regional council covering half the country and there may well be a return to single-tier local government. In that case, Strathclyde would disappear but its leaders would no doubt resurface in Edinburgh in a Scottish government. A general repoliticisation of Scottish society might stimulate political competition and open up new avenues for radical policy initiatives.

A heavy responsibility for the state of Glasgow lies with central government. The almost obsessive concern of the Scottish Office with the problems of Glasgow in the 1945-75 period has altogether disappeared while the remorseless process of centralisation has reduced the attractiveness of local government service and the ability of local leaders to address problems and deliver solutions. So not only does central government not do anything for the city—it prevents the city from helping itself, an attitude which must seem strange to American or Continental readers. The idea of purposive local government of the 1970s, meanwhile, has given way to a view of councils as mere administrative agents, devoid of political responsibility.

At the same time as reducing local discretion, central government has increased the financial pressure. All the major initiatives examined in this book have been the result of public initiative or public funding. Yet the post-1979 Conservative Government behaved as though public spending were inherently bad (their Labour predecessors were not entirely blameless in this regard). Even in the city centre, where conditions are relatively favourable, the major private economic and housing initiatives have required government help and funding. In the periphery, with no indigenous industrial or financial sector, public expenditure is still more vital for economic as well as physical and social regeneration.

Then there is the private sector. The decline of Scottish capitalism is clearly visible in Glasgow's history since the First World War. *Glasgow Action* aims to mobilise business concern behind regeneration yet, without a regeneration of the business community itself—a return to the innovative and entre-preneurial style of the past—its impact may be confined to spelling out new ways of spending public funds. So far, there are few signs of the entre-preneurial revival of which central government has dreamed.

In Glasgow, in the SDA, in *Glasgow Action* and in the regional council, many people have looked to the example of American cities which have apparently pulled themselves round (Boyle and Rich, 1984). Transplanting ideas out of their own social and economic context is always risky and assessment of Glasgow's success or failure may have to await the end of the century but American experience does allow us to pose some issues. In the post-war years, Glasgow relied almost exclusively on the state and municipal bureaucracy—there were successes, but there were gigantic failures, notably in the peripheral estates. Now the accent is on private and business leadership in transforming the city centre, the pattern may repeat itself. There will no doubt be successes to be trumpeted but the private sector does not have the resources and skills to undertake the task of urban management. Nor are its goals that of the community as a whole. A thriving business environment in the city centre may have little spin-off in employment for large sections of the population. To ensure such a spin-off will require elaborate and expensive public policies, including a return to spatial planning and the integration of spatial planning policies with social priorities. Otherwise, the local councils will be left with the responsibility for coping with the social problems of the periphery while the SDA and the private sector take credit for the revival of the centre. So we must ask not only what kind of city we will have in the year 2000 but whose city it will be?

# References

Bain, A.D., Ashcroft, B.K., Love, J.H. and Scouller, J. (1987), 'The Economic Effects of the Inward Acquisition of Scottish Manufacturing Companies, 1965 to 1980', *Economics Statistics Unit Research Papers* (Edinburgh: Industry Department for Scotland).

Baird, R. (1958), 'Housing' in J.Cunnison and J.B.S.Gilfillan (eds.), *Third Statistical Account of Scotland. Glasgow*. (Glasgow: Collins).

Baker, B. (1958), 'The Glasgow Overspill Problem', in R. Miller and J. Tivy (eds.), *The Glasgow Region* (Glasgow: British Association).

Balsillie, D. (1986), *Garden Festivals—Propagation or Propaganda*, M.Sc. dissertation, Department of Urban and Regional Planning, University of Strathclyde.

Bochel, J. and Denver, D. (1975), *The Scottish Local Government Elections, 1974. Results and Statistics* (Edinburgh: Scottish Academic Press).

Boddy, M. and Fudge, C. (eds.) (1984), *Local Socialism ?* (London: Macmillan).

Booth, S., Pitt, D. and Money, W. (1982), 'Organisational Redundancy? A Critical Appraisal of the GEAR Project', *Public Administration*, 60.1.

Boyle, R. and Rich, D. (1984), 'In Pursuit of the Private City. A Comparative Assessment of Urban Policy Orientations in Britain and the United States.', *Strathclyde Papers in Planning, 3* (Glasgow: University of Strathclyde).

Bailey, M.J. (1984), 'Management and Participation in Locally-Based Housing Associations' in D. Maclennan and M.J.Brailey, 'Housing Associations and Rehabilitation in Scotland', *Centre for Urban and Regional Research Discussion Paper no. 13*, University of Glasgow.

Brand, J. (1968), 'Politics in Glasgow', unpublished manuscript (University of Strathclyde).

Brennan, T. (1959), *Reshaping a City* (Glasgow: House of Grant).

Bruce, R. (1945), *First Planning Report to the Highways and Planning Committee of the Corporation of the City of Glasgow* (Glasgow: Corporation of Glasgow).

Budge, I., Brand, J.A., Margolis, M. and Smith, A.L.M. (1972), *Political Stratification and Democracy* (London: Macmillan).

Bulpitt, J. (1983), *Territory and Power in the United Kingdom* (Manchester: Manchester University Press).

Butler, D. and Stokes, D. (1969), *Political Change in Britain* (London: Macmillan).

Butt, J. (1983), 'Working Class Housing in Scottish Cities, 1900-1950', in G Gordon and B. Dicks (eds.), *Scottish Urban History* (Aberdeen: Aberdeen University Press).

Cable, J.V. (1974), 'Glasgow's Motorways. A Technocratic Blight', *New Society*, 30.

Cairncross, A. (1958), 'The Economy of Glasgow', in R. Miller and J. Tivy (eds.), *The Glasgow Region* (Glasgow: British Association).

Campbell, I. (1984), 'Glasgow's Peripheral Estates' unpublished M.Sc. project, University of Strathclyde.

Campbell, R.H. (1958), 'Iron and Steel', in J.Cunnison and J.B.S.Gilfillan (eds.), *Third Statistical Account of Scotland. Glasgow* (Glasgow: Collins).

Cameron, G. (1980), 'The Economies of the Conurbations', in G. Cameron (ed.), *The Future of the British Conurbations. Policies and Prescriptions for Change* (London: Longman).

Carter, C. (n.d.), *The Development of Regional Planning in Scotland* (Dundee: Duncan of Jordanstone College of Art).

Carter, C. and Keating, M. (1986), 'The Designation of Cumbernauld New Town. A Case Study of Central-Local Relationships during the 1950s', Open University Faculty of Social Sciences, *Working Paper no. 2* (Milton Keynes).

Castells, M. (1978), *City, Class and Power* (London: Macmillan).

Checkland, S.G. (1976), *The Upas Tree. Glasgow 1875-1975* (Glasgow University Press).

Clyderail (1974), A development study and cost benefit analysis produced by British Railways: Scottish Region and Greater Glasgow Transportation Study Team.

Craig, F.W.S. (1984), *City and Royal Burgh of Glasgow Municipal Election Results, 1949-73* (Chichester, Parliamentary Research Services).

CVRPAC (1946), Clyde Valley Regional Planning Advisory Committee, *The Clyde Valley Regional Plan, 1946* (Edinburgh: HMSO).

Daiches, D. (1982), *Glasgow* (London: Granada).

Dearlove, J. (1979), *The Reorganisation of British Local Government* (Cambridge University Press).

Dunleavy, P. (1980a), *Urban Political Analysis* (London: Macmillan).

Dunleavy, P. (1980b), 'The Political Implications of Sectoral Cleavages and the Growth of State Employment', *Political Studies, XXVIII*.

Dyer, I. (1982), 'Housing Associations in Glasgow', in B. Allen (ed.), *Making the City Work. Enterprise and Democracy in Urban Europe* (Glasgow: City of Glasgow District Council).

Franklin, M. (1985), *The Decline of Class Voting in Britain* (Oxford University Press).

Franklin, M. and Page, E. (1984), 'A Critique of the Consumption Cleavage Approach in British Voting Studies', *Political Studies, XXXII*.

Fraser of Allander Institute (1985), *Some aspects of Britoil's contribution to the communities of Strathclyde and Scotland* (Glasgow: University of Strathclyde).

GGTS (1967), *Greater Glasgow Transportation Study*.

GGTS (1971), *Greater Glasgow Transportation Study. Planning for Action*.

Geekie, J. and Keating, M. (1983), 'The Labour Party and the Rise of Activist Democracy', Glasgow Fabian Society, *Discussion Papers*.

Gibb, A. (1983), *Glasgow. The Making of a City* (London: Croom Helm).

Gilfillan, J.B.S. (1958a), 'The Site and its Development', in J.Cunnison and J.B.S. Gilfillan (eds.), *Third Statistical Account of Scotland. Glasgow.* (Glasgow: Collins).

Gilfillan, J.B.S. (1958b), 'The Historical Setting', In J.Cunnison and J.B.S.Gilfillan (eds.), *Third Statistical Account of Scotland. Glasgow.* (Glasgow: Collins).

Glasgow (1951), *Development Plan, 1951.* (Glasgow: Corporation of Glasgow).

Glasgow (1954), *Development Plan. Written Statement as Modified by City of Glasgow Development Plan Approval Order, 1954.* (Glasgow: Corporation of Glasgow).

Glasgow (1959), *Industry on the Move* (Glasgow: Corporation of Glasgow).

Glasgow (1972), *Second Review of the Development Plan. Areas of Need in Glasgow,* R.D. Mansley, Director of Planning.

Glasgow (1975), Corporation of the City of Glasgow, *Planning Policy Reports. Transportation,* March 1975.

Griffith, J.A.G. (1974), *The Parliamentary Scrutiny of Government Bills* (London: Allen and Unwin).

Gyford, J. (1985), *The Politics of Local Socialism* (London: George Allen and Unwin).

Harvie, C. (1981), *No Gods and Precious Few Heroes. Scotland, 1914-80*. (London: Edward Arnold).

Harvie Anderson, B. and Johnston, R. (1969), 'Note of Reservation', in Royal Commission on Local Government in Scotland, *Report*, Cmnd. 4150 (Edinburgh: HMSO).

Heald, D. (1981) 'Territorial Equity and Public Finance. Concepts and Confusion', *Studies in Public Policy*, no. 75 (Glasgow: University of Strathclyde).

Heald, D. (1983), *Public Expenditure* (Oxford: Martin Robertson).

Heidenheimer, A.J., Heclo, H. and Adams, C.T. (1983), *Comparative Public Policy. The Politics of Social Choice in Europe and America*, 2nd edn (New York: St. Martin's Press).

Henderson, R. (1974), 'Industrial Overspill from Glasgow, 1958-68', *Urban Studies*, 11.1.

Higgins, J., Deakin, N., Edwards, J. and Wicks, M. (1983), *Government and Urban Poverty* (Oxford: Blackwell).

Holman, R. (1978), *Poverty. Explanations of Social Deprivation* (London: Martin Robertson).

Hood, N. and Young, S. (eds.) (1984), *Industry, Policy and the Scottish Economy* (Edinburgh University Press).

Johnston, T.L. (1971), *Structure and Growth of the Scottish Economy* (Glasgow: Collins).

Jordan, G. and Reilly, G. (1981), 'Enterprise Zones. The Clydebank EZ and Policy Substitution', in H.M. Drucker and N.L. Drucker (eds.), *The Scottish Government Yearbook, 1982* (Edinburgh: Paul Harris).

Keating, M. (1975), 'The Scottish Local Government Bill', *Local Government Studies*, Jan. 1975.

Keating, M. 1975a), *The Role of the Scottish MP*, Ph.D. thesis, CNAA.

Keating, M. (1978), 'The Battle of the Western Approaches. A Study in Local Pressure Politics and Amenity in Glasgow', Glasgow College of Technology, Policy Analysis Research Unit, *Discussion Paper, no. 4.*

Keating, M. (1985a), 'Local Government Spending and Central Control', *Fraser of Allander Institute Quarterly Economic Commentary*, May.

Keating, M. (1985b), 'Whatever Happened to Regional Government?', *Local Government Studies*, 11.6.

Keating, M. (1985c), 'Bureaucracy Devolved', *Times Educational Supplement (Scotland)*, 5 April.

Keating, M. (1986), 'Regional Results are Bad News for Conservatives', *Municipal Journal*, 30 May.

Keating, M. and Bleiman, D. (1980), *Labour and Scottish Nationalism* (London: Macmillan).

Keating, M. and Boyle, R. (1986), *Remaking Urban Scotland. Strategies for Local Economic Development* (Edinburgh University Press).

Keating, M. and Midwinter, A. (1983a), *The Government of Scotland* (Edinburgh: Mainstream).

Keating, M. and Midwinter, A. (1983b), 'Region-District Relationships. Lessons from Glasgow', in D.McCrone (ed.), *Scottish Government Yearbook, 1983* (Edinburgh University).

Keating, M. and Waters, N. (1985), 'Scotland in the European Community', in M. Keating and B. Jones (eds.), *Regions in the European Community* (Oxford University Press).

Kendall, W. (1969), *The Revolutionary Movement in Britain, 1900-21* (London: Weidenfeld and Nicolson).

Kernaghan, J. (1982), 'Harnessing the Resources of the Private Sector: The New

Challenge for Housing Policy', in B. Allen (ed.), *Making the City Work. Enterprise and Democracy in Urban Europe* (Glasgow: City of Glasgow District Council).

Labour Party (1973), *Scotland and the National Enterprises Board* (Glasgow: Scottish Council of the Labour Party).

Leclerc, R. and Draffan, D. (1984), 'The Glasgow Eastern Area Renewal Project', *Town Planning Review*, 55.3.

Leser, C.E.V. (1958), 'Industries—Preliminary Survey', in J.Cunnison and J.B.S.Gilfillan (eds.), *Third Statistical Account of Scotland. Glasgow*. (Glasgow: Collins).

Lever, W. and Mather, F., 'The Changing Stucture of Business and Employment in the Conurbation', in W. Lever and C. Moore (eds.), *The City in Transition. Public Policies and Agencies for the Economic Regeneration of Clydeside* (Oxford University Press).

Lindsay, M. (1971), *Portrait of Glasgow* (London: Robert Hale).

Lythe, C. and Majmudar, M. (1982), *The Renaissance of the Scottish Economy* (London: George Allen and Unwin).

McAllister, I. and Rose, R. (1984), *The Nationwide Competition for Votes* (London: Frances Pinter).

McAthur, A. and Kingsley Long, H. (1935), *No Mean City* (Spearman).

McFadden, J. (1982), 'Participation and Decentralisation: The Contribution of Area Management', in B. Allan (ed.), *Making the City Work. Enterprise and Democracy in Urban Europe* (Glasgow: City of Glasgow District Council).

McGregor, A. and Mather, F. (1986), 'Developments in Glasgow's Labour Market', in W. Lever and C. Moore (eds.), *The City in Transition. Policies and Agencies for the Economic Regeneration of Clydeside* (Oxford University Press).

McLean, I. (1974), 'Red Clydeside, 1915-1919', in J.Stevenson and R.Quinault (eds.), *Popular Protest and Public Order* (London: Allen and Unwin).

McLean, I. (1983), *The Legend of Red Clydeside* (Edinburgh: John Donald).

Maclennan, D. (1983), 'Housing Rehabilitation in Glasgow. Progress and Impacts since 1974', *Housing Review*, November-December.

Maclennan, D. (1984), 'Rehabilitating Scotland's Central Cities' in D. Maclennan and M.J.Brailey, 'Housing Associations and Rehabilitation in Scotland', Centre for Urban and Regional Research *Discussion Paper no. 13*, University of Glasgow.

Martlew, C. (1986), 'Democracy, Policy and Implementation: Decentralisation in Strathclyde Regional Council', *Occasional Paper, no.23*, Planning Exchange, Glasgow.

Midwinter, A. (1982), 'Management Reform in Scottish Local Government', Department of Administration, University of Strathclyde (Glasgow).

Midwinter, A. (1984), *The Politics of Local Spending* (Edinburgh: Mainstream).

Miller, W. (1985), 'Politics in the Scottish City', in G.Gordon (ed.), *Perspectives on the Scottish City* (Aberdeen University Press).

Moon, J. and Richardson, J.J. (1984), 'Policy Making with a Difference ? The Technical and Vocational Education Initiative', *Public Administration*, 62.1.

Nairn, A. (1983), 'GEAR—Comprehensive Redevelopment or Confidence Trick?', *Fraser of Allander Quarterly Economic Commentary,*, 2.

Oakley, C.A. (1937), *Scottish Industry Today* (Edinburgh: Murray Press).

Oakley, C.A. (1975), *The Second City*. 3rd edn. (Glasgow: Blackie).

Page, E. (1978), 'Why Should Central-Local Relations in Scotland be Different to Those in England?', *Public Administration Bulletin*, December.

Paterson (1973), *The New Scottish Local Authorities, Organisation and Management Structure* (Edinburgh: HMSO).

Purkiss, E., Mason, T. and Hamilton Oldfather, I. (1983), 'Homesteading at Glenelg

Quadrant, Glasgow, *Research Memorandum no.2,* Glasgow District Council Housing Department.

Rae, J. (1977), *Multiple Deprivation. A Report by Officers of the Strathclyde Regional Council. Observations by the Director of Planning, Glasgow District Council.*

Ranson, S., Jones, G. and Walsh, K. (1985), *Between Centre and Locality* (London: George Allen and Unwin).

Rhodes, R.A.W. (1981), *Control and Power in Central-Local Relations* (Aldershot: Gower).

Robb, A.M. (1958), 'Shipbuilding and Marine Engineering', in J.Cunnison and J.B.S.Gilfillan (eds.), *Third Statistical Account of Scotland. Glasgow.* (Glasgow: Collins).

Robertson, D.J. (1958), 'Population, Past and Present', in J.Cunnison and J.B.S.Gilfillan (eds.), *Third Statistical Account of Scotland. Glasgow.* (Glasgow: Collins).

Roger Tym (1984), *Monitoring Enterprise Zones. First Year Report* (London: Roger Tym and Partners).

Roger Tym (1984b), *Integrated Development Operation for Strathclyde. Final Report Preparatory Study* (London: Roger Tym and Partners).

Rose, R. (1982), *Understanding the United Kingdom* (London: Longman).

Rosengard, A. (1984), '*The Development of Community Based Housing Associations in Glasgow; an experiment in the social control of housing*', unpublished Ph.D. thesis, University of Strathclyde.

Ross, J. (1980), 'Local Government in Scotland: Some Subversive Reflections', mimeo, University of Strathclyde.

Ross, J. (1981), 'The Secretary of State for Scotland and the Scottish Office', *Studies in Public Policy, 87,* University of Strathclyde.

RSA (1983), Regional Studies Association, *Report of an Inquiry into Regional Problems in the United Kingdom* (Norwich: Geo).

SAPT et.al. (1974), *A Better Glasgow. Transport and Environment.* Statement issued jointly by Scottish Association for Public Transport, Transport 2000, Scottish Rapid Transit Group, Public Transport Action Group, New Glasgow Society, Glasgow-East Kilbride Railway Development Association.

SCDI (1969), *Centralisation. Scotland's Nine of Diamonds* (Edinburgh: Scottish Council, Development and Industry).

SCDI (1973), *A Future for Scotland* (Edinburgh: Scottish Council, Development and Industry).

SOCRU (1986), *A Review of Community Councils in Scotland* (Edinburgh: Scottish Office Central Research Unit).

Scott, J. and Hughes, M (1980), *The Anatomy of Scottish Capital* (London: Croom Helm).

Saunders, P. (1979), *Urban Politics. A Sociological Interpretation* (London: Hutchinson).

Saunders, P (1981), *Social Theory and the Urban Question* (London: Hutchinson).

Sim, D. (1984), 'Glasgow's Special Housing Initiatives. Ways of Dealing with Difficult to Let Estates', *Research Memorandum no. 3,* Glasgow District Council Housing Department.

Sim, D. *et al.* (1984), 'Clearance in the 1980s. The Experience of Barlanark', *Research Memorandum, no. 4,* City of Glasgow District Council.

Smith, R. and Farmer, E. (1985), 'Housing, Population and Decentralisation', in R. Smith and U. Wannop (eds.), *Strategic Planning in Action. The Impact of the Clyde Valley Plan, 1946-82* (Aldershot: Gower).

Starkie, D. (1982), *The Motorway Age. Road and Traffic Policies in Post-war Britain* (Oxford: Pergamon).

Stewart, J. (1974), *The Responsive Local Authority* (London: Charles Knight).

Stewart, J. (1985), 'The Functioning and Management of Local Authorities', in M. Loughlan, M.D.Gelfand and K.Young (eds.), *Half a Century of Municipal Decline, 1935-85* (London: Allen and Unwin).

Strathclyde (1976), *Regional Report*, Strathclyde Regional Council.

Strathclyde (1977), *Multiple Deprivation*, Strathclyde Regional Council.

Strathclyde (1982), *Social Strategy for the Eighties*, Strathclyde Regional Council.

Strathclyde (1984), *Areas for Priority Treatment*, Chief Executive's Department, Strathclyde Regional Council.

Strathclyde (1985), *Strathclyde Economic Trends, 10*. Chief Executive's Department, Strathclyde Regional Council.

Strathclyde (1987), *Strathclyde Economic Trends, 15*, Chief Executive's Department, Strathclyde Regional Council.

Taylor, S. (1981), 'The Politics of Enterprise Zones', *Public Administration*, 59.

Thomson, G.M. (1935), *Scotland that Distressed Area* (Edinburgh: Porpoise Press).

TPP (1975-), *Transport Policies and Programmes*, Strathclyde Regional Council, issued annually.

WCSP (1974), West Central Scotland Plan Steering Committee, *West Central Scotland Plan—a programme of action*. (Glasgow).

Wheatley (1969), Royal Commission on Local Government in Scotland, 1966-69, *Report*, Cmnd. 4150 (Edinburgh: HMSO).

Worsdall, F. (1979), *The Tenement. A Way of Life*. A Social and Architectural Study of Housing in Glasgow. (Edinburgh: Chambers).

# Index